TOXIC
TALK

ALSO BY BILL PRESS

Eyewitness

Spin This!

Bush Must Go

How the Republicans Stole Religion

Trainwreck

TOXIC TALK

How the
Radical Right
Has Poisoned
America's Airwaves

BILL PRESS

THOMAS DUNNE BOOKS
ST. MARTIN'S PRESS
NEW YORK

THOMAS DUNNE BOOKS.
An imprint of St. Martin's Press.

TOXIC TALK. Copyright © 2010 by Bill Press. All rights reserved. Printed in the United States
of America. For information, address St. Martin's Press, 175 Fifth Avenue, New York,
N.Y. 10010.

www.thomasdunnebooks.com
www.stmartins.com

ISBN 978-0-312-60629-9

10 9 8 7 6 5 4 3

To Milo and Prairie

CONTENTS

*There can be no higher law in journalism
than to tell the truth and shame the devil.*

—WALTER LIPPMANN

INTRODUCTION:
THE POWER OF TALK

"You can't just listen to Rush Limbaugh and get things done."

On January 23, 2009, three days after taking the oath of office, President Barack Obama invited congressional leaders of both parties to the White House.

It was more than just a house-warming party. Obama asked the assembled Democrats and Republicans to join in supporting his plan to bring the nation back from the brink of economic disaster.

But House Minority Whip Eric Cantor threw cold water on any hope of bipartisanship, telling the president bluntly he wasn't sure the stimulus package was something Republicans could get behind.

Everyone held their breath, waiting for Obama's reaction. After pausing for a few seconds, the president began by repeating his pledge to reach across the aisle and seek bipartisan support. But then he warned the Republicans present he was willing to enact the stimulus package without them, if necessary. We just had an election, he reminded them. "I won. I'm the president."

At which point, Obama turned directly to Cantor and fired his final salvo: "You can't just listen to Rush Limbaugh and get things done."

A nd so the battle was joined. Between a newly elected, immensely popular president and the longtime, and still influential, king of right-wing talk radio.

Nothing better illustrates the power of conservative talk radio today, or the prominent place it commands in American political discourse.

No doubt about it: Talk radio is the most powerful force in the media today. Especially conservative talk radio. It is more powerful than newspapers, the television networks, or cable news—all of which take their cues from the right-wing radio bigmouths.

It's also more powerful than the Internet. For all the buzz about bloggers, none of them yet have the power, reach, or viselike grip over segments of the electorate exercised by right-wing radio talkers Rush Limbaugh, Glenn Beck, Sean Hannity, Michael Savage, and others.

Conservative talk radio is even more powerful than conservative politicians. Not so long ago, conservative talk radio hosts considered it their job to drum up support for policies or legislation initiated by Republican politicians in Washington.

Today, it's just the opposite. The tables have been turned. With such a vacuum in leadership among Republicans in Washington, conservative talk show hosts have rushed in to fill the void. In this new world of conservative media and politics, talk show hosts set the agenda—and both public and politicians follow their lead, no matter how crazy.

Rush Limbaugh, for example, no longer listens to John Boehner or Mitch McConnell to know what to talk about that day on his program. Instead, Boehner and McConnell listen to Limbaugh, Hannity, Beck, or Savage to decide what the big issues are and what they should be focusing on.

When Lou Dobbs insisted there were still unanswered questions about Barack Obama's birth certificate, ten Republican members of Congress sponsored legislation requiring all future candidates for president to produce valid proof of birth before filing.

When Glenn Beck accused White House "czars" of plotting the overthrow of the government, Republican leaders in Congress requested release of all background information gathered during the administration's vetting process for presidential appointees who did not require Senate confirmation.

When Glenn Beck called President Obama a "racist" on national television, South Carolina congressman Joe Wilson felt empowered to call the president a liar on the floor of the House of Representatives during Obama's State of the Union address.

When Fox News headlined irregularities at a collection of community-based organizations called ACORN as the biggest news story of the decade, House Republican Leader John Boehner demanded that President Obama tell the nation where he personally stood on ACORN.

Right-wing talk show hosts are so proud of their new power to set the agenda that Glenn Beck could even boast: "If it wasn't for Fox or talk radio, we'd be done as a republic."

The battle between Obama and right-wing radio talkers had, in fact, been brewing for some time. Crisscrossing Illinois as a long-shot candidate for the U.S. Senate in 2002, Obama asked voters what the most important issues were in their own lives. As he recounts in his memoir, *The Audacity of Hope,* Obama was surprised to discover that some people merely "recited what they had heard on Rush Limbaugh or NPR."

In May 2007, as a brand-new senator, Obama joined forty other Democratic senators in signing a letter written by Senate Majority Leader Harry Reid to Mark Mays, CEO of Clear Channel Communications (which broadcasts *The Rush Limbaugh Show*), demanding an apology for Limbaugh's reference to Iraq veterans critical of the war in Iraq as "phony soldiers."

And, during his campaign for president, Obama often singled out Limbaugh for criticism. Addressing a Florida fund-raiser on May 22, 2008, for example, Obama told the crowd: "A certain segment has basically been feeding a kind of xenophobia. There's a reason why hate crimes against Hispanic people doubled last year. If you have people like Lou Dobbs and Rush Limbaugh ginning things up, it's not surprising that would happen."

For his part, just two days before Obama's White House meeting, Limbaugh had chastised fellow Republicans, including John McCain, for expressing their hope that Obama succeed as president. Limbaugh strongly disagreed. "We are being told we have to hope he succeeds, that we have to bend over and grab our ankles . . . because his father was black, because he's the first black president, we've got to accept this," he told his loyal listeners.

Limbaugh, who proudly proclaimed himself the new, de facto leader of the Republican Party, preached just the opposite. He put it bluntly: "I hope he fails."

And with that verbal salvo, Limbaugh launched a war against Obama, soon joined by all other right-wing talk show hosts, that continues to this day: a war that has only intensified in the level of ugly, hateful, personal rhetoric—to the point where anything goes, no insult is considered over-the-line, and name-calling has become the standard fare of conservative talk radio and television.

In late 2009, the hostility broke out into open warfare between the Obama White House and Fox News. Tired of the nonstop attacks from Fox hosts Glenn Beck, Bill O'Reilly, and Sean Hannity, the administration struck back. In an interview with CNBC, Obama himself singled Fox out for criticism: "I've got one television station [network] that is entirely devoted to attacking my administration." And on September 20, when he scored what Beltway pundits call the "Full Ginsburg," named after Monica Lewinsky's attorney, William Ginsburg, the first to appear on five Sunday morning talk shows the same day, Obama shut out Fox, granting an interview to Univision instead.

Fox News Sunday anchor Chris Wallace responded by calling Obama press aides "the biggest bunch of crybabies I have dealt with in my thirty years in Washington." In response, a few weeks later, White House communications director Anita Dunn dismissed Fox News as little more than "a wing of the Republican Party." They "take their talking points, put them on the air; take their opposition research, put them on the air. And that's fine," she told CNN host Howard Kurtz on *Reliable Sources.* "But let's not pretend they're a news network the way CNN is."

Indeed, for the most part, what we see on Fox News are lies that have already been tested on right-wing talk radio—and by many of the same people. They're singing from the same hymnal, and reading from the same set of talking points.

It's a far cry from the robust but fair debate of issues originally envisioned as the goal of the format. Indeed, rather than encourage honest debate, most conservative talk radio hosts today have an extremely corrosive impact on our public discourse: engaging in personal attacks, spreading lies, fanning the flames of bigotry, and slamming the door on legitimate differences of opinion.

But it doesn't stop there. This toxic cloud of hate, bluster, and deceit spewed forth by Limbaugh and conservative radio talkers has also poisoned our politics. First cable television hosts, and then Internet bloggers, adopted the arguments and rhetoric of right-wing talk radio; conservative politicians soon followed. As a result, our political dialogue has become increasingly polluted, and the opportunities for true bipartisan leadership and real, critical debate in Washington have been diminished, if not destroyed.

Make no mistake: The genie of right-wing talk, unleashed by Limbaugh and his compatriots, is destroying our democratic process. As the old saying goes, "A lie can get halfway around the world before the truth can get its boots on." And that's particularly true when blowhards like Rush Limbaugh and Glenn Beck attract such large audiences—and when Republican politicians gladly spew the same ugly rhetoric and employ the same dirty tactics.

Strangely, what many Republicans don't seem to realize is that the hateful rhetoric of right-wing talk radio is not only hurting this country, it's also hurting the Republican Party. Republicans have allowed themselves to be defined by their most extreme element—the loudest, most strident, most hateful voices.

Yes, the hatred and intolerance oozing from conservative talk radio energizes and reinforces the party's hard-core base. But at the same time, it alienates more and more moderates and independents—the very people the Republican Party is going to need if it's ever to fight its way back from the political wilderness.

Meanwhile, average Americans are increasingly turned off by the intellectual bankruptcy of the GOP's toxic talk arguments.

With America facing the worst financial crisis since the Great Depression, tired, old attacks on "tax-and-spend liberals" sounded totally off-key. After watching an unregulated Wall Street lead us over the cliff, nobody took seriously any more talk radio platitudes about free, "self-correcting" markets. When our nation is clearly suffering from a broken health insurance system, the Republican cries of "socialized medicine," "rationing," and "death panels" rang increasingly false. And after the tragic cost in lives and dollars of two protracted wars in Iraq and Afghanistan, few Americans took seriously the old, simplistic right-wing cry that you either support any U.S. war, anywhere, anytime, or you're an al Qaeda sympathizer.

The conservative dog-and-pony show was fun for a while. But in these tough times, Americans have come to realize certain fundamental truths about the whole right-wing talk radio enterprise: Yelling louder doesn't make ideas better. And repeating lies over and over again doesn't make them true.

It's a lesson we learned once, and then forgot.

THE ORIGINS OF RIGHT-WING TALK

Sad but true, the excesses and intolerance of today's conservative radio personalities are nothing new. We've seen it all before.

While principled conservative William F. Buckley, Jr., once fostered legitimate dialogue and debate on television with his show, *Firing Line,* right-wing talk radio was toxic from the very beginning. Cases in point: Father Charles Coughlin and Joe Pyne, the founding fathers of conservative talk.

In his day, Father Coughlin, the "Radio Priest," made Rush Limbaugh look like a small-town disc jockey. During the 1930s, more than 40 million people, one third of the nation at that time, tuned in to his weekly broadcasts from the National Shrine of the Little Flower in Royal Oak, Michigan.

Coughlin started out a strong supporter of Franklin Roosevelt and the New Deal—rallying audiences in 1933 to believe in "Roosevelt or Ruin!"

and arguing that "The New Deal is Christ's Deal!" But later, feeling the president hadn't taken him seriously enough, particularly when it came to Coughlin's pet issue of remonetizing silver, the radio priest turned on FDR and began to rally opposition to the New Deal. "We were supposed to be partners," a bitter Coughlin later ruminated about FDR. "He said he would rely on me. That I would be an important adviser. But he was a liar."

Even more troubling, Coughlin began to praise the Fascist policies of Germany's Adolf Hitler and Italy's Benito Mussolini. He even adopted their anti-Semitic language, blaming the Great Depression on an "international conspiracy of Jewish bankers" and arguing that the Russian Revolution "was launched and fomented by distinctively Jewish influence."

As news of Nazi atrocities against Jews reached America, Coughlin dismissed them or explained them away. "Jewish persecution only followed after Christians first were persecuted," he insisted. Thankfully, at this point, Coughlin was losing his audience by 1942. With the outbreak of World War II, Coughlin's popularity sank and Catholic Church authorities finally forced him to give up his radio broadcasts.

Even though Father Coughlin talked a lot on the radio, he was not a true talk show host in the sense of giving opinions and interacting with listeners. That honor falls to Joe Pyne, who debuted as a talk show host on WILM-AM in Wilmington, Delaware, in 1950.

Because making a call on a pay phone then cost five cents, Pyne called his show *It's Your Nickel*. Every night, Pyne would give his opinion on the hot issues of the day and invite listeners to call with their five cents. His insults to callers became legendary, like telling listeners to "go gargle with razor blades."

In many ways, Pyne was a precursor to Limbaugh, devoting much of his program to insulting hippies, gays, and feminists. But Pyne didn't necessarily win every argument. In one verbal duel he insulted musician Frank Zappa by suggesting, "So I guess your long hair makes you a woman." Zappa responded: "So I guess your wooden leg makes you a table." And, even back then, there was no point in arguing with a dining room table.

Despite Pyne's success and popularity, however, his in-your-face brand of talk radio remained the rare exception on the AM dial until the 1970s, and the emergence of competitive programming on the FM band. Given the option of a clearer signal on the FM dial, more and more listeners abandoned AM and started turning to FM for music. Indeed, for a while, it looked like the AM dial might actually disappear. But in 1987, when the FCC abandoned the Fairness Doctrine, thereby relaxing restrictions on local programming, AM program directors seized the opportunity to put more talkers on the air—and talk radio exploded as a popular format.

At first, talk stations provided a smorgasbord of opinion, in order to attract listeners of any political persuasion. At San Francisco's powerful KGO-AM, for example, moderate talker Ronn Owens was followed by once liberal, now conservative Dr. Laura, while late nights were filled by liberals Bernie Ward and Ray Taliaferro. The classic talk show format was also heard over KABC-AM in Los Angeles, where top talker Michael Jackson dutifully presented both sides of any issue before asking listeners for their opinions, while seldom giving his own. (Later, after leaving KABC, Michael became a strong progressive voice on Southern California talk radio.)

That balanced—"on the one hand, on the other hand"—format changed abruptly in 1988 with the debut of Rush Limbaugh. Balance went out the window. There was never any doubt where Limbaugh stood on any issue. He was all conservative, all the time. He made sport of liberals, environmentalists, and "feminazis." Absent the Fairness Doctrine, radio programmers were no longer under any obligation to present an opposing, liberal, opinion. And Limbaugh's three-hour midday program soon rocketed to appear on six hundred local stations, reaching over 16 million listeners a week.

Conservative talk radio now dominated the AM dial—and still does. As noted by the Center for American Progress in its 2007 survey of national talk radio:

- In the spring of 2007, of 257 news-talk stations owned by the top five commercial station owners, 91 percent of the total weekday talk radio programming was conservative. Only 9 percent was progressive.

- Each weekday, 2,570 hours and 15 minutes of conservative talk were broadcast on those 257 stations, compared to 254 hours of progressive talk. That's ten times as much conservative talk as progressive talk.
- 76 percent of the news-talk programming in the top ten radio markets is conservative, while only 24 percent is progressive.

TOXIC TALK IN FULL FLOWER

Father Coughlin and Joe Pyne notwithstanding, radio talk was rarely more virulent than during the long presidential election campaign of 2008. And no hosts spewed more poison than right-wing radio's big four: Rush Limbaugh, Sean Hannity, Glenn Beck, and Michael Savage.

Rush Limbaugh, the aging but still undisputed king of conservative talk radio, encouraged his listeners to join in "Operation Chaos." By reregistering as Democrats and voting for Hillary Clinton, Limbaugh explained, they could help prolong the closely contested Democratic primary well after Obama's victory was mathematically assured. But not enough followed his call.

His one-man crusade for chaos having failed, Limbaugh blamed Clinton's loss on liberal guilt. Obama won the Democratic primary, the right-wing megaphone insisted, not because he ran a better campaign, but only because "nobody had the guts to stand up and say no to a black guy."

On a daily basis, Limbaugh also accused Obama and fellow liberals of being antimilitary. "They hate the military anyway," he asserted. "Liberals do not trust the military. Don't think the military's any good." This, of course, from a man who never served a day in the military, thanks to student deferments in college and a subsequent physical deferment due to what he claims was either for a "football knee from high school" or a "pilonidal [anal] cyst."

Then there's poor Sean Hannity. Every day, he tries hard to be as outrageous, obnoxious, and funny as Rush Limbaugh. But he never quite makes it. Because he's simply not as talented.

Hannity is second only to Limbaugh in radio audience, appearing on almost five hundred stations and reaching 12 million listeners a week. But, evidently, size of audience does not correlate with truth of message.

During 2008, Hannity spent weeks of his nationally syndicated radio program on attempts to brand Barack Obama as a dangerous supporter of terrorism, if not an out-and-out terrorist himself. On radio and TV, he aired the unsubstantiated claim of conservative blogger Andy Martin that Obama's work as a community organizer in Chicago was in fact "training for a radical overthrow of the government." Martin also made the dubious assertion that Obama's entire political career had been planned and directed by former Weather Underground member William Ayers: a total fabrication that Hannity embraced and preached as gospel truth, despite zero supporting evidence.

Challenging Limbaugh and Hannity for media stardom, nationally syndicated talk show host Glenn Beck took one look at Barack Obama and declared: "There's a socialist agenda there for America." But Beck didn't stop there. He was soon accusing Obama of being not only a socialist, but a communist. "The thing that I do find about Barack Obama," he told his audience, "is that—and I think America's starting to catch on to this—this guy really is a Marxist. He believes in the redistribution of wealth."

Earlier, Beck had leveled the same charge against Hillary Clinton, labeling her "Comrade Clinton" and a "liberal fascist . . . who wants to redistribute the wealth in this country the way she believes is good for everybody." Obama? Clinton? What the hell? Why not paint John Edwards with the same brush? Which Beck proceeded to do: "Now, put a red star on his furry head. He's a communist."

Sadly, Beck is living proof that toxic talk pays off. He was so good at stirring up hatred on his radio program that he landed a brief gig on CNN Headline News before migrating to his nightly perch on Fox News, where, of course, he belongs—in the company of Sean Hannity and Bill O'Reilly.

In some ways Limbaugh, Hannity, and Beck were pussycats compared to hate-monger Michael Savage. On the Talk Radio Network, Savage daily stirred up fears about an Obama presidency. "He's an Afro-Leninist, and

I know he's dangerous," Savage warned listeners. Not only that, "I fear that Obama will stir up a race war . . . in order to seize absolute power."

And, despite Obama's somewhat controversial twenty-year membership in a Christian church, Savage warned listeners: "Now we have an unknown stealth candidate who went to a madrassa in Indonesia and, in fact, was a Muslim." Obama had only been in the White House seventy-five days, with no sign of a race war on his agenda, when Savage accused him of taking down a painting of George Washington and replacing it with a portrait of Malcolm X!

NATIONAL COMRADES-IN-ARMS

Of course, Limbaugh, Hannity, Beck, and Savage—the Big Four of Hate Talk—are not alone. They've spawned a whole army of wannabes, both at the local and national level, who also deal in lies and personal attacks.

Classic example: Mark Levin, who started out as an acolyte to Sean Hannity but was given his own talk show on ABC Radio, where his brand of ugly talk soon made him the fastest-growing conservative talk show host in the country.

During the 2008 campaign, Levin repeatedly linked Barack Obama to Adolf Hitler. Obama, he sneered, was "into these big, German-like events that he creates in this country." Even after Obama was in the White House, Levin continued spreading rumors about the authenticity of his birth certificate and questioned whether Obama was really an American citizen.

Among other targets, Levin also made waves by rebranding the National Organization for Women as the "National Organization of Really Ugly Women" and declaring that the United Nations was no different from the KKK.

Breaking news, Mark: U.N. members don't wear hoods, lynch people, or firebomb churches.

If Levin's the newest kid on the right-wing block, G. Gordon Liddy's one of the oldest. But the convicted Watergate felon is still at it, and has only grown meaner with age. Having broken the law himself, Liddy doesn't hesitate to encourage listeners to do likewise, especially when it comes to guns. He counseled his audience in November 2008: "The first thing you do is, no matter what law they pass, do not—repeat, not—ever register any of your firearms."

Which is probably still more benign than his April 1995 advice to shoot to kill: "Well, if the Bureau of Alcohol, Tobacco and Firearms comes to disarm you and they are bearing arms, resist them with arms. Go for a head shot; they're going to be wearing bulletproof vests." Later, Liddy suggested aiming, instead, "twice for the body and then the groin." Gee, thanks.

By the way, despite all the right-wing attacks on Obama's long-ago fund-raiser in the home of ex-Weatherman William Ayers, Liddy's invitation to murder didn't stop John McCain from holding a fund-raiser in Liddy's Scottsdale home in 1998 and appearing frequently on his radio show.

Then there's Neal Boortz.

Trying to distinguish himself from Limbaugh, Hannity, Savage, Beck, and others, Boortz calls himself a libertarian. Which is really an insult to libertarians, who, unlike Boortz, distrust big government without necessarily hating their fellow human beings. Boortz, on the other hand, appears to despise anyone who is poorer than he is, or happens to have a different skin color.

In his eyes, if you're unlucky enough to make only the minimum wage, you're a pure loser. "How incompetent, how ignorant, how worthless is an adult that can't earn more than the minimum wage?" Boortz asked his radio audience on August 3, 2006. "You have to really, really, really be a pretty pathetic human being to not be able to earn more than . . . the minimum wage."

In Boortz's warped world, the failures of local, state, and federal governments were not to blame for the disastrous response to Hurricane Katrina. "The primary blame," Boortz insisted, "goes on the worthless parasites who lived in New Orleans, who . . . couldn't even wipe themselves, let alone get out of the way of the water when that levee broke."

As for illegal immigrants, Boortz's solution is to deport all 11 million to Mexico, and then: "Give 'em a little bag of nuclear waste as your lovely parting gift. AMF, which means 'Adios, my friend.' Send them all back across the border to Mexico. Tell 'em it's a tortilla warmer. . . . And you'll be able to find them at night, too, because they'll glow."

LOCAL, BUT NO LESS LETHAL

While right-wingers from Limbaugh to Boortz were poisoning the national airwaves, there's an even greater army of toxic talkers, either not yet big enough or good enough to have their own nationally syndicated show, stalking the local airwaves. Which doesn't mean they're any less lethal.

Unlike Limbaugh and his cohorts, a handful of conservative talk show hosts don't aim all their venom at Democrats. They're more than willing to destroy fellow conservatives they believe have strayed from the straight-and-narrow. Leading the anti-establishment pack: John Kobylt and Ken Chiampou, longtime hosts of *The John and Ken Show*, the most listened to local talk show in the country.

John and Ken first teamed up in New Jersey, where they helped send Governor Jim Florio packing for raising taxes. In 1992, they took their antitax crusade to KFI-AM in Los Angeles. They helped lead the successful recall campaign against Democratic governor Gray Davis in 2003. But by 2009, they had turned against his successor, Republican Arnold Schwarzenegger. For putting a new tax measure on the ballot, John and Ken called Schwarzenegger and fellow Republicans "nothing but a bunch of weak slobs"—and threatened to recall him, too.

Cincinnati talk show host Bill Cunningham was one of the first to warm up a crowd for candidate John McCain by calling his opponent "Barack *Hussein* Obama"—his deliberate repetition of the middle name, Cunningham admitted, intended to portray Obama as a "Muslim, un-American, terrorist."

McCain at first condemned Cunningham's inflammatory language, but later in the campaign, when his chances had dwindled to nothing,

McCain remained silent while other speakers made similar sport with Obama's middle name.

During this same period, *Radio & Records* magazine decided to present its 2008 Lifetime Achievement Award to veteran conservative talker Bob Grant. *R&R* decided to honor Grant, even though he'd been fired from New York's WABC-AM for regretting, on air, that Commerce Secretary Ron Brown had most likely survived the airplane crash that killed him. Earlier, he'd prayed for Magic Johnson "to go into full-blown AIDS" and suggested how authorities might prevent a gay rights march in Manhattan: "Ideally, it would have been nice to have a few phalanxes of policemen with machine guns and mow them down."

WABC later rehired Grant. He's still on the air. Old haters never die. They just sign new contracts.

DECONSTRUCTING TOXIC TALK

And that's just the tip of the iceberg. Thanks to this army of venom-spewing blowhards, political dialogue has never been more poisonous, and talk radio is its driving force. The heated rhetoric of right-wing talk has even spilled over onto network and cable television. Some conservative radio hosts, including Sean Hannity and Glenn Beck, also host their own TV cable shows. Other TV hosts have simply adopted both their style and pattern of personal attacks.

On virtually every political show on cable, from Fox to MSNBC to CNN, conservative commentators now indulge in the same kind of wild charges, irrespective of the facts, once only heard on talk radio. In this new poisoned political climate, Republican pundits succeed because they're outrageous and obnoxious, not because they're factually accurate or honest. Such are the fruits of right-wing radio.

Yet, even though it's so powerful and so much in the news, conservative talk radio has received relatively little critical analysis—in part because so much of our attention is now focused on the Internet and bloggers. While Weblogs are an intriguing phenomenon to be sure, their reach in politics is still in its incipient stages, and very far from full flower. Talk radio, on the other hand, has never been stronger, and is still growing in influence.

This book, then, is an in-depth examination of right-wing talk radio and its destructive impact on American culture and politics. With right-wing talkers exerting so powerful an influence on national politics, this is the perfect time to take a critical look at conservative talk radio: who the major players are; why conservatives dominate talk radio; and what damage they've done, both to the American political scene and, eventually, to their own movement.

Like every book by every author, this is one is built both on my own experience and bias.

I know talk radio inside out. My broadcasting career began as a television commentator on KABC-TV in Los Angeles in September 1980. Within a year, I had also become a radio talk show host on KABC-AM 790, and soon moved to the king of Los Angeles talk radio, KFI-AM 810. After relocating to Washington to co-host CNN's *Crossfire* and *The Spin Room* and, later, MSNBC's *Buchanan and Press,* I continued to broadcast on radio as well, first on WMAL-AM 630, and later with my own nationally syndicated program.

The Bill Press Show is heard daily, 6–9 A.M. EST, on Sirius and XM Satellite Radio and syndicated on dozens of major stations across the country, including Seattle, Portland, San Francisco, Los Angeles, Denver, Dallas, Minneapolis–St. Paul, Madison, Chicago, Detroit, Buffalo, Asheville, Jacksonville, and Washington, D.C. And I make frequent appearances on various shows on MSNBC, CNN, CNBC, and Fox News.

I also know politics inside out. I've worked in the California State Legislature and the California governor's office. I've volunteered for more campaigns than I can remember—at the local, state, and national level. I've walked countless precincts. I've managed state and local campaigns, served as campaign press secretary, and run for statewide office in California. For three years, I was the Democratic state chair of California, and raised millions of dollars for California politicians and for Bill Clinton's 1996 reelection campaign.

In both my broadcasting and political careers, I've never tried to hide where I'm coming from. I'm a Democrat. I'm a liberal. And proud of it. That's my political bias.

My broadcast bias is: I believe talk radio should inform, not inflame. I think it should entertain, not demean. I think it should elevate political discourse, not debase it. I am a firm believer in, and practitioner of, the First Amendment. I believe a talk show host should be free to express whatever opinions he holds and to make a total ass of himself on a daily basis. At the same time, I think that political debate, whether it ends up veering right or left, should at least start from a foundation of truth, not rumor, speculation, or lies.

Indeed, that's the way it worked when I was getting started. During my career, I've duked it out with some of the toughest and brightest conservatives in the business: Bob Novak, Pat Buchanan, John Sununu, Mary Matalin, and Tucker Carlson, among others. They are not only adversaries, they became friends. While we tend to disagree on almost every policy issue, I still have great respect for them, even a certain affection. Because, while tough, our debates were always civil, well prepared, argued from reason, and based on facts, not personal attacks.

Regretably, as we will see, that's not the way it is on conservative talk radio today. Civility is the exception, not the rule. Tolerance of differing opinions has given way to fear, contempt, and hatred. Reason and rational discourse have been replaced by toxic talk.

RUSH LIMBAUGH: THE BIG FAT LIAR

In the beginning, there was Rush.

There is still nobody bigger in talk radio, and probably never will be.

Conservative talk radio didn't begin with Rush. As we saw in the Introduction, Father Charles Coughlin and Joe Pyne established the format long before Rush got anywhere near a microphone.

But with Rush Limbaugh, right-wing radio really came into its own. Not for nothing was El Rushbo invited by President George H. W. Bush to spend the night in the Lincoln Bedroom, made an Honorary Member of Congress by Speaker Newt Gingrich, and declared by some to be the leader of the Republican Party in 2009.

Rush Limbaugh enjoys a bigger audience, sells more advertising, makes more money, pisses more people off, and wields more political clout—by far—than any other talk show host in the country, conservative or liberal. Indeed, most other talkers, whether they admit it or not, strive to imitate him. The airwaves hum with Rush wannabes.

More than anyone else, Limbaugh has honed talk radio into the lethal weapon it is today. Echoes of his technique may be heard in the patter of

Glenn Beck, Sean Hannity, Michael Savage, Mark Levin, or countless other disciples, but the undiluted essence of right-wing talk—and everything that's so corrosive about it for our democracy—can only be found, minute by minute, in the original Rush.

You don't even have to listen long. Back when I was broadcasting at KFI-AM in Los Angeles, on Saturdays from 12–3 P.M., I followed a rerun of the *Best of Rush* from the previous week. After brainstorming the best way to lure Limbaugh's audience into staying tuned for my show, program director David Hall and I came up with two ideas. First, we changed my name from Bill Press to "Bill Press, True American" and ran promos during Rush's three hours, challenging listeners to stay tuned for a different point of view.

Producer Tim Kelly also prepared a whole series of riffs on the "True American" theme just to annoy Rush's loyal listeners—known as "ditto-heads" because they usually just happily swallow, without thinking, whatever garbage Rush comes out with. "He still helps old ladies across the street," ran one promo. "Of course, he's Bill Press, True American!" And again: "He baked his wife a cherry pie. Of course, he's Bill Press, True American!"

Our second ploy was to feature a "Now Hear the Truth" segment to my show. Every Saturday, I'd play a clip of some outrageous statement Rush had made the previous week and refute it: "Here's what Rush said this week, now hear the truth!"

In order to prepare for that segment, I at first rearranged my schedule so I could listen to at least an hour of Rush's show every day and dutifully make notes on what I might respond to. But I soon learned that was a complete waste of time. It wasn't necessary to suffer through an hour or two of Rush in order to hear something outrageous. Any five minutes would do. Any five minutes was bound to contain either a big lie, a total misrepresentation of the facts, or a personal attack. The man is nothing if not predictable.

Rush responded by dissing me as a "mere entertainer"—which I took, coming from him, as a sublime compliment. Years later, he put me down as "no intellectual giant" and just your "average media liberal."

Where to start? Maybe the best place is where Limbaugh himself started. In 1988, the year he moved from local to national talk radio, Limbaugh published in *The Sacramento Union* a rundown of what he called "35 Undeniable Truths." Loaded with warnings about the threat of the Soviet Union at the time, his list also included the following aphorisms:

- Peace does not mean the absence of war.
- There is only one way to get rid of nuclear weapons—use them.
- The peace movement in the United States, whether by accident or design, is pro-communist.
- Evolution cannot explain creation.
- Feminism was established so as to allow unattractive women access to the mainstream of society.
- There will always be poor people.
- This is not the fault of the rich.

In 1994, after the collapse of the Soviet Union, Limbaugh came back down from the mountaintop with an updated list of "Undeniable Truths," including:

- The earth's ecosystem is not fragile.
- The most beautiful thing about a tree is what you do with it after you cut it down.
- Evidence refutes liberalism.
- Condoms only work during the school year.
- Women should not be allowed on juries where the accused is a stud.
- Liberals attempt through judicial activism what they cannot win at the ballot box.
- You could afford your house without the government—if it weren't for your government.

It's classic Limbaugh. Even though his listeners embraced them as gospel, every single one of Limbaugh's "Undeniable Truths" is neither undeniable nor true. Their supposed irrefutability exists only in the make-believe world in which he broadcasts.

In the real world, of course, even the possibility of engaging in nuclear warfare is rejected by rational people everywhere, and there's a growing movement to get rid of nuclear weapons altogether. Yet, in September 2009, when the United Nations Security Council, under President Obama's leadership, unanimously called on all nuclear states to scrap their nuclear arsenals, Limbaugh warned: "This may be the most dangerous development yet, and I hope he fails."

On other fronts, feminism has won women the right to vote and pay equity in the workplace; evidence of global warming has proven how extremely fragile the earth's ecosystem really is; and millions of Americans would have lost their homes were it not for the intervention of the federal government. And, as for *liberals* trying to use the court to circumvent the ballot box, I have only two words for Rush: Florida 2000!

Of course, the thin-skinned Limbaugh has little patience for those who might express a different point of view. As far as he's concerned, they should remove themselves from the same planet—starting with Andrew Revkin, global climate reporter for *The New York Times*. "This guy from *The New York Times*, if he really thinks that humanity is destroying the planet, humanity is destroying the climate, that human beings in their natural existence are going to cause the extinction of life on earth—Andrew Revkin. Mr. Revkin, why don't you just go kill yourself and help the planet by dying?"

We could spend the rest of the chapter repudiating all seventy of Limbaugh's twice-told lists of "35 Undeniable Truths," but why take the time? Even at face value, like almost every word he says, they are manifestly untrue.

Instead, let's simply borrow the format to tell some undeniable truths about Rush. For which we don't need thirty-five pronouncements. Eight will do.

EIGHT UNDENIABLE TRUTHS ABOUT RUSH

1. RUSH LIMBAUGH IS A BIG FAT LIAR.

Al Franken—now Senator Al Franken!—was the first to methodically expose Limbaugh's pathological dishonesty in his entertaining book, *Rush Limbaugh Is a Big Fat Idiot.*

Of course, liar's a tough word. Senator Franken didn't use it lightly, and neither do I.

We all know what lying means, because we all do it occasionally— either deliberately or carelessly. It's not just failing to tell the truth. We all do that, occasionally, sometimes without even knowing it. You might tell a friend that a certain stock's a good buy, for example, simply because you heard Jim Cramer tell you as much on CNBC. When, in fact, it's a dog. You didn't tell the truth. But that's still not a lie.

No, to tell a lie you either have to know the truth, and then deliberately tell someone the direct opposite. Like George W. Bush, knowing the CIA could not confirm the existence of WMDs in Iraq, but nevertheless telling the American people that Saddam Hussein had piles of them. That was a big fat impeachment-worthy lie.

Or, speaking of impeachment—and in the spirit of bipartisanship—it was like Bill Clinton's insisting "I did not have sexual relations with that woman, Miss Lewinsky." As we all know, that was another big fat lie, even though lies about sex are a lot less harmful than lies about why we should go to war. Whatever damage President Clinton caused to his marriage, his lying about his relationship with Monica Lewinsky didn't result in thousands of lives being lost. Or, as the popular bumper sticker put it: "When Clinton lied, nobody died."

The other kind of lie, more common among talk radio hosts, is simply not taking the time to verify the truth of what you're saying before repeating it.

But either way, whether you know it's not true but say it anyway, or don't bother to check whether it's true or not before saying it, you're not telling the truth. You're telling a lie. A big fat lie.

And big fat lies are what Rush tells every day on his *EIB*, or *Excellence in Broadcasting* network. Which, come to think of it, is itself a big fat lie. As we know, lies are powerful because, coming from people we trust, they sound so real, they spread so fast, and suckers—aka listeners—so easily believe them.

When he first burst onto the national scene, Limbaugh was able to spit out his lies with impunity. Enjoying the field to himself, there was nobody around to track and refute them, and nobody yet knew how quickly and doggedly Limbaugh would make dishonesty his bread-and-butter. Fortunately, thanks to two great liberal media watchdog organizations, that's no longer the case. FAIR, or Fairness and Accuracy in Reporting, was first on the scene. They were joined a couple of years ago by the bigger and better-known Media Matters for America, founded by David Brock. Thanks particularly to Media Matters, no sooner does a lie escape Limbaugh's lips these days than it is duly chronicled and corrected. I'm proud to acknowledge that Media Matters has been the primary source for much of the material commented on in this book.

The list of Limbaugh falsehoods is virtually limitless. Here are just a few of the more egregious ones, both old and new. The old ones, of course, just prove how long Rush has been butchering the truth.

President Obama's Stimulus Package

Frantic over its inevitable passage, Limbaugh told so many patent untruths about the Obama stimulus plan that it's hard to keep track of them. On several occasions, for example, he asserted that the legislation would provide tax cuts to illegal immigrants. "Do you know that in this 'Porkulus' bill," he asked his audience on January 29, 2009, "it has been learned, in addition to everything else, illegal immigrants will also be given checks of $500 to $1,000 as tax credits?"

That was a big fat lie, and Limbaugh must have known it.

As passed by Congress and signed by President Obama, the $787 billion economic recovery legislation clearly stated that, in order to qualify for Obama's middle-class tax cuts, individuals had to comply with Section 32(c)(1)(E) of the Internal Revenue Tax Code. Check it out. That's the section requiring a valid Social Security number—for which people in this country illegally do not qualify.

Parroting the Republican Party talking points, Limbaugh also asserted that small-business owners would be hardest hit by Obama's allowing George Bush's tax cuts for the wealthy, those making over $250,000 a year, to expire in the year 2011. He fulminated in February 2009: "This is a massive—in the midst of a recession—tax increase on small business. It is not a tax on the wealthy. I mean, it is, but it's that—it's going to hit far many more small-business people than it's going to hit the wealthy."

That was a big fat lie, and Limbaugh must have known it.

In 2007, according to the Tax Policy Center, only 2 percent of tax returns reporting small-business income were in the top two tax brackets, those making over $250,000 a year. And, of course, Limbaugh failed to point out that such taxes are paid only on taxable income, not gross income, and that, under Obama's plan, the higher tax rate would apply only to that portion of *net* income *over* $250,000 a year.

Who's he kidding? We all know Limbaugh's real problem with watching Bush's tax cuts for the wealthy disappear was that he himself would end up a big loser. Limbaugh takes home about $38 million a year. Which means Bush's tax cuts saved him a fat $1.5 million annually. Clearly, Limbaugh's not motivated by concern for small business. He's motivated by pure, personal greed!

On the stimulus bill, Limbaugh also claimed it would cost taxpayers $275,000 for every job created. The actual cost, according to most economists, was closer to $60,000, less than 25 percent of Limbaugh's scary figure—and that's not even counting additional benefits the package would create in terms of energy efficiency, health care, or new schools.

In addition, Limbaugh accused Obama of hiding inside the stimulus package a $4.19 billion direct, no-bid gift to ACORN (Association of Community Organizations for Reform Now), the grassroots organization Republicans accused of massive voter fraud during the 2008 campaign.

More on ACORN later, which somehow turned out to be a favorite buga-
boo of the wacko right. Meanwhile, in this case, Limbaugh was wrong on
both counts. Despite some irregularities, all too common in every voter
registration campaign, widespread voter fraud by ACORN was never
proven. And no money for ACORN was either secretly or openly contained in the stimulus bill. Nevertheless, Limbaugh tried his best to link
Obama with ACORN, telling listeners: "He *is* ACORN. Barack Obama *is*
ACORN."

We've already unmasked a number of easily refutable lies, all revolving
around just one piece of legislation! But this is nothing new. Limbaugh's
been doing it for years! So now a few oldies, but still goodies.

Tobacco

On his radio show of April 29, 1994, Limbaugh boldly asserted: "It has not
been proven that nicotine is addictive, the same with cigarettes causing
emphysema [and other diseases]."

That was a big fat lie, and Limbaugh must have known it. As noted by
FAIR, the addictiveness of tobacco had been reported in medical literature dating from the beginning of the twentieth century. In 1988, Surgeon
General C. Everett Koop erased any remaining doubts with his seminal
Koop Report: "Today, the scientific base linking smoking to a number
of chronic diseases is overwhelming, with a total of 50,000 studies from
dozens of countries."

Native Americans

Is America's record toward Native Americans anything to be ashamed of?
Not according to the Rushmeister. "There are more American Indians
alive today than there were when Columbus arrived or at any other time in
history," Limbaugh wrote in his 1993 book, *See, I Told You So.* "Does this
sound like a record of genocide?"

That was a big fat lie, and Limbaugh must have known it.

As reported by FAIR, Carl Shaw of the Bureau of Indian Affairs estimates the pre-Columbian population of what later became the United States ranged somewhere between 5 and 15 million. By the late nineteenth century, due to rampant disease and genocidal practices, there were roughly 250,000 natives left. Today, there are 2 million Native Americans, most of them still stranded in poverty on Indian reservations—except those wily enough to have built casinos in order to turn the tables and fleece paleface for a change.

Election of JFK

Right-wingers so hate the Kennedy family, they still refuse to believe that John F. Kennedy won, albeit barely, his election against Richard Nixon. And, of course, Limbaugh helps fan the flames. "And it was only four thousand votes that—had they gone another way in Chicago—Richard Nixon would have been elected in 1960," he declared on the April 28, 1994, broadcast of his television show.

That was a big fat lie, and Limbaugh must have known it.

Or would have known it, had he done the least bit of research. Kennedy beat Nixon in the Electoral College, 303–219. Even without the twenty-seven electoral votes of Illinois, JFK would still have been elected president.

Iran-Contra

For El Rushbo, the Second Coming was the election of Ronald Reagan. Or, at least, he likes to pretend as much. In the real world, Rush never voted for Reagan—he didn't even register to vote until he was thirty-five.

Nevertheless, even after members of the Reagan White House, with or without the doddering president's knowledge, were found guilty of selling arms to terrorists, Limbaugh still refused to believe there was anything to the Iran-contra scandal and continued to keep his followers in denial.

On his short-lived TV show, Rush dismissed the investigation led by special prosecutor Lawrence Walsh: "This Walsh story basically is, we just spent seven years and $40 million looking for any criminal activity on the part of anybody in the Reagan administration, and guess what? We couldn't find any. These guys didn't do anything, but we wish they had so that we could nail them. So instead, we're just going to say, 'Gosh, these are rotten guys.' They have absolutely no evidence. There is not one indictment. There is not one charge."

That was yet another big fat lie, and Rush must have known it.

Check the facts. Walsh actually won indictments against fourteen people in the Iran-contra scandal, including: Defense Secretary Caspar Weinberger; National Security Advisers Robert McFarlane and John Poindexter; and top White House aide Ollie North. Of those fourteen, eleven were convicted or pleaded guilty.

I could go on, but you get the picture. From the election of 1960 to Iran-contra to the stimulus bill of 2009 to pretty much any other political issue you can think of, Rush Limbaugh lies like a rug. It seems almost pathological.

There's only one conclusion you can draw from all of this: As entertaining as he may be, you can't believe a word you hear on the Rush Limbaugh program. In fact, every time you hear Limbaugh say "I'm not making this up, folks" you can be pretty sure he is.

2. RUSH LIMBAUGH IS A HYPOCRITE.

Hypocrisy—the fine old art of accusing someone else of wrongdoing while engaged in the same practice, or worse, yourself—is a Republican specialty.

Indeed, if Bill Bennett were to write yet another book about right-wing "virtues," hypocrisy would have to be at the top of the list. And when Peggy Noonan or some other conservative pundit drones on endlessly about good old Republican "character," what they usually mean is the capacity to be flagrantly hypocritical while maintaining a straight face.

We remember Newt Gingrich leading the charge to impeach Bill Clinton for having sex with a White House staffer—while he happened to be enjoying carnal relations with his own congressional staffer.

We remember Antonin Scalia and Clarence Thomas preaching the importance of respecting states' rights—and then rushing to deny Florida the right to count its own votes in the presidential election of 2000.

We remember Dick Cheney solemnly warning the nation that the projected deficit in President Obama's 2010 budget would destroy the economy—several years after, as vice president, he assured fellow Republicans that "deficits don't matter."

But, when it comes to hypocrisy, Rush Limbaugh is once again the standard-bearer of his party.

Throughout the presidency of Bush II, the recurring theme of his show was accusing Democrats of wanting George W. Bush to fall flat on his face. "I'm getting so sick and tired of people rooting for the defeat of the good guys," he complained in July 2006. With typical gusto, Limbaugh almost daily charged Democrats with rooting for Bush to fail, wanting the war in Iraq to fail, and, by extension, hoping for America to fail.

In the gospel according to Rushbo, circa 2000–2008, no matter how you voted, once the president was in office, wanting him to fail was out-and-out un-American. Shame on you!

But that was then, this is now. Even before Barack Obama walked into the Oval Office, Limbaugh had rewritten his gospel and turned it upside down. "I disagree fervently with the people on our side of the aisle who have caved and who say 'Well, I hope he succeeds,'" Limbaugh declared on Friday, January 16, 2009.

Limbaugh explained that he had been asked by a national magazine to submit a four-hundred-word statement outlining his "hope for the Obama presidency." In words that soon became infamous, he spurned the offer.

"So, I'm thinking of replying to the guy: Okay, I'll send you a response, but I don't need four hundred words, I need four: 'I hope he fails.' (interruption by producer) What are you laughing at? See, here's the point. Everybody thinks it's outrageous to say that. Look, even my staff. 'Oh, you can't do that.' Why not? Why is it any different? What's new? What is unfair about my saying I hope liberalism fails? Liberalism is our problem. Liberalism is what's gotten us dangerously close to the precipice here. Why do I want more of it? I don't care what the drive-by story is. I would be honored if the drive-by media headlined me all day long: 'Limbaugh: I Hope Obama Fails.' Somebody's gotta say it."

Once Obama was in the White House, Limbaugh continued to wish for his failure. In fact, he said that only by Obama's failure could America be "saved." "Barack Obama's policies and their failure is the only hope we've got to maintain the America of our founding," he told listeners after the (ultimately successful) auto industry bailout. In September 2009, Limbaugh went one step further. He not only repeated his desire that Obama fail, he accused Obama himself of wanting America to fail: "I'm wondering if maybe that Obama wants America to fail so he can rebuild and remake it."

This is one area of attack where even some of Rush's most loyal acolytes refused to follow him. "You're irrational if you don't want the new president to succeed," Newt Gingrich countered on *Meet the Press*. "I don't think anyone should want the president of the United States to fail; I want some of his policies to be stopped."

But, for Limbaugh, this hypocrisy is nothing new. His rules were different for the Clinton era as well. Starting in January 1993, he began each show with a dramatic "America Held Hostage" announcement, counting down the days left till the end of the Clinton presidency.

In other words, it's un-American to want a president to fail—except when the president is a Democrat.

Drugs Hit Home

Forget politics. Limbaugh's most public, and most embarrassing, display of hypocrisy was his passionate love affair with hillbilly heroin.

For years, nobody was a bigger cheerleader for America's often ill-advised "war on drugs." On the radio, on TV, in print, Limbaugh railed against both those who used illegal drugs and those who would decriminalize them. Drug use was not a sickness, he insisted. It was a deliberate choice to commit a criminal act and drug offenders should face the maximum punishment.

"There's nothing good about drug use," Limbaugh told television viewers in October 1995. "We know it. It destroys individuals. It destroys families. Drug use destroys societies. Drug use, some might say, is destroying this country. And we have laws against selling drugs, pushing drugs, using drugs, importing drugs. And the laws are good because we know what happens to people in societies and neighborhoods which become consumed by them. And so if people are violating the law by doing drugs, they ought to be accused and they ought to be convicted and they ought to be sent up."

The solution to the problem of illegal drug use was simple, he concluded. "What this says to me is that too many whites are getting away with drug use. Too many whites are getting away with drug sales. Too many whites are getting away with trafficking in this stuff. The answer to this disparity is not to start letting people out of jail because we're not putting others in jail who are breaking the law. The answer is to go out and find the ones who are getting away with it, convict them, and send them up the river, too."

Earlier, Limbaugh quoted basketball coach and owner Jerry Colangelo in disputing the notion that drug abuse was a disease and should be treated with rehabilitation: "The first time you reach for a substance you are making a choice. Every time you go back, you are making a personal choice. I feel very strongly about that." To which Rush added his own endorsement: "And Colangelo is right."

As Limbaugh knew well. Because, when it came to OxyContin, he had made thousands of personal choices of his own.

News of Limbaugh's own drug problem was first reported in the October 2003 edition of the *National Enquirer*, where a former housekeeper claimed the talk show host paid her tens of thousands of dollars to procure painkillers. Although her claim was never substantiated, state investigators did determine that Limbaugh had obtained multiple prescriptions of the drugs OxyContin, Lorcet, Norco, and hydrocone through illegal "doctor shopping" in Florida, New York, and California. Court records showed he had thus acquired more than two thousand pills over one five-month period.

At first, Limbaugh responded by taking out full-page ads in *The Palm*

Beach Post and Fort Lauderdale *Sun-Sentinel*, accusing State Attorney Barry Krischer of pursuing him for political reasons. But then he finally fessed up, admitted his addiction, and checked himself into an Arizona treatment facility.

Once back on the air, Limbaugh admitted he could not have overcome his drug addiction without professional help. But he has yet to admit that he was wrong—indeed, a big hypocrite—in demanding that, rather than undergo rehabilitation, all other drug addicts should instead be hunted down, convicted, and sent "up the river." Limbaugh, of course, never served a day.

3. RUSH LIMBAUGH IS A PARTISAN HACK.

One big difference between conservative and progressive talkers: You will often hear liberal hosts criticize fellow Democrats. But you will seldom, if ever, hear conservative hosts criticize fellow Republicans. Most of the time, in fact, they sound like they're broadcasting from the bowels of the Republican National Committee.

Want to know what the Republican Party talking points are on any given day? Tune in to Rush Limbaugh.

During debate over Obama's $787 billion economic stimulus package, for example, the comments of Limbaugh and congressional Republicans amounted to a carefully orchestrated echo chamber of criticism. Their first line of attack was to claim that "stimulus" was just a euphemism for "spending"—ignoring the fact that any stimulus program is, by definition, a spending program.

"This is a spending bill. This is not a stimulus bill," said House Minority Whip Eric Cantor on Limbaugh's January 28, 2009, program. Obama's economic recovery legislation was "not a stimulus package. It's a spending package," echoed Senator John McCain a couple of days later on the *CBS Evening News*.

For his part, on January 29, Limbaugh read from the same talking points: "If we're going to stimulate the economy, there's got to be something in here that stimulates, and there just isn't. It is just traditional typical Democrat [sic] spending."

And, speaking of GOP talking points, notice how Limbaugh adds insult to injury by joining immature Republicans who deliberately use the noun "Democrat" where they should use the adjective "Democratic"—as in "Democrat Party," instead of the grammatically correct "Democratic Party." Among certain brain-dead politicians and pundits, this is considered clever. I guess because they heard it on the radio.

Operation Chaos

During the 2008 campaign, Limbaugh's radio show eventually became a full-service arm of the McCain campaign.

At first, Rush tried to convince Republican primary voters to oppose John McCain because he was not conservative enough and could not win the general election. When those efforts failed (so much for Limbaugh's supposed "political power"), he switched gears and launched Operation Chaos, aimed at convincing Republicans to re-register as Democrats and vote for Hillary Clinton in the remaining primaries in order to stop Obama from running away with the nomination. In fact, he bragged that by the time he'd finished working his electoral mischief, both candidates "will be so bloodied and brought down to earth that neither can win in the general."

Did some Republicans play Limbaugh's game? Yes, some. But there's no way to calculate how many. There's not even any way to prove he influenced the outcome of one state primary. Nor is there any way to prove how many of those Republicans who did change parties did so out of loyalty to Rush or out of disgust with George W. Bush. Nevertheless, even though Operation Chaos was a manifest failure, Limbaugh declared it a huge success. And in the Republican tradition of such dubious declarations, he hung a virtual "Mission Accomplished" banner over his radio broadcast. "We have been successful beyond our wildest dreams," he crowed to his listeners. "Obama is no longer the Messiah." And he predicted that Obama would "lose and lose big come November." Mr. Limbaugh, repeat after me: "President Barack Obama."

Mr. Limbaugh, please repeat after me: "Secretary of State Hillary

Clinton." As a matter of fact, the only "mission accomplished" was more publicity for the Rushmeister. Meanwhile, luckily for him, nobody took his efforts seriously enough to investigate their questionable legality. In many states, you can't just switch parties back and forth for the fun of it—or because a fat, drug-addled media personality tells you to. In Ohio, for example, party switchers are supposed to sign a form stating, under penalty of election fraud—a felony—that they support the principles of the party they are joining.

But the law is rarely invoked or enforced, and was not in 2008. Just in case, Limbaugh told his listeners not to worry about it. He was willing to fall on his sword—for them and for the TV cameras. "I wouldn't worry about it. Look at this as a badge of honor, ladies and gentlemen. If anybody gets indicted, if anybody has to go to jail, it will be me—and I'll do my program from jail for the short amount of time I will be there before I am excused and the charges dismissed." Of course, as Rush knew from the OxyContin episode, his chances of ever going to jail for breaking the law were slim to none.

Riots in Denver

Having failed to serve his party by preventing the nomination of Barack Obama, Limbaugh next tried to prevent his election by inciting riots at the Democratic National Convention. Riots in Denver, he declared, would be one way to ensure a Democrat was not elected president. And he told his listeners they had a responsibility to make that happen.

"Riots in Denver, at the Democratic convention, will see to it that we don't elect Democrats," he bellowed on April 23, 2008. "And that's the best damn thing that can happen to this country, as far as I can think."

There was no worry that the same thing might happen a week later in the Twin Cities, he assured his audience. "We don't riot. We don't burn our cars. We don't burn down our houses. We don't kill our children. We don't do half the things the American left does."

After Denver mayor John Hickenlooper and Colorado, U.S. senator Ken Salazar complained to Clear Channel about their star talk show host's inciting illegal activity, Limbaugh backed off. "I am not inspiring or inciting riots," he insisted. "I am *dreaming* of riots in Denver."

Now, attempting to incite riots at the opposition convention goes a bit further than most Republican elected officials would dare in public. Nevertheless, Rush's radio show remains basically the official propaganda arm of the Republican National Committee—as biased, over-the-top, and patently untrue as the old Soviet *Pravda*.

When it comes to repeating the official GOP talking points as independent fact, as we'll see, nobody's more craven to his Republican handlers than radio host turned Fox News anchor Sean Hannity. But give credit where credit's due. Hannity is just another disciple of Rush. He learned well at the feet of his master.

4. RUSH LIMBAUGH IS A MISOGYNIST.

It may be going too far to say Rush Limbaugh dislikes women. After all, he's been married, and divorced, three times and is scheduled to add number four. As the old joke goes, when Rush defends the institution of marriage—which one of his marriages is he defending?

But it is fair to say that Limbaugh has a problem with women. Just look at all the ugly things he's said about them.

Among all his outrageous statements over the years, Limbaugh is perhaps best known for branding feminists as "feminazis"—an insult he still delights in to this day. "Women were doing quite well in this country before feminism came along," he insists. Even though, he fails to add, they couldn't vote, didn't get paid the same salary as men for doing the same job, and couldn't even legally challenge their pay inequity until President Obama signed the Lilly Ledbetter legislation in 2009.

Far from helping women achieve their equal rights under the Constitution, Limbaugh asserts, the feminist movement was only established "as to allow unattractive women easier access to the mainstream of society." And, for feminists, the most important thing in life remains "ensuring that as many abortions as possible occur."

Despite his multiple marriages, Limbaugh doesn't seem to have learned much about women. In fact, he brags that whatever he knows about women, he learned from a pet. November 20, 2006: "My cat's taught me more about women than anything in my whole life."

She "comes to me when she wants to be fed," he explained. "And she's smart enough to know she can't feed herself. She's actually a very smart cat. She gets loved. She gets adoration. She gets petted. She gets fed. And she doesn't have to do anything for it."

Women Leaders

Maybe Rush's cat also taught him to dismiss the significant achievements of America's female leaders. "Women still live longer than men because their lives are easier," he observed in March 2005.

This is yet another patently stupid remark by Limbaugh. Even putting aside less pay for equal work, horrifying rates of domestic and sexual violence, all the chronic and lingering social expectations that argue women should remain in the home and/or still diminish their role in the workplace, and everything else women have to deal with on a daily basis, it sounds like Rush is aware of neither the rigors of childbirth nor life in high heels.

It also sounds like he never heard Ann Richards's great line in her address to the 1992 Democratic convention in New York: "Ginger Rogers did everything Fred Astaire did, except backwards and in high heels."

Limbaugh frequently dismisses, for example, the leadership of Nancy Pelosi, the first female speaker of the House of Representatives. To him, she is nothing but a glorified, spoiled, housewife: "Look at Ms. Pelosi," he brayed on January 5, 2007, the day after she was sworn in for her first term as speaker. "Why, she can multitask. She can breast-feed, she can clip her toenails, she can direct the House, all while the kids are sitting on her lap at the same time."

In the same vein, Limbaugh ridiculed the candidacy of Hillary Clinton (before he fired up Operation Chaos). Even though she was then leading the Democratic pack for president, Limbaugh dismissed her campaign and her supporters as nothing but the final act of a frustrated feminist movement: "You have to understand the mind-set of a lot of these feminists and women. . . . These women have paid their dues. They've been married two or three times; they've had two or three abortions; they've done everything that feminism asked them to do. They have cut men out of their lives; they have devoted themselves to causes and careers. And this—the candidacy of Hillary Clinton—is the culmination of all of these women's efforts."

Of course Rush didn't let up, even after Senator Clinton became the new secretary of state. She remained the target of his ridicule and merciless personal attack.

In September 2009, while Obama was weighing whether to send more troops to Afghanistan, Limbaugh questioned what possible advice Clinton could offer the president, given "her many years of military experience and training." This, I remind you again, from the man who claims that an anal cyst or high school football knee prevented him from serving even one day in the military.

Actually, as a young woman, Hillary Clinton had tried to enlist in the Marines, only to be rejected because of poor eyesight. But Mr. Anal Cyst didn't buy her story. "That wasn't the reason," he told his radio listeners. "They didn't have uniforms or boots big enough to fit that butt and those ankles."

I don't mean to flog a dead horse, but—if I were Rush, I wouldn't make fun of anybody else's big butt.

Long before Hillary, one of the first women he trashed, of course, was Anita Hill. Limbaugh portrayed her as nothing but Clarence Thomas's rejected and scornful former girlfriend.

"Anita Hill followed Clarence Thomas everywhere," he said on May 4, 1994. "Wherever he went, she wanted to be right by his side, she wanted to work with him, she wanted to continue to date him. . . . There were no other accusers who came forth after Anita Hill did and said, 'Yeah, Clarence Thomas, he harassed me, too.' There was none of that."

Not true. As FAIR reports, Anita Hill could not have continued to date Thomas, because they never dated in the first place. And two other women, Sukari Hardnett and Angela Wright, did, in fact, come forward during the Clarence Thomas confirmation hearings with similar sexual harassment charges.

Nonetheless, we know what side Rush was on, and he was duly repaid for it. In 1994, Clarence Thomas presided over Limbaugh's third wedding—which was held in the justice's own home.

Breasts in Show

Maybe there's a ready explanation for Rush's confusion when it comes to women. He himself may have unwittingly revealed it, back in 1994, when he told viewers about a 1972 study allegedly conducted at Boston's Tufts University—on bra sizes!

It was a "three-year study of five thousand coeds and they used a benchmark of a bra size of 34-C," he breathlessly explained to his TV audience. "They found that the—now wait. It's true. The larger the bra size, the smaller the IQ."

There's only one problem with that study: It never happened. Reporters could find no evidence or copies of the report. And Dr. Burton Hallowell, president of Tufts at the time, said he had absolutely no recollection of such a study. "I surely would have remembered that!" he added.

As reported by FAIR, a search of Nexis turns up no information on the alleged Tufts study (nor, today, does Google), but does cite several women who believe that the presence of large breasts does indeed cause a lowering of IQ in some males. Especially radio talk show hosts?

5. RUSH LIMBAUGH IS A NEAR-RACIST.

I'm not going to call Rush Limbaugh a racist. Because I don't really think he is. You see how charitable I am?

I honestly believe that Limbaugh supports equal rights for all Americans, regardless of race. I don't believe he'd deny anybody a job, just because he or she happened to be black. I even think he'd vote for an African-American, as long as he was a Republican—and wasn't either Michael Steele or Colin Powell.

At the same time, as is apparent by his many public statements on race, the nation's number-one talkmeister clearly has a problem with some people of color. He can't accept blacks as qualified players in the NFL, which is why he was blocked from buying the St. Louis Rams. And he certainly can't accept blacks as equal players on the American scene. Not even the current occupant of the Oval Office.

Barack Obama won the 2008 election with 53 percent of the vote. He trounced John McCain in the Electoral College, 365–173. But according to Limbaugh, Obama won for one reason only. His victory had nothing to do with his campaign skills, his positions on the issues, or the fact that most Americans felt it was well past time for a change in leadership. No, no, no. According to Rushbo, Obama won both his party's nomination and the general election—only because he's black. When not playing the parody song "Barack, the Magic Negro," Rush often referred to Obama as the "affirmative action candidate" and accused General Colin Powell of endorsing Obama only because he was a fellow African-American.

"It is striking how unqualified Obama is," Limbaugh complained on August 19, just before the Democratic convention, "and how this whole thing came about within the Democrat [sic] Party. I think it really goes back to the fact that nobody had the guts to stand up and say no to a black guy."

Of course, Limbaugh's got it backward. The historical significance of the 2008 election is not that Obama won *because* he's black, but that Obama won *despite* being black. Let's be honest. No matter how tolerant we pride ourselves on being, few of us expected to see an African-American president in our lifetime.

Still, ignoring the persistent reality of racial prejudice in this country, Limbaugh insisted Obama benefited from being black: "It's—you know, it's just—it's just we can't hit the girl. I don't care how far feminism's saying, you can't hit the girl—and you can't—you can't criticize the little black man-child. You just can't do it, 'cause it's just not right. It's not fair. He's such a victim. "

Even after Obama was in the White House, Limbaugh continued to insist that any support he earned was due, not to the strength of his ideas, but only to the color of his skin. Rush even accused some of his fellow Republicans of falling into the trap of wishing Obama well, just because he was our first black president: "We are being told that we have to hope he succeeds, that we have to bend over, grab the ankles, bend over forward, backward, whichever, because his father was black, because this is the first black president."

Had Obama not been black, Rush insisted, he would never have made the big time: "If Barack Obama were Caucasian, they would have taken this guy out on the basis of pure ignorance long ago." (Oh, if only that were true of Rush!)

Nope, according to Rushbo, Obama's only in the White House today because of white guilt. "He was elected by a bunch of whiners who wanted him to take care of them. That's who voted for the guy. Well, it's some white people who thought they could get rid of the nation's racist past by voting for the guy."

You still think Rush Limbaugh doesn't have a problem with blacks?

What about his analysis of the situation in Darfur? Again, according to Rush, there was only one reason Democrats wanted to withdraw American troops from Iraq and send forces to Darfur: not to stop the genocide in Sudan, but to appease black voters. "What color is the skin of the people in Darfur? It's black. And who do the Democrats really need to keep voting for them? If they lose a significant percentage of this voting bloc, they're in trouble." For the record, the original champion of American assistance to Darfur was a conservative white Republican, Congressman Henry Hyde. Still not convinced? What about Limbaugh's dismissal of black contestants on the CBS program *Survivor*?

On August 23, 2006, discussing the new season of *Survivor*, where participants were divided into ethnic tribes, Rush suggested the competition would not be fair if there were a lot of water events, because "blacks can't swim." He based his comments on a study reporting that young black males were more likely to die in public swimming pools. Therefore, he insisted, "it is not a racial or racist comment at all."

At the same time, Limbaugh couldn't resist placing his money on Latino contestants because they had demonstrated great "survival tactics." Illegal immigrants "have shown a remarkable ability to cross borders," they can go "without water for a long time, they don't get apprehended, and they will do things that others will not do." Need more evidence? Consider Limbaugh's brief career as a color commentator for ESPN.

In 2003, Limbaugh ridiculed the skills of Philadelphia Eagles quarterback Donovan McNabb. Appearing on ESPN's *Sunday NFL Countdown*, Rush insisted there was only one reason McNabb was getting such positive publicity: his skin color. "The media has been very desirous that a black quarterback do well," Limbaugh insisted, and therefore McNabb "got a lot of credit for the performance of this team that he didn't deserve."

After the ensuing outrage, Limbaugh resigned his position with ESPN, but still refused to back down. "If I wasn't right, there wouldn't be this cacophony of outrage that has sprung up in the sportswriter community."

His McNabb put-down came back to bite Limbaugh in the ass in October 2009, when he—briefly!—entertained the idea of becoming an owner of the St. Louis Rams. As soon as word got out that Limbaugh had been asked to join an investors team headed by St. Louis Blues chairman Dave Checketts, strong reservations were expressed by several owners, NFL commissioner Roger Goodell, and at least seven NFL players, in addition to DeMaurice Smith, head of the NFL Players Association. Players, especially, were still smarting from his January 2007 comment that "The NFL all too often looks like a game between the Bloods and the Crips without any weapons."

So many voices were heard in opposition that Checketts promptly announced Limbaugh had been dropped from the investors group. At which point, a bitter Limbaugh again proved why he had no business being a team owner. He blamed "race hustlers" DeMaurice Smith, Rev. Al Sharpton, Rev. Jesse Jackson, and the Congressional Black Caucus for Checketts's decision and complained he was a victim of "Obama's America on full display." Without him, he warned, the NFL would just continue to be a bed of "racism and liberalism."

Now, that's really rich: After all his racist comments about football players, Rush Limbaugh accusing the NFL of racism.

His reaction to two other events shows that Rush is so obsessed with race he sees racist overtones everywhere, even when there aren't any.

In Ohio's 2006 Senate race, Limbaugh commented on the withdrawal of Iraq veteran Paul Hackett from the race—effectively ceding the Democratic nomination to Congressman Sherrod Brown. "And don't forget, Sherrod Brown is black," Limbaugh reminded his listeners. "There's a racial component here, too." He added that he'd been reading about the latest developments in the race in *The New York Times* "and they, of course, don't mention that."

There's a good reason why the *NYT* didn't mention that Congressman Brown is black: Because he was, is, and always will be, *white*. Obviously, Limbaugh assumed that anybody with the first name "Sherrod" must be black, or at least brown.

And in September 2009, he again assumed that any dispute between whites and blacks must be racially motivated. What prompted his comment this time was a video that exploded on the Internet of two black high school students in Belleville, Illinois, beating a fellow white student on a school bus. The Belleville police originally speculated publicly that the dispute must have been about race. But they later apologized, explaining that the altercation actually started when the white student, looking for a seat on the bus, threw another student's book bag on the floor.

Not only did Limbaugh refuse to accept the police department's explanation, he urged a return to the days of Rosa Parks and Birmingham, Alabama—and, of course, blamed it all on Barack Obama. "I think the guy's wrong," Rush harrumphed the next day. "I think not only it was racism, it was justifiable racism. I mean, that's the lesson we're being taught here today. Kid shouldn't have been on the bus anyway. We need segregated buses—it was invading space and stuff. This is Obama's America." Only Limbaugh could get away with demanding a return to the day of segregated buses, thereby turning the civil rights movement—which, in effect, started with Rosa Parks and the Montgomery Bus Boycott—on its head. I guess Rush just wants to bring back the "good old days."

And speaking of good old days, what does he mean by "justifiable racism"? Now, there's a novel concept. Exactly what kind of racism is "justifiable"? According to Rush, all racism is. Because, like homosexuality, that's just the way we're born, not the way we choose to be. "If homosexuality being inborn is what makes it acceptable, why does racism being inborn not make racism acceptable?" he asked, in talking further about the bus beating incident. "Apparently now we don't choose racism, we just are racists. We are born that way. We don't choose it. So shouldn't it be acceptable, excuse . . . this is according to the way the left thinks about things."

But, of course, racism is never acceptable or justifiable. And that's not the way "the left thinks about things." Anybody on the left could easily point out the difference between following one's sexual orientation and choosing to deny another person equal rights solely because of the color of his skin.

6. RUSH LIMBAUGH IS A BULLY.

What do you do if you have the most powerful microphone in the world? Do you use it to enlighten? Inform? Inspire? No, you use it to attack or make fun of others. And for the most part, like any other bully, Limbaugh prefers beating up on those who can't defend themselves.

Among those he likes to insult, gays and lesbians are probably at the top of his list. He's always ready for a cheap shot at openly gay Congressman Barney Frank. In January 2009, for example, in the middle of the subprime mortgage crisis, he called Frank the "Banking Queen." And that summer, when Frank poked fun at a woman holding an Obama/Hitler poster at a town meeting—"On what planet do you spend most of your time?"—Limbaugh couldn't resist the cheap homophobic slur. "Isn't it an established fact," he asked, "that Barney Frank himself spends most of his time living around Uranus?"

Limbaugh even took advantage of a natural disaster to bash lesbians. When historic floods threatened Fargo, North Dakota, in March 2009, he opened the second hour of his radio show with this lament: "I heard some top-of-the-hour news and it made me feel uncomfortable. It's about the flooding in Fargo, North Dakota, brought on by the melting snowpack and icepack. (reading news item) 'As the Red River threatens to overflow, they're filling in the dikes.'"

He continued: "Isn't there a more appropriate word? Do we have to say, I mean, we don't have any dikes here. The 'dykes' are over there. . . . They're filling in the dikes. Couldn't we change that to 'they're filling in the contingencies' or something?"

According to Limbaugh and his more virulent disciples, like Michael Savage, gays and lesbians control the Democratic Party. Unlike Republicans, who were willing to alienate their Christian base, he argued in 2008, Democrats would never alienate their gay base. "You want to know why Republicans are willing to say 'Screw you' to 30 percent of their voters and yet Democrats will bend over, grab the ankles, and say, 'Have your way with me,' for 10 and 2 percent of the population?"

Strangely enough, it's the same analogy Limbaugh used to defend angry mobs that turned up at congressional town hall meetings in the summer of 2009. Protesters were vilified simply for exercising their First Amendment rights, Limbaugh insisted: "So we get tarred and feathered as Nazis 'cause we just don't bend over, grab the ankles, and let you guys ram whatever down our throats that you want."

Rush, in fact, seldom mentions gays and lesbians without using the "bend over and grab your ankles" reference. He also once observed: "When a gay person turns his back on you, it is anything but an insult; it's an invitation." Notice, again, the above reference to Barney Frank's "living around Uranus."

And then there's his apparent obsession with "anal poisoning." As on April 1, 2009, warning that if British prime minister Gordon Brown keeps "slobbering" over President Obama, he'll "come down with anal poisoning and may die from it."

And again on May 15, referring to President Obama's first hundred days in office: "He knows that he's being followed around by a bunch of sycophants who are going to die of anal poisoning before the year's out."

Yet again on September 22, commenting on Obama's appearance the night before on David Letterman's show. Letterman, claimed Rush, was "in full anal poisoning mode, meaning if he keeps this up he's gonna die of it."

Note: I will leave it to another author to probe Limbaugh's obvious fixation on anal sex. For the time being, it seems that everything Rush knows about gays and lesbians he learned from watching *Deliverance*!

Women and Minorities

As noted above, women, young and old, are a favorite Limbaugh target for insult and ridicule.

In February 1994, when *Time* featured on its cover the face of a five-thousand-year-old man found buried in the ice, Limbaugh insisted the magazine was wrong. The frozen face really belonged to Sally Jesse Raphael. "This is just what Sally Jesse Raphael looks like without makeup," he explained.

Not even teenage girls are spared his bullying. Early in the Clinton administration, Limbaugh showed a picture of Socks, the White House cat, on his TV show. "Did you know there's a White House dog?" he next asked his audience—and immediately showed a photo of First Daughter Chelsea.

Chelsea Clinton was only thirteen at the time. When widely condemned for his insensitivity, Limbaugh, a real profile in courage, blamed his producer for posting Chelsea's photo without his knowledge. But take it from me as a longtime talk show host, nothing happens on Limbaugh's program without his advance knowledge.

In Limbaugh's world, minorities are always fair game for attack. For him, there was no secret why a Mexican won the 1992 New York Marathon: "An immigration agent chased him for the last ten miles." And he questioned why California would consider creating a state holiday to honor labor leader César Chávez: "This is asinine! Wasn't he convicted of a crime?"

Even the disabled aren't exempt from Limbaugh's hate talk, as Michael J. Fox discovered. When the actor taped commercials supporting several Democratic senatorial candidates in 2008, Rush accused him of faking his affliction with Parkinson's disease. "He is exaggerating the effects of the disease," Limbaugh told listeners. "He's moving all around and shaking and it's purely an act. . . . This is really shameless of Michael J. Fox. Either he didn't take his medication or he's acting." He had to be acting, Limbaugh added, because "this is the only time I've ever seen Michael J. Fox portray any of the symptoms of the disease he has."

In this case, response to Limbaugh's screed was immediate and angry. For perhaps the first and only time in his career, he apologized before the end of the same show. "Now people are telling me they have seen Michael J. Fox in interviews and he does appear the same way in the interviews as he does in this commercial," Limbaugh fessed up. "All right then, I stand corrected. . . . So I will bigly, hugely admit that I was wrong, and I will apologize to Michael J. Fox, if I am wrong in characterizing his behavior on this commercial as an act."

Limbaugh may have been moved to apologize quickly because he suffers from a disability himself. The right-wing radio king went deaf in 2001 as a result of an autoimmune ear disease, and can now only hear his callers with the aid of a cochlear implant. You'd think that would instill some compassion in the man. But old habits die hard. In the same breath, Rush immediately leveled a different attack against the actor: "Michael J. Fox is allowing his illness to be exploited and in the process is shilling for a Democratic politician."

Limbaugh simply can't believe that anyone who supports a Democratic candidate for public office might be doing so because he or she sincerely believes in what that candidate stands for. Only those who support Republican candidates, of course, do so out of pure, unquestionable motives.

7. RUSH LIMBAUGH IS THE INTELLECTUAL LEADER OF THE GOP.

Scary, isn't it? But true. And true for a long time.

Ronald Reagan was the first national Republican leader to worship at the shrine of El Rushbo, calling the talk show host "the number-one voice for conservatism in our country." But Reagan wasn't alone.

In 1992, President George H. W. Bush called Limbaugh a "national treasure" and invited him to bunk out for the night in the Lincoln Bedroom. In 1995, Speaker Newt Gingrich made him an Honorary Member of the House Freshman Republican class. And, before he left office in January 2009, President George W. Bush hosted Limbaugh for lunch and birthday cake in the Oval Office. The king of talkers then stood by in the East Room while Bush awarded the Medal of Freedom to former Prime Ministers Tony Blair of the U.K. and John Howard of Australia.

By this time, of course, Limbaugh was more than the number-one voice of conservatism. He was the self-proclaimed leader of the Republican Party—a position of honor Democrats were more than happy to acknowledge. White House chief of staff Rahm Emanuel even described him as "the voice and the intellectual force and energy behind the Republican Party."

But heaven help any Republican who disagreed. Several tried, and were burned at the stake for their heresy.

Georgia's Republican congressman Phil Gingrey was the first victim of the Obama era.

After President Obama had warned congressional Republicans not simply to follow Limbaugh's lead, Rush accused Obama of fearing him more than he feared Senate Republican Leader Mitch McConnell or House Minority Leader John Boehner. Loyal acolyte that he is, Gingrey rose to defend his congressional leaders.

"I mean, it's easy if you're Sean Hannity or Rush Limbaugh or even sometimes Newt Gingrich to stand back and throw bricks. You don't have to try to do what's best for your people and your party. You know you're just on these talk shows and you're living well and plus you stir up a bit of controversy and gin the base and that sort of thing. But when it comes to true leadership, not that these people couldn't be or wouldn't be good leaders, they're not in that position of John Boehner or Mitch McConnell," Gingrey—correctly!—observed.

But how dare he suggest that Rush Limbaugh take a back seat to anybody? Gingrey was pummeled by calls and e-mails from outraged dittoheads. One day later, Gingrey said he regretted his "stupid remarks" and groveled for Limbaugh's forgiveness. "I regret and apologize for the fact that my comments have offended and upset my fellow conservatives—that was not my intent," he insisted.

Then, just to be sure he was fully redeemed, Gingrey appointed himself head of the Rush Limbaugh Fan Club: "Rush Limbaugh, Sean Hannity,

Newt Gingrich, and other conservative giants are the voices of the conservative movement's conscience. Every day, millions and millions of Americans—myself included—turn on their radios and televisions to listen to what they have to say, and we are inspired by their words and by their determination."

The next member of the "I'm Sorry, Rush, Stampede" was Kansas congressman Todd Tiahrt. Asked by a member of the *Kansas City Star* editorial board if Limbaugh was the de facto head of the Republican Party, Tiahrt refused to take the bait. "No, no, he's just an entertainer," the congressman observed.

But, once again, the proverbial stuff hit the fan. This time, it was Tiahrt's turn to crawl on his knees before the mighty Rush. "The congressman believes Rush is a great leader of the conservative movement in America," said a spokesman for Tiahrt. "Nothing the congressman said diminished the role Rush has played and continues to play in the conservative movement."

Not even Republican leaders of the House of Representatives were allowed to say or do anything without first checking with their "boss," as Congressman Eric Cantor, number-two top GOP dog in the House, learned the hard way. In May 2009, he and other GOP leaders announced a series of town halls across the country "so we can get back to listening to the people." Former presidential candidate Mitt Romney, on stage with Cantor, gleefully joined in: "Listening to people can make a difference. That's what we're talking about here, we're listening to people."

The next day, "Chairman" Rush threw cold water on the whole project: "We do not need a listening tour," he lectured Cantor. "We need a teaching tour. That is what the Republican Party, or, slash, the conservative movement needs to focus on. Listening tour ain't it."

Wouldn't you know? Cantor dropped the entire project. It's never been heard of since. The listening tour never happened.

But no one felt Rush's wrath more strongly, nor was forced to bow more deeply, than RNC chair Michael Steele. Rush might even suggest that he forced the chairman to bend over and grab his ankles.

Having just been elected chair of the Republican National Committee, Steele understandably bristled at the suggestion—encouraged by Rush—that he, Steele, was just a figurehead, and that Limbaugh was the *real* head of the party. Appearing on CNN, he decided to set the record straight. "So let's put it into context here. Rush Limbaugh is an entertainer," he explained to viewers. "Rush Limbaugh—his whole thing is entertainment. Yes, it's incendiary. Yes, it's ugly."

Ugly? You bet it got ugly when Rush fired back, accusing Steele of launching "an attack on me even though the premise of what was said to him was false." Limbaugh bitingly dismissed the new chairman as part of the gutless Washington crowd who are afraid of taking on President Obama: "They chicken out when I happen to articulate exactly what their agenda really is. They don't have the guts to admit it, and I do." As proof of Steele's lack of backbone, Limbaugh further accused him of committing the unpardonable (in Rush's eyes) sin of wanting Obama to succeed: "Why do you claim to lead the Republican Party when you seem obsessed with seeing to it President Obama succeeds?"

Whereupon, Steele crawled on his belly to apologize to, yes, the undisputed, *real* intellectual head of the Republican Party. The last thing he wanted to do, Steele whined, was give the impression that Republicans had any other leader than Rush. "My intent was not to go after Rush—I have enormous respect for Rush Limbaugh," he insisted. "I was maybe a little bit inarticulate. . . . There was no attempt on my part to diminish his voice or his *leadership*."

Check—mate!

The only top Republican to get away with saying anything critical about Limbaugh without being forced to apologize is Colin Powell. Asked on CNN if Republicans should continue to follow the lead of Rush Limbaugh, Powell expressed his own grave doubts. "Is this really the kind of party we want to be, where these kinds of spokespersons seem to appeal to our lesser instincts rather than our better instincts?" When Powell refused to back down from his comments, Limbaugh—in his secure position as unofficial head of the GOP—summarily threw the good general out of the party. "What Colin Powell needs to do is close the loop and become a Democrat," Rush decreed from his radio perch, "instead of claiming to be a Republican interested in reforming the Republican Party. He's not. He's a full-fledged Democrat."

So, there's no doubt who is the Republicans' top dog, and no one had dare suggest otherwise. But that does not mean it's good for the party. Limbaugh is, after all, but a radio talk show host. And talk show hosts, by definition, are ill-equipped to lead a political party.

Take it from me. I am one. On a much smaller scale, granted. But, nonetheless, I am one of hundreds of daily radio talk show hosts. And, whether liberal or conservative, we all have two goals: to make noise and to make money. In other words, to get publicity and to get ratings. We are all in it for ourselves. We may talk politics, we may support candidates, we may espouse one particular political point of view, and we may even wear our party affiliation on our sleeve. But we are not there as the official voice of either the Republican or Democratic Party, and we shouldn't be.

There is at least one conservative who understands that reality, and had the courage to express it. In a March 16, 2009, cover story for *Newsweek*, David Frum, former speechwriter for George W. Bush, noted that President Obama and chief of staff Rahm Emanuel had effectively branded Limbaugh as the unofficial head of the Republican Party.

That's just what Republicans don't need, lamented Frum: "A man who is aggressive and bombastic, cutting and sarcastic, who dismisses the concerned citizens in network news focus groups as 'losers.' With his private plane and his cigars, his history of drug dependency and his personal bulk, not to mention his tangled marital history, Rush is a walking stereotype of self-indulgence—exactly the image that Barack Obama most wants to affix to our philosophy and our party. And we're cooperating!"

Frum then accurately described the inherent problem in picking a talk show host as your leader. Limbaugh, he pointed out, "claims 20 million listeners per week, and that suffices to make him a very wealthy man. And if another 100 million people cannot stand him, what does he care? What can they do to him other than . . . not listen? It's not as if they can vote against him."

All well and good, Frum concluded. However, even if those who hate Rush can't hurt him, they can hurt Republicans. "But they can vote against Republican candidates for Congress. They can vote against Republican nominees for president. And if we allow ourselves to be over identified with somebody who earns his fortune by giving offense, they will vote against us."

It's good to have a popular talk show host on your side, in other words. But he's the last person you should count on to lead your political party out of the wilderness. Despite warnings by Frum and others, Republicans seem to have chosen Rush Limbaugh and fellow talker Glenn Beck as their leaders. And they are more than willing to follow them, right over the cliff. As *New York Times* conservative columnist David Brooks noted, "Every single leader of the Republican Party is afraid to take on Rush and Glenn Beck."

8. RUSH LIMBAUGH IS AN ENTERTAINER.

What's funny is that, in the end, critics Frum, Steele, Tiahrt, and Gingrey were right: Rush *is* an entertainer. Every successful talk show host is. If your show is not entertaining, as well as informative, no one will listen.

Remember: Before he was "Rush Limbaugh," he was "Rusty Sharpe" and then "Jeff Christy," spinning records on the radio like any good DJ. He knew his job then, as he knows it now. As an entertainer, Limbaugh's job is to—well, to entertain. So you can expect him to say some funny things. Even outrageous things. Some of which are tongue-in-cheek. It's part of his shtick.

Was he really serious, for example, when he alone defended the torture of prisoners at Abu Ghraib? Even George W. Bush apologized for our brutal treatment of prisoners of war. But not Limbaugh. He compared it to a frat party. A frat party held, incidentally, at Bush's own former fraternity: "This is no different than what happens at the Skull and Bones initiation and we're going to ruin people's lives over it and we're going to hamper our military effort, and then we are going to really hammer them because they had a good time. You know, these people are being fired at every day. I'm talking about people having a good time, these people, you ever heard of emotional release? You ever heard of the need to blow some steam off?"

With that over-the-top defense, Limbaugh, as he clearly intended, didn't convince anybody—but he sure made headlines. Which is the goal of any entertainer. Just like he turned people's heads when he once admitted: "I had a dream, I had a dream that I was a slave building a Sphinx in a desert that looked like Obama." For years, psychiatrists will have a dream analyzing that statement!

And, of course, the whole Operation Chaos campaign was pure performance art. The media may have taken it seriously. Clearly, Rush never did. He changed from asking listeners to vote against McCain, to asking them to re-register and vote for Clinton, to asking them to vote for Obama—whatever was necessary to keep the gimmick alive and keep people talking about it. P. T. Barnum would have been proud. What's surprising is that, as an entertainer, Rush has been so commercially successful—yet remains so politically unpopular. There's a good reason Limbaugh's never run for public office: He couldn't win!

In March 2009, smack-dab in the middle of his public spat with Michael Steele, CBS News took a national poll to test Limbaugh's popularity. The results were not what you might expect.

For a talk show host who brags about appearing on over five hundred radio stations, with 20 million listeners a week, 41 percent of Americans had no opinion of him. Only 19 percent had a favorable opinion. And 40 percent registered an unfavorable opinion. CBS's findings mirrored a concurrent survey of one thousand 2008 voters conducted for Democracy Corps by the polling firm Greenberg Quinlan Rosner. In their findings, voters viewed Limbaugh negatively by a two-to-one ratio, 53 to 26 percent—with 45 percent viewing him very negatively. Perhaps more significantly, by almost two to one, 57 to 32 percent, voters said Rush does not "share their values."

Limbaugh dismissed the significance of both polls. Which he should. Because those numbers, no matter how abysmal, mean nothing to an entertainer—as long as he continues to attract an audience.

But the negative findings reinforce David Frum's warnings about the perils Republicans face in embracing Limbaugh as their political savior. Democrats could wish for nothing better.

There is, however, one consolation for Limbaugh. He is no longer alone. He is now surrounded by a whole galaxy of right-wing talk show hosts who are every bit as reckless with the truth as he is.

Rush is not jealous about all the competition on conservative talk radio. Instead, he takes credit for having "spawned" them—starting with Glenn Beck.

2

GLENN BECK, THE BIG CRYBABY

In the world of right-wing talk, after Rush Limbaugh, there is Glenn Beck.

In fact, whether you're talking ratings or headlines, Beck has been so successful in his relatively brief time at Fox News, he even threatens to overtake Rush himself. Christopher Ruddy, president of *Newsmax*, one of the top conservative blogs, calls Beck "the No. 1 populist, conservative voice in the media." But Limbaugh insists he's not worried. In fact, he takes all the credit for Beck's success.

In her interview for NBC's *Today* show, correspondent Jamie Gangel asked Rush, "Do you worry about the new kid on the block?"

"No," responded Rush. "Look. In 1988, I'm the only national conservative voice. Now look at conservative media. Look what I have spawned. Glenn Beck to me is right on, daddy-o. Glenn Beck is a result of my success."

Now, it is true that Glenn Beck is Rush Limbaugh's most successful acolyte. But there's a big difference between the two.

Rush Limbaugh is so sure of himself, he could never admit he was wrong about anything. Glenn Beck is just the opposite. He's so unsure of himself, he looks like he could break down in tears at any minute—and often does.

Rush Limbaugh is cocky. Glenn Beck is needy.

Rush Limbaugh's in charge. Glenn Beck's in therapy.

Yet, say whatever you want about him—and don't worry, I will!—Beck is also an amazing success story. After eking out a living as a Top 40 DJ while struggling with alcoholism and various drug addictions, he cleaned himself up and got his start as a radio talk show host in 2000 on WFLA-AM in Tampa, Florida.

Two years later, he leaped into national radio syndication with Premiere Radio Networks and moved his show to Philadelphia. In 2006, CNN recruited him to host his own evening show on Headline News. After only two years at CNN, he bounced onto the prime-time lineup on Fox News, where he soon catapulted right up there with Bill O'Reilly and Sean Hannity, and far outperformed his competition on CNN or MS-NBC. In his new slot on Fox, Beck also emerged as a powerful new political force. Not even Rush Limbaugh was able to embarrass President Obama into firing two members of his White House team.

That's a long way to go for a guy who calls himself an "alcoholic rodeo clown" and for a talk show host whom *Time* magazine, in a glowing cover story profile, could only describe as a "pudgy, buzz-cut, weeping phenomenon of radio, TV, and books."

Yet Beck's brand of tearful paranoia seems to fit perfectly the mood of today's beleaguered conservatives, much as Sean Hannity was the perfect voice for the early, headstrong days of the George W. Bush administration, and Rush Limbaugh's optimism just what the doctor ordered for conservatives when Reagan was in the White House. He lives by sowing fear and stoking outrage. First: "Here's what I'm scared of, and you should be, too." And then: "Here's what we gonna do about it, dammit." In a way, he resembles no one so much as Howard Beale, the mad anchorman in *Network*, standing up in the middle of his newscast and screaming, "I'm mad as hell, and I'm not going to take this anymore." The difference, of course, is that Beale implodes because he gets sick of spewing standard-issue media bullshit. Beck never tires of it. The formula works in more ways than one, winning both audience and income for Glenn Beck. He has the third-highest-rated radio talk show and is the third-highest-paid performer. And on Fox, even with an unenviable 5 P.M. time slot, he sometimes beats the numbers Bill O'Reilly and Sean Hannity pull in prime time. A devoted reader and promoter of thriller novels, he sells so many books he's been called the "Conservative Oprah." And he's even launched his own political action network, "The 9/12 Project."

Beck appears as uncomfortable with his success as his critics, as if he can't believe where he is or what he's saying. He comes across like a guy who just broke into the studio and is always looking over his shoulder for the security guard to throw him off the set. And you sometimes have to wonder if he's so perceptive that he sees things the rest of us would never pick up on—or if he's just flat-out schizophrenic.

On May 29, 2009, for example, he asked his viewers: "When did we get to the place in America to where we can't have disagreements without demonizing each other?" Now, you might expect that statement from Barack Obama. But Glenn Beck? This is the man who does more demonizing on television than anybody else, with the possible exception of Sean Hannity.

It was, after all, Glenn Beck who appeared on *Fox & Friends* on July 28, 2009, and called President Obama a "racist."

Beck had been invited on the lively morning program to talk about the big flap surrounding President Obama's comments on the arrest of Harvard professor Henry Louis Gates in Cambridge, Massachusetts. The well-known American history scholar, a friend of Obama's, had been reported to police on suspicion of breaking and entering, after forcing open the front door to his house upon returning from a trip to China. But even after proving he was, in fact, in his own home, Gates was arrested by Cambridge police and taken to police headquarters. At a prime-time news conference, Obama said—correctly, if not so artfully—that the police officer had acted "stupidly."

Asked for his reaction, Beck volunteered: "This president, I think, has exposed himself as a guy, over and over and over again, who has a deep-seated hatred for white people, or the white culture, I don't know what it is."

That was too much even for the conservative Fox anchor. To his credit, Brian Kilmeade immediately challenged Beck: "You can't say he doesn't like white people. David Axelrod's white, Rahm Emanuel, his chief of staff, is white. I think 70 percent of the people we see every day are white. Robert Gibbs is white." (Kilmeade might also have reminded him that Obama's mother was white.)

But Beck wouldn't let go: "I'm not saying that he doesn't like white people. I'm saying he has a problem. He has a . . . *This guy, I believe, is a racist.*"

This kind of personal attack is very much the pattern for Beck. He is, in fact, a serial name-caller.

He called Hillary Clinton a "stereotypical bitch."

He called Cindy Sheehan a "tragedy slut."

He called Jimmy Carter a "waste of skin."

And, just two months earlier, he had also called Obama's Supreme Court nominee Sonia Sotomayor a racist. But calling the president of the United States a racist?

That's kind of extreme, don't you think? Even for Fox News, and especially coming from a Fox anchor, and not just some wacky guest.

After years of ugly personal attacks by Bill O'Reilly, Sean Hannity, and others, you might have thought there was no limit on what Fox anchors could say and get away with, no line they could cross without getting away with it. But Glenn Beck may finally have found it.

Later that same day, Fox News put out a statement disclaiming any ties to Beck's comments. A Fox spokesperson told *TVNewser* blog that Beck had "expressed a personal opinion, which represented his own views, not those of the Fox News Channel." Yet Beck continues on the air with his own program, and frequently pops up on other Fox shows.

He may not be making as much money for Fox, however. Two days after he called the president a racist, Color of Change, a coalition of African-American political organizations, began a campaign directed at Beck's commercial sponsors. It asked its 600,000 members to contact advertisers and demand that they stop running ads on *The Glenn Beck Program*. The overwhelmingly positive response surprised even the leaders of Color of Change.

Most boycotts never get off the ground. This one took off. Within weeks, over eighty major retailers ordered their spots withdrawn from *The Glenn Beck Program*. Giant ConAgra led the way, explaining: "We are firmly committed to diversity, and we would like to prevent the potential perception that advertising during this program was an endorsement of the viewpoints shared." Other firms that pulled their spots included: Geico, Procter & Gamble, Roche, Sanofi-Aventis, RadioShack, GMAC Financial Services, Men's Wearhouse, State Farm, Progressive Insurance, Walmart, Sprint, Clorox, CVS, Capital One, Discover, HSBC, Infiniti, Mercedes-Benz, and Best Buy.

Glenn Beck responded to the boycott in typical right-wing fashion: He doubled-down. Instead of apologizing for calling President Obama a "racist," which would have been the decent thing to do, he stepped up his attacks, accusing Obama of filling his administration with communist agitators to help him turn America into a communist state like Cuba, and—get this!—doing so quietly, through the ruse of an election. Imagine that! On November 4, 2008, we didn't participate in an election to choose a new president and change the direction of America. We were duped. We signed on to a coup d'état! At least, if you're crazy enough to believe Glenn Beck. "There is a revolution," he warned his viewers, "and they think they can get away with it quietly. They think they—and they—they—you know what? At this point, gang, I'm not sure, they may be able to because they are so far ahead of us. They know what they're dealing against; most of America does not yet. Most of America doesn't have a clue as to what's going on. There is a coup going on. There is a stealing of America, and the way it is done, it has been done through the—the guise of an election, but they lied to us the entire time."

How could so many millions of us have been so naive to have been tricked into a revolution disguised as an election? But when we do, someday, finally wake up and realize what's happened, Beck says: Don't say I didn't warn you! "Some of us knew! Some of us, we're shouting out, you were: 'This guy's a Marxist!' 'No, no, no, no, no, no.' And they're gonna say, 'We did it democratically,' and they're going to grab power every way they can. And God help us in an emergency."

At this point, it's worth pointing out that the one national election that did, indeed, constitute a coup d'état happened in 2000, when five conservative members of the Supreme Court seized power and anointed George W. Bush the president of the United States. Funny, I don't remember Glenn Beck or other conservatives manning the ramparts against revolution back then.

You will also remember that, following the heroic example of Al Gore, Democrats accepted the court's deeply dubious decision and allowed the new administration to take over, even though they still disagreed with Bush's policies. That's a far cry from how conservatives treated the new and democratically elected Obama administration.

It's a big and dangerous leap from disagreeing with an incumbent president's policies to accusing him of being a traitor and turning the country into a communist dictatorship. And it's such a big lie, you would think it would be hard for anyone to believe. Just the opposite. Professional liars know that the bigger the lie, the more gullible the audience. It's the little lies nobody believes, as another odious character once wrote:

> The broad masses of a nation are always more easily corrupted in the deeper strata of their emotional nature than consciously or voluntarily; and thus in the primitive simplicity of their minds they more readily fall victims to the big lie than the small lie, since they themselves often tell small lies in little matters but would be ashamed to resort to large-scale falsehoods. It would never come into their heads to fabricate colossal untruths, and they would not believe that others could have the impudence to distort the truth so infamously. Even though the facts which prove this to be so may be brought clearly to their minds, they will still doubt and waver and will continue to think that there may be some other explanation. For the grossly impudent lie always leaves traces behind it, even after it has been nailed down, a fact which is known to all expert liars in this world and to all who conspire together in the art of lying.

Just to prove that both sides can play this invoking-the-Nazis game, that was Adolf Hitler, writing in *Mein Kampf.*

If, indeed, we are in the middle of a Fascist, socialist, Marxist, and/or communist takeover of our government, you might fairly ask: How could Obama even pull off such a coup? Beck has the answer to that, too. He's further accused Obama of planning to force his radical agenda on Americans by creation of a "National Civilian Security Force"—as strong, and as well armed, as the military. Beck warned that this would be a Gestapo-like force of heavily armed, uniformed goons that he actually compared to Hitler's SS troops and Saddam Hussein's paramilitary force, the fedayeen.

That's enough to put the fear of God into anyone listening. Until you realize that what President Obama was talking about when he called for expansion of a "national civilian security force" was expanding the size of such volunteer, public service projects as the Peace Corps, Ameri-Corps, Go Teach America, and the Green Jobs Corps. In so doing, Obama was continuing the tradition of volunteerism advocated by every American president, Republican and Democrat, since FDR created the Civilian Conservation Corps, inspired by William James's call for the "moral equivalent of war." Only a very sick man could compare young Americans repairing trails in our national parks or teaching in inner city classrooms to Hitler's ruthless, trained killers. But, then again, Glenn Beck is a very sick man.

Finally, and most blatantly, Glenn proceeded to charge Obama with filling the White House with "czars"—known "communists" and "revolutionaries"—who had no other purpose than to deliver Obama's own radical agenda. His first target: a relatively low-level environmental adviser named Van Jones.

Jones hardly fits the profile of a dangerous radical, unless saving the environment is your definition of subversive activity. Actually, he fits the profile of a new generation of African-American leaders like Barack Obama, Cory Booker, and Deval Patrick, who have risen from difficult circumstances to positions of leadership in their communities.

A pioneer in the development of "green jobs," he led creation of the nation's first Green Jobs Corps in Oakland, California, in 2005. That same year, he also helped found the Web-based Color of Change—which, as noted above, spearheaded the 2009 sponsor boycott of *The Glenn Beck Program*. But Jones had left the organization in 2007. One year later, in January 2008, he launched "Green for All," a national NGO whose mission is to help lift people out of poverty through green jobs—work for which he was recognized by *Time* magazine as one of its "Environmental Heroes" and one of the hundred most influential people in the country. In March 2009, he joined the Obama administration as a special adviser for Green Jobs, Enterprise and Innovation at the White House Council on Environmental Quality—where he was singled out for praise by presidential adviser Valerie Jarrett and First Lady Michelle Obama.

Yet all that good work was for nothing. Beck bore down on two relatively harmless mistakes in Jones's past. Years ago, he had, strangely enough, signed a petition urging an investigation into the bizarre theory that George Bush and Dick Cheney had actually staged the September 11 attacks. Even though Californians are known for signing any petition shoved in their face, that was a stupid and inexplicable mistake on Jones's part. But is just asking for an investigation really a fireable offense?

And, more recently, Jones had referred to Republicans who were trying to derail Obama's health care reform as "assholes." Hey, if the shoe fits . . .

Which means, of course, that I will never qualify for a job in the Obama administration. I've called many Republicans "assholes," as well as a few Democrats. But what you and I might be able to get away with proved too much of a burden for Van Jones.

A mere two weeks after Beck launched his personal attack on him, Jones resigned from the Obama White House, citing a campaign of "lies and distortions" that he feared would distract from the president's legislative agenda.

Van Jones thus became Victim No. 1 of the Glenn Beck purge. And suddenly McCarthyism was back, with a vicious and reckless new leader, but the same old, ugly smear tactics. Through the lies he spread about Jones, painting him as a dangerous, violent radical planted in the very heart of the administration, Beck—with no help from Congress (on vacation) and little help from other conservative talk show hosts—was single-handedly able to force the resignation of a talented young Obama aide.

Followed, shortly, by another one. Yosi Sergant served briefly in the Obama administration as communications director of the National Endowment for the Arts—until he, too, came under fire from Glenn Beck.

Sergant's sin was participating in a conference call in which artists were encouraged to support, and perhaps create artwork supporting, President Obama's call for national service. Again, as noted above, most people don't see national service as a subversive activity. But, for Glenn Beck, it is pure evil. He accused Sergant and the NEA of engaging in Nazi-like propaganda. "Your government is trying to trick you, use your tax dollars to change your mind," he told his television audience. "It's called propaganda. The people involved in the conference call, including the White House, knew that this was on the fence if not outright illegal." After Beck raised the issue, Sergant was first reassigned and then voluntarily resigned. Glenn Beck had struck again.

That was scary. And nobody believed that, having twice tasted blood, vampire Beck would stop there. Indeed, the next day he sent out a message to his followers on Twitter: "FIND EVERYTHING YOU CAN ON CASS SUNSTEIN, MARK LLOYD AND CAROL BROWNER."

Apparently, they didn't find much. Because Sunstein remained director of the Office of Information and Regulatory Affairs in OMB; Lloyd continued as diversity chief at the FCC; and Browner hung on as Obama's top energy and environmental adviser in the White House. Beck also misfired when he tried to take down John Holdren. An expert on renewable energy and former professor of environmental policy at Harvard's Kennedy School, Holdren was appointed director of the White House Office of Science and Technology Policy. In short, he is President Obama's science and technology adviser.

Beck's beef with Holdren was a book on population control, *Ecoscience*, which he co-authored back in 1977, with Stanford professors Paul and Anne Ehrlich. At that time, early in the development of the conservation movement, population control—not global warming—was considered the most serious environmental issue facing the planet. Holdren and the

Ehrlichs speculated about what might happen if indeed, as feared, the world's population exploded to the point where it endangered the survival of the human species. If that ever happened, they surmised—a big IF—some governments might resort to such measures as compulsory abortion or mandatory sterilization.

Note: In their book, they did not call for or endorse such steps. Again, they merely conjectured what might follow *if* the worst projections about rapid population growth actually came true.

In the meantime, of course, the population growth rate has decreased, rather than increased. All their doomsday predictions failed to come true. And Holdren and the Ehrlichs now focus on other, more real and pressing environmental issues.

Holdren's over-three-decades-old musings are so out-of-date, in fact, that they were hardly even mentioned in his confirmation hearings before the United States Senate. The extent of discussion on this topic is summed up in the following exchange with Republican David Vitter of Louisiana:

"Vitter: Do you think determining optimal population is a role of government?"

"Holdren: No, Senator, I do not."

Holdren was unanimously confirmed in his job by the U.S. Senate. And, at this point, Holdren still has his job.

That hasn't stopped Glenn Beck. He continues to warn of a communist conspiracy in the Obama White House. He's still targeting Obama White House staffers. He's still demanding that every Obama appointee answer the question: "Are you now, or have you ever been . . ." And, sad to say, he still pulls in over 2 million viewers a night, and there are still plenty of amoral advertisers willing to air their commercials on his program.

But the controversies he's stirred up should serve as a warning to Fox News that they now have a ticking time bomb on their hands. Like Senator Joseph McCarthy, whose tactics he employs, it's only a matter of time before Glenn Beck goes too far and blows himself up. Indeed, he's already almost done so on several occasions.

KILLER INSTINCT

Actually, President Obama is probably lucky. At least, Glenn Beck only called him a racist. He didn't say he wanted to kill him. (Of course, had he done so, the Secret Service might have done us all a favor and put him in prison.) Instead, Beck cast his death threat at a much less well-protected target: Michael Moore.

Back in 2005, Beck was musing aloud about what some people might be willing to do for $50 million. With an alacrity that will fascinate generations of psychiatrists, Beck immediately thought about strangling filmmaker Moore.

"Would you kill someone for that? I'm thinking about killing Michael Moore, and I'm wondering if I could kill him myself, or if I would need to hire someone to do it . . . No, I think I could. I think he could be looking me in the eye, you know, and I could just be choking the life out. Is this wrong?" Yes, it's wrong. And yes, it's weird.

Ever since he stopped wearing his "What Would Jesus Do" band, Beck confessed, he'd lost all sense of right and wrong. "I used to be able to say 'Yeah, I'd kill Michael Moore,' and then I'd see the little band: What Would Jesus Do? And then I'd realize, 'Oh, you wouldn't kill Michael Moore. Or at least, you wouldn't choke him to death.' And you know, well, now I'm not sure."

Of course, the Bible says that even lusting in your heart is as bad as doing the act. Same with murder. But we'll leave that up to Beck and his Creator. For now.

Michael Moore isn't Beck's only death target, by the way. He just has a different fate in mind for an Ohio congressman: "Every night I get down on my knees and pray that Dennis Kucinich will burst into flames."

And an equally brutal end for New York's Congressman Charles Rangel: "We've been sitting here for the last few minutes trying to come up with a list of people that I want to kill with a shovel, people that I'd just like to whack over the head with a shovel. . . . How many people have I said let's kill with a shovel, huh? How many people have I said let's light 'em up and shoot 'em in the head? I think quite a few. You know, every-body who has a stinkin' opinion now seems to be an extremist. There doesn't seem to be anybody that actually makes any sense that can get any face time on television. It's all people like Jesse Jackson or Charles Rangel. Now, there's a guy. There's where we start, Charles Rangel. Do you have any sound effects for me? (sound effects) Charlie Rangel. See, I feel better already. There's a time for everything. To every purpose there is a season. And let me tell you, baby, today the season is: clubbin' people over the head with shovels."

Now, I don't think threatening to club people over the head with shov-els is quite what our Founding Fathers had in mind when they wrote the First Amendment. But maybe I'm just old-fashioned.

BLAMING THE VICTIMS

When Hurricane Katrina struck New Orleans in September 2005, most Americans were appalled by the disastrously slow government response and felt sorry for the thousands stranded and herded into the Astrodome. But not Glenn Beck. He joined Neal Boortz and other right-wing talk show hosts in attacking the victims of Hurricane Katrina because they were too dumb to get out of town ahead of the storm.

Of course, most of those left behind in New Orleans had no car, or could not afford transportation, to get out of Dodge. But Beck didn't care. He still called them "scumbags" and blasted them for not queuing up like the British when rescue workers showed up to hand out $2,000 ATM cards.

As if that wasn't insensitive enough—fasten your seat belts!—while thinking about how much he hated the victims of Katrina, Beck was re-minded how much he also loathed the victims of September 11: "I didn't think I could hate victims faster than the 9/11 victims." Like the stranded families in New Orleans, Beck despised the families who lost loved ones on 9/11 because they wouldn't just shut up and go away. "This is horrible to say, and I wonder if I'm alone in this," he admitted, "you know it took me about a year to start hating the 9/11 victims' families? Took me about a year. And I had such compassion for them, and I really wanted to help them, and I was behind, you know, 'Let's give them money, let's get this started.' All of this stuff. And I really didn't—of the three thousand victims' families, I don't hate all of them. Probably about ten of them. And when I see a 9/11 victim family on television, or whatever, I'm just like, 'Oh, shut up!' I'm so sick of them because they're always complaining."

Using the same tortured reasoning, Beck lashed out at the father of Nick Berg, the young American contractor in Iraq beheaded by al Qaeda operatives on videotape. While Nick Berg supported Bush's war in Iraq, his father, Michael, did not—and said so even after his son was killed. Still, the Bush White House sent the president's condolences to the Berg family. Glenn Beck wasn't so generous: "I find this guy despicable. Everything in me says that. The want-to-be-a-better-person-today-than-I-was-yesterday says he's a dad, he's grieving, but I don't buy it. I think he is grieving, but I think he's a scumbag as well. I don't like this guy at all."

Spoken like a true compassionate conservative.

MUSLIMS HATE AMERICA

Do you think maybe we're seeing a recurring theme here? Glenn Beck sees the world in clearly defined blocks: All hurricane victims are lazy; all blacks and Latinos are racists; all Democrats are socialists; and, of course, all Muslims hate America.

He admitted as much when he interviewed Minnesota's Keith Ellison, shortly after he'd become the first Muslim elected to the U.S. Congress. That should have been an occasion to celebrate America's diversity and the fact that, while some Muslims were fanning the flames of hatred against the United States, most—like Keith Ellison—were devoted Americans, working hard to protect and serve this country.

Not so for Glenn Beck. Simply because of Ellison's religious faith, Beck lumped him in with Osama bin Laden. Insisting he meant "no offense," Beck nonetheless began his interview: "I have to tell you, I have been nervous about this interview with you, because what I feel like saying is, 'Sir, prove to me that you are not working with our enemies.'" (Reminder: The man had just been elected to Congress!) Beck continued: "I'm not accusing you of being an enemy, but that's the way I feel, and I think a lot of Americans will feel that way."

A lot of Americans feel the same way about all Muslims? As Jon Stewart quipped the next day: "Finally, a guy who says what people who aren't thinking are thinking."

Ellison showed a lot of class in his response. Rather than blowing up at Beck (which any self-respecting terrorist would have done) or break down in tears (which Glenn Beck would have done), Ellison coolly replied: "The people of the Fifth Congressional District know that I have a deep love and affection for my country. There's no one who is more patriotic than I am. And so, you know, I don't need to . . . need to prove my patriotic stripes."

"And I'm not asking you to," insisted Beck. But, of course, he just had. A couple of days later, Beck defended himself by saying he only asked the question because nobody talks in this country "about who the bad guys are and who the good guys are." And, naturally, since Ellison is a Muslim, he's a bad guy.

GORING AL GORE

Every radio talk show host has his or her favorite topics or targets: issues they're excited about, or issues that drive them crazy. Two things, among many others, drive Beck crazy: ACORN and global warming.

Even George W. Bush finally admitted that global warming is real. Glenn Beck's not only still in denial, he believes that people like Al Gore, who are trying to get the United States to do something about climate change, are evil. He even accused Gore, in warning about the dangers facing the planet because of global warming, of practicing Hitler's aforementioned Big Lie theory: "It was Goebbels or Hitler that talked about lies. The bigger, the more audacious the lie, the easier it is for people to buy." See, when it comes to lies, Beck knows whereof he speaks. That being said, talk about paranoia. Beck actually believes the global warming movement is not about saving the planet, but about eliminating people. Because people cause pollution, he argues, cutting back on pollution means cutting back on people. In his sick mind, it's the ultimate form of population control.

And again, the comparison to Hitler: "Al Gore's not going to be rounding up Jews and exterminating them. It is the same tactic, however. The goal is different. The goal is globalization. The goal is global carbon tax. . . . You need to have fear. You needed to have the fear of starvation. You needed to have the fear of the whole place going to hell in a handbasket. . . . And you must silence all dissenting voices. That's what Hitler did. That's what Al Gore, the U.N., and everybody on the global warming bandwagon are doing."

Attempts by Democrats in Congress to reduce emissions of greenhouse gases through a free market "cap and trade" system are, in Beck's paranoid worldview, nothing less than a direct attack on the American way of life. On climate change legislation, he agreed with the assessment of crazy Minnesota congresswoman Michele Bachmann—"You're either for freedom, or you're not." And he called supporters of the legislation "either the dumbest people to ever walk the face of the earth, which I think some of them are. They are just greedy, and just want their own power and their own control. . . . Or they believe in a different system other than the Republic, which I think some of them do. They have exposed themselves as incompetent, they have exposed themselves as wicked, they have exposed themselves, quite honestly, as treasonous. I think some of them are treasonous."

Beck has a different idea of how to save the planet: by destroying it. On April 22, 2009, he rejoiced in a call from a listener outside Cleveland who was celebrating Earth Day by using his chain saw to cut down trees. "This is nirvana here, this is pure eroticism," Beck purred, as the chain saw whirred away in the background.

I can just imagine the bumper sticker on Glenn Beck's Hummer: "Save the Whales, Cut Down a Tree."

THE MIGHTY ACORN

Once the 2008 election was over and Barack Obama was safely settled into the White House, conservatives forgot all about ACORN. Right?

Wrong! For some of them, ACORN—the Chicago-based community activist organization Barack Obama never belonged to, but once represented in court—remained the number-one target of criticism, manufactured outrage, and downright paranoia. And, after Sean Hannity, no one seemed more obsessed with ACORN than Glenn Beck.

Indeed, once Obama was in the White House, rather than leave ACORN behind him, Beck accused the new president of trying to lure the entire country into ACORN's thrall. "Our president is not just bankrupting our country, he is fundamentally transforming it as he promised, and he is doing it to the core. In the next few years, I promise you America will look more like ACORN in structure and less like anything our Founders had in mind."

Once again seeing an evil conspiracy in the making, Beck declared that ACORN had joined forces with SEIU, the nation's biggest labor union, to create a giant "thugocracy"—and it's all done with Obama's blessing. "Their chief organizer is the president of the United States," he asserted, again with zero supporting evidence. "SEIU is part of ACORN." (*Not true.*) "ACORN and SEIU—stop separating them in your head. They are the same group of people. SEIU is the one that is pushing health care through. They're the ones that met with the drug companies. They're the ones—these are the people that are strong-arming. When Walmart decides to meet and decide on whether or not they're for health care, who meets with them? SEIU. These people are thugs." True to the old McCarthy game, Beck did everything but call them card-carrying members.

There is, of course, a smidgen of truth here. Long before Obama ever got to the White House, the SEIU did mount a very successful campaign to pressure Walmart into providing health insurance to its employees. And Walmart ended up doing the right thing, for which SEIU organizers get the credit. There were meetings. There were ads. There were pickets. But there was no violence. Where's the thugocracy?

In Beck's scary world, the conspiracy doesn't end there. He claims Obama allowed the economy to collapse in order to force young people to join ACORN and AmeriCorps. He accuses Obama of using the combined forces of the student loan program, the census, ACORN, SEIU, and AmeriCorps to create a "modern-day slave state" that will be better funded than the military. He asserts that their goal is nothing short of transforming the United States into a "socialist-Marxist state." And, in perhaps the most bizarre conspiracy theory of all, he insists that ACORN inspired Obama to arrange for Lynn Sweet of the *Chicago Sun-Times* to ask about the arrest of Professor Gates in order to rally community organizers to support his health care reform legislation.

Paranoia, thy name is Glenn Beck. He makes the black-helicopter crowd seem almost sane by comparison. At times, he even makes Michael Savage seem sane—and that, as we will see shortly, is no small feat.

Often in the news business you hear the phrase: "You can't make this stuff up." Which is true, for most people. The problem is that Glenn Beck *does* make stuff up. Indeed, his show offers little more than a pure neurotic, on camera, expressing his worst possible fears: based, not on reality, but on his own sick imagination. If anybody truly believed Glenn Beck, they'd think the world was going to end tomorrow!

POLITICAL PROVOCATEUR

One thing that makes Glenn Beck's show unique is that he is more than willing to use his radio and television megaphone to promote political activity.

It's a tactic frowned upon by many other talkers. Rush Limbaugh dismisses it as either phony or unnecessary. "I don't rally people and haven't since the first year of my radio show," he told *Politico* (even though he reveled in launching Operation Chaos during the 2008 primary campaign). But Beck enjoys whipping up the masses, appealing to the Ross Perot or Ron Paul, hate-government crowd—and has done so with considerable success.

He encouraged Fox viewers to turn out for so-called Tea Parties on April 15, 2009, and spoke to the crowd assembled at the Alamo. He helped fan the flames of anger that drove people to congressional town halls in August 2009. And he personally called for, helped organize, and relentlessly promoted a Tea Party March on Washington on September 12 for which, according to him, 1.7 million people showed up. D.C. police estimated the crowd at only seventy thousand, but still nothing to sneer about.

As noted above, Beck's political activity has won him praise from some fellow conservatives, but scorn from others. Talk show host Mike Gallagher paid him the ultimate compliment: "People have asked me, 'Who's the next Rush,' because Rush is the gold standard. The answer seems to be Glenn." And Washington Republican lobbyist Grover Norquist gives Beck credit for "playing more of a rallying role than Limbaugh has or is."

Other conservatives think just the opposite. Peter Wehner, a former adviser to President George W. Bush, wrote that Beck is "harmful to the conservative movement" because he's so "erratic," "bizarre," and too obsessed with "conspiracy theories." And MSNBC's Joe Scarborough, former Republican congressman from Pensacola, does not hide his disdain for Beck: "You cannot preach hatred. You cannot say the president is racist. You cannot say things that have very deadly consequences."

New York Times columnist David Brooks doesn't buy any of it. He believes the political strength or appeal of conservative talk show hosts like Limbaugh and Beck is pure media hype, which, unfortunately, Republican politicians fall into—to the detriment of the party. In 2008, despite all the media attention, they weren't successful either in preventing the primary victory of John McCain or the general election victory of Barack Obama, Brooks points out. And, no matter how much noise they make, they won't succeed in derailing Obama's presidency or rebuilding an ever-shrinking Republican Party.

"The rise of Beck, Hannity, Bill O'Reilly and the rest has correlated almost perfectly with the decline of the G.O.P.," Brooks wrote in a scathing *New York Times* column entitled "The Wizard of Beck." "But it's not because the talk jocks have real power. It's because they have illusory power, because Republicans hear the media mythology and fall for it every time." Appearing later on *Meet the Press*, Brooks actually called out "Glenn Beck, Rush Limbaugh, Mark Levin, and all these guys" as "loons" and "harmful for America." Contrary to what the talk show hosts would have us believe, says Brooks, "they have actually no power over real Americans. It's all a media circus."

Republican strategist Mike Murphy, who directed McCain's 2000 primary campaign, followed Brooks on *Meet the Press* and agreed: "The noisiest parts of kind of the conservative media machine have far less influence than the mainstream media machine that covers the Republican world thinks they do," Murphy noted. "These radio guys can't deliver a pizza, let alone the nomination."

WHITE HOUSE WAR

While Brooks and Murphy may have discounted their influence, Beck, Hannity, and O'Reilly proved just the opposite. They managed to spew out so much anti-Obama bile that the White House was finally forced to respond, starting at the very top.

In an interview with John Harwood of CNBC, as noted earlier, President Obama admitted that he knew what he was up against in the world of cable television: "I've got one television station [network] that is entirely devoted to attacking my administration." When Harwood said he assumed the president was talking about Fox News, Obama didn't even pretend otherwise: "Well, that's a pretty big megaphone, and you'd be hard-pressed if you watched the entire day to find a positive story about me on that front."

The White House war on Fox continued on September 20 when President Obama appeared on every Sunday morning show except Fox and, later, when Communications Director Anita Dunn stepped up on CNN's *Reliable Sources*. Pressed by Howard Kurtz for the Obama administration's honest appraisal of the level of treatment they received from Fox News, she didn't hold back: "Let's be realistic here, Howie. They are widely viewed as, you know, a part of the Republican Party. Take their talking points, put them on the air. Take their opposition research, put them on the air, and that's fine. But let's not pretend they're a news network the way CNN is."

In response, Fox News was relatively quiet—except for Glenn Beck. He first accused the Obama White House of being "more worried about the war on Fox than the actual war in Afghanistan." Which was kind of strange, given Beck's own priorities. As Media Matters for America noted, he hadn't paid much attention to Afghanistan, either. From the launch of his show on Fox until October 14, 2009, Beck had talked about ACORN some 1,224 times, and only talked about the Taliban thirty-eight times. He had attacked green jobs czar Van Jones 267 times, yet only condemned former Taliban leader and wanted terrorist Mullah Omar twice.

Next, true to form, Beck went where he always goes when trying to make a point. He compared the Obama White House to the Nazis. In an almost comic twist on Pastor Martin Niemöller's classic poem about the indifference of German intellectuals during the Nazi rise to power, Beck warned his viewers:

"When they're done with Fox, and you decide to speak out on something. The old, 'first they came for the Jews, and I wasn't Jewish.' When you have a question, and you believe that something should be asked, they're a—totally fine with you right now; they have no problem with you.

"When they're done with Fox and talk radio, do you really think they're going to leave you alone if you want to ask a tough question? Do you really think that a man who has never had to stand against tough questions and has as much power as he does—do you really believe after he takes out the number one news network, do you really think that this man is then not going to turn on you? That you and your little organization is going to cause him any hesitation at all not to take you out?

"If you believe that, you should open up a history book, because you've missed the point of many brutal dictators. You missed the point on how they always start."

One thing's for sure. If Beck felt rejected by the Obama White House, he could also join other Fox hosts in feeling showered with love by the Republican National Committee. With good reason. He worked hard to serve them. But nobody at Fox carried the Republican Party banner higher and prouder than the wannabe Republican candidate—for Senate? For president?—Sean Hannity.

3

SEAN HANNITY, PARTY HACK

If your church is looking for a new altar boy, Sean Hannity might not be a bad choice. If your community's looking for a new Boy Scout leader, might I suggest Sean Hannity. If you're looking for a cute, Irish husband for your daughter, Sean Patrick Hannity might just do the trick.

But if you're looking for an independent thinker who speaks the truth about the important issues of the day, Sean Hannity is the last person you'd want for the job. Because, boyish good looks aside, Sean Hannity is little more than the loyal, fast-talking parrot of the Republican National Committee, trained to repeat whatever outrageous new talking points they deposit in the bottom of his bird cage every morning. As we will see, his willingness to embrace, embellish, and then broadcast every lie the Republicans put forth about Barack Obama and Hillary Clinton in 2008 earned him the title "Misinformer of the Year" from Media Matters for America. And, given the tough competition from Rush, Beck, Savage, and the rest of his talk radio peers, that's quite an accomplishment.

Of all the Rush Limbaugh wannabes, Hannity is by far the most successful. He appears on more stations, reaches more people, and makes more money than any conservative talk show host, other than Rush. He has his own television show on Fox News. He even has his own dating service.

But compared to Rush, Hannity will always be the bridesmaid, and never the bride. If he were a drug, he'd be the close, but nowhere near as good, generic substitute. Rush is the real thing. Hannity is basically Rush blow-dried and spruced up for popular consumption by the GOP.

Hannity's meteoric rise in radio began when the college dropout from Long Island, working as a general contractor in Santa Barbara, started calling talk shows to defend Ollie North during the Iran-contra hearings. Producers at the University of California's volunteer college station, KCSB-FM, liked the brash young caller so much they gave him his own radio show, which lasted only a few months. But Hannity cleverly parlayed that experience into landing other talk show host gigs, first in Huntsville, Alabama, and then Atlanta. Fox News discovered him there in CNN's backyard in 1996 and offered him a nightly TV spot against a yet-to-be hired liberal, who turned out to be Alan Colmes.

Hannity & Colmes debuted in October 1996 and soon grew to be one of Fox's highest-rated programs, second only to *The O'Reilly Factor*. After twelve years, however, both Fox and Hannity were tired of sharing the platform with a liberal—even a polite, relatively harmless, domesticated liberal like Colmes. So Hannity pushed Colmes overboard and took the wheel by himself. His new show was named, of course, simply *Hannity*.

Meanwhile, Hannity continued his talk radio career, moving to New York's powerful WABC-AM—first as their late-night talent, then their afternoon drive host, a spot he has successfully filled since January 1998. *The Sean Hannity Show* began national syndication on September 10, 2001, over the ABC Radio Network, to over five hundred stations nationwide. In 2008, he reportedly signed a five-year deal with ABC Radio (now owned by Citadel Media) for $100 million.

Give him his due. Hannity was the first right-wing talk show host to master radio and TV both. Rush and Savage tried TV and failed; Bill O'Reilly, whom we'll see up close in Chapter 5, tried radio and failed.

Hannity maintains high ratings on both, every day of the week. He's one of the most successful radio and TV broadcasters ever.

With all that exposure, all that reach, all that power, what do you get for your listening buck? True, from Hannity you don't get the same white-hot hate you hear from Savage, nor the same sneering, frat-boy sexism or racism you hear from Limbaugh, nor the same apocalyptic nonsense you hear from Beck. But you get nothing new or original, either.

Instead, you get . . . Propaganda! Whether on radio or TV, the Hannity show is where Republicans come together to hear the official Republican message of the day and gulp down the GOP Kool-Aid right from the source. Indeed, sometimes I wonder whether Hannity's required to file transcripts of his broadcasts with the Federal Election Commission as contributions to the Republican National Committee.

THE PROPAGANDA MACHINE

I have to admit, it bugs the hell out of me. Sean Hannity has it too easy these days.

As a talk show host myself, I can tell you: Doing three hours of talk radio every day is a lot of work. You have to survey all the papers and Web sites to find out what's going on, decide what topics you want to cover, do research on each topic so you know what you're talking about (or at least pretend to), book guests, and plan the proper flow of the show.

For every other talk show host, it's a lot of work, too—except for Sean Hannity. All he needs to do is log onto his e-mail and snare the daily memo from the Republican National Committee. "Dear Sean: Here's what President Obama said and did today. And here's why it's wrong. There's your show." On point after point, day after day, Hannity delivers just what his GOP handlers want. And for that, he's paid over $10 million a year. Nice work if you can get it.

Other conservative talk show hosts or commentators may occasionally stray from the path. Rush Limbaugh blasts Republicans who voted for the stimulus package. Tom Tancredo abandons his own party on immigration reform. Newt Gingrich breaks with Republicans and sits down with Obama to help craft health care reform legislation. Bill O'Reilly said a public health insurance option made sense.

Not Hannity. His creed is simple. No matter the issue, he reads what the GOP puts in front of him. And, if there's any doubt on the matter, he just follows his backup rule of thumb: If Obama's for it, he's against it.

HANNITY VERSUS THE PRESIDENT

As we'll soon see, Hannity lied like a rug about Barack Obama during the 2008 campaign. Did he cease and desist once Obama became president? No. He just told a different pack of lies.

He accused Obama of apologizing for the war on terror, for example, when he told the Turkish parliament that the United States "is not and never will be at war with Islam." In fact, President George W. Bush had made the same statement, shortly after September 11, 2001.

He blamed the president for misrepresenting America when, in a news conference in Turkey, Obama said: "One of the great strengths of the United States is . . . we have a very large Christian population—we do not consider ourselves a Christian nation or a Jewish nation or a Muslim nation. We consider ourselves a nation of citizens who are bound by ideals and a set of values."

He's wrong, insisted Hannity, because this country is founded on the Declaration of Independence, which argues we are endowed "by our creator" with certain inalienable rights. And because, according to Hannity— a college dropout, remember—*all* of our Founding Fathers looked to the Judeo-Christian ethic as the foundation of this country.

Actually, it's Hannity who's wrong. The Constitution, not the Declaration of Independence, is the document on which the United States is founded—a document in which neither the word "God" nor "creator" appears. And *none* of our Founding Fathers actually states anywhere that the United States is founded on the Judeo-Christian ethic. Several of them were not even Christians, but Deists.

Hannity also accused the president, in a speech at Cairo University, of giving the green light for Iran to develop nuclear weapons, claiming that Obama "gives in this speech pretty much the go-ahead, as he did the day before, that Iran can now pursue their nuclear ambitions." The truth is, Obama has made persuading Iran to abandon its nuclear weapons program a top priority. In Cairo, what he actually said was: "any nation—including Iran—should have the right to access peaceful nuclear power if it complies with its responsibilities under the Nuclear Non-Proliferation Treaty"—which bans Iran from acquiring nuclear weapons.

On the economic front, Hannity tore into President Obama for wanting to cap executive salaries, even for companies that were not getting a bailout. In fact, Treasury Secretary Tim Geithner explicitly stated that restrictions on executive compensation applied only to "financial institutions that are receiving government assistance."

Hannity accused Obama of making drastic cuts in the defense budget and demanded that Defense Secretary Robert Gates resign for agreeing to them. What cuts? As sent to Congress, Obama's first budget actually requested $533.7 billion for 2010, an *increase* of 4 percent over the $513.3 billion budgeted for 2009. And that's not counting the additional $130 billion for operations in Iraq and Afghanistan.

That wasn't the only Hannity lie about President Obama's spending priorities. Among other prevarications, Hannity told his television and radio audience that Obama had included funds in the stimulus package for a "Frisbee golf course" and a high-speed rail line to Las Vegas. No such funds existed.

He also claimed that $4 billion in Obama's economic recovery plan were earmarked expressly for ACORN, the voter registration organization that Hannity and other Fox News hosts spent so much airtime on during the 2008 campaign. In fact, there was no such allocation to ACORN. What about those $4.19 billion designated for "neighborhood stabilization activities"? Weren't they designed especially for ACORN? No. Those grants would be allocated according to a competitive bidding process, which CEO Bertha Lewis said ACORN wouldn't even take part in because "we are not eligible in the first place."

Finally, Hannity almost daily repeated the most pernicious lie of all: that

Obama can't be trusted because he's not a true American. "Is there anything that he likes about this country?" Hannity asked RNC chair Michael Steele on April 17, 2009. No, Sean, he campaigned twenty hours a day for eighteen months so he could preside over a nation he hates.

Even though Obama was doing little more than following the lead of his freedom-loving predecessor Bush in bailing out Wall Street and Detroit, Hannity accused Obama of being on "a mission to hijack capitalism in favor of collectivism." He called Obama "Commissar-in-Chief," and warned his listeners that the forty-fourth president was pushing "the single biggest power grab and move toward socialism in the history of the country."

When even most conservative commentators credited Obama with one of the most ambitious and productive first hundred days in office since FDR, Hannity saw instead "one hundred days of America going down the drain." On April 30, 2009, he lamented: "I don't think anybody that understands economic systems can deny that America is moving from a free market economy to a socialist economy."

Of course, Hannity failed to inform his audience that it was under George W. Bush, in October 2008, that the federal government assumed 30 percent of the ownership of America's nine biggest banks. Will the real socialist please stand up? Nor did he take any notice of the fact that by June 2009, ten banks, already well on the road to financial recovery, paid the government back the $68 billion they had received in federal bailout funds—plus almost $2 billion in interest! In December 2009, Bank of America repaid an additional $145 billion. In the end, those loans to the banks weren't socialism at all. They proved to be a good example of wise and prudent capitalism!

CZARS IN HIS EYES

No sooner was Obama in the White House than the loudmouths of Fox News declared war on various administration officials who, because they were appointed directly by the president and did not require Senate confirmation, were informally known as "czars." Although you would never know it from watching Fox, the appointment of so-called White House czars was nothing new. It started with Franklin Roosevelt and flourished under George W. Bush—who, depending on your definition of terms, created as many as thirty-one different czar positions. But, of course, Fox never had a problem with Bush's czars.

As we saw in the previous chapter, Fox's anti-czar crusade was actually launched and led by Glenn Beck, with his initial attack on green jobs "czar" Van Jones. But Hannity soon got into the act—maybe because he was nervous, or jealous, about Beck's soaring ratings. The difference is that where Beck scored, forcing Jones out of a job, Hannity bombed.

Like Beck, Hannity reached way back in the past to uncover things that Obama staffers had done or said, on the basis of which they should be fired. He targeted three rather low-level administration officials: State Department legal adviser Harold Koh; science and technology adviser John Holdren; and safe schools chief Kevin Jennings. In each case, Hannity got his facts wrong. But that didn't stop him from trying to destroy their careers.

On Harold Koh. As a California professor of law, Hannity charged, Koh had once said in a speech that "sharia law can be applied in American courts." But, of course, Hannity never had any evidence of such a statement. Koh, as well as the organizer of the event, denied the charge. Another UC Davis law professor noted that Koh had published seventy-one articles in the *Westlaw Law Review*, only one of which even mentions sharia. In that article, Koh denounces the government of Iran for "imposing a strict form of Sharia law that denies basic rights to women and minorities." Did Hannity not know the truth or simply ignore the truth?

Same question for John Holdren, director of the Office of Science and Technology Policy, whom Hannity, echoing Beck, charged with advocating forced sterilization. As we saw, Holdren did no such thing. He did, however, co-author a 1977 science textbook in which compulsory sterilization and abortion were listed as possible consequences for countries that did not voluntarily slow down population growth.

Hannity saved his most scurrilous attacks for Kevin Jennings, assistant deputy secretary of education for safe and drug-free schools, whom he accused of covering up statutory rape.

A former teacher, openly gay man, and founder of the Gay, Lesbian and Straight Education Network, Jennings is recognized as a national leader in working to make schools safe and comfortable for all students, regardless of gender or sexual orientation. What captured Hannity's sick imagination was a 1988 incident Jennings related in his memoirs, published in 1994. As teacher and counselor at a Concord, Massachusetts, high school, he met with a male sophomore who came seeking his advice after meeting an older man on a bus and going home with him. Jennings told him he hoped he'd had enough sense to use a condom.

As related by Hannity and other Fox anchors, the kid was only fifteen and therefore underage. According to them, Jennings had a legal duty to report the incident to authorities and not doing so amounted to being an accessory to statutory rape. Actually, as documented by Media Matters for America, the student was sixteen, not fifteen—which, under Massachusetts law at the time, meant he had reached the age of consent. According to the law, Jennings was under no obligation to report the matter unless there was evidence of coercion or injury, of which there was none.

Indeed, the last words on this matter should have been those of the student himself, who provided Media Matters with the following statement:

"Since I was of legal consent at the time, the fifteen-minute conversation I had with Mr. Jennings twenty-one years ago is of nobody's concern but his and mine. However, since the Republican noise machine is so concerned about my 'well-being' and that of America's students, they'll be relieved to know that I was not 'inducted' into homosexuality, assaulted, raped, or sold into sexual slavery.

"In 1988, I had taken a bus home for the weekend, and on the return trip met someone who was also gay. The next day, I had a conversation with Mr. Jennings about it. I had no sexual contact with anybody at the time, though I was entirely legally free to do so. I was a sixteen-year-old going through something most of us have experienced: adolescence. I find it regrettable that the people who have the compassion and integrity to protect our nation's students are themselves in need of protection from homophobic smear attacks. Were it not for Mr. Jennings' courage and concern for my well-being at that time in my life, I doubt I'd be the proud gay man that I am today."

But again, the facts mattered not to Sean Hannity. He refused to believe the man's assertion that he was sixteen at the time. And he was willing to try to destroy Kevin Jennings's career based on allegations of a crime he did *not* commit over twenty years ago—as long as it gave him one more hook for attacking Barack Obama.

Following Hannity's cue, fifty-three House Republicans wrote a letter to President Obama demanding that he fire Jennings for all the reasons wrongly stated on Fox. Obviously, they didn't do their own research, either. Or just didn't care.

HANNITY VERSUS JUDGE SOTOMAYOR

Given his long record of strident attacks against the president, it came as no surprise when Sean Hannity led the conservative charge against Sonia Sotomayor, Obama's first nominee to the Supreme Court. After all, he had denounced her in principle even before Obama nominated her.

On May 1, 2004, the day David Souter announced his resignation from the court, Hannity predicted that Obama's first nominee would be "somebody extremely radical," since his policies as president so far had been purely "socialist." Three days later, still twenty-two days before Sotomayor's nomination, Hannity declared that the "chances . . . are zero" that "radical activist" Obama would select a justice who would "follow the law and the Constitution."

Fast-forward. I was in the East Room of the White House on May 26 when President Obama introduced Sonia Sotomayor to the nation. She was still a relatively unknown appeals court judge from New York. Her decisions on the bench were as yet unexamined in depth by anybody outside of the White House counsel's office.

But that didn't stop Sean Hannity. His fax machine had already told him what to think. That very night on his TV show he accused President Obama of "turning his back on America" and denounced his nominee, a "left-wing judge," as "the most divisive nominee possible." In fact, he hyperventilated, Sotomayor might very well be "the most activist nominee in the history of the high court."

By nominating her, Hannity charged, Obama was exhibiting "the arrogance of hope"—a cheap poke at Obama's best-selling book on politics, *The Audacity of Hope*. Again, Hannity didn't show much originality or depth in his barrage of attacks against Sotomayor. He simply and repeatedly focused on one court decision and one sentence from one speech—which is probably all that the boys in the basement of the Republican National Committee had time to dig up for him.

Of over four thousand decisions Sotomayor participated in during her seventeen years' experience on the bench, the most controversial—and the subject of Hannity's wrath—involved a group of white firefighters in New Haven, Connecticut. In 2003, the city's Civil Service Board held an exam for promotions in the fire department. When results were tabulated, no African-Americans and only one Latino qualified for promotions. The board subsequently ruled that the exam was flawed and refused to honor it. Twenty white firefighters, who had scored well on the exam, sued for discrimination.

Sotomayor joined two other judges in upholding a lower court's rejection of the plaintiffs' claim. Whatever the merits of the firefighters' case, the judicial panel unanimously ruled, the laws on affirmative action were clear. The board had followed the law and they, as judges, were bound to uphold it.

For Hannity, Limbaugh, and many other conservative commentators, this was an out-and-out case of reverse racism: denying whites a job simply because they were white. Perhaps. But Hannity and others didn't seem to understand that by zeroing in on this one case, they were undermining their own argument that Sotomayor was a judicial activist. In fact, the New Haven decision proved just the opposite. In deciding for the city, she had refused to legislate from the bench. She applied the law. No activism there.

In June 2009, even before Sotomayor's confirmation hearings began, a divided U.S. Supreme Court voted 5–4 to reinterpret the doctrine of affirmative action, overturn the appeals court ruling, and support the reverse racism complaint of New Haven's white firefighters—a clear case of judicial activism.

More compelling evidence of racism, or "reverse racism" on Sotomayor's part—according to Hannity, Limbaugh, Beck, Pat Buchanan, Charles Krauthammer, Bill O'Reilly, Newt Gingrich, and every other white male conservative you can think of, all singing from the same hymnal—was her now famous 2001 statement about judging: "I would hope that a wise Latina woman with the richness of her experiences would more often than not reach a better conclusion than a white male who hasn't lived that life."

"This would never be tolerated by a white male," Hannity thundered on behalf of the oppressed white masses. "If a white male ever said 'My experience as a white man makes me better than a Latina woman,' he would never be considered for the court."

Now, as a white male, I don't feel the least bit threatened by what Sotomayor said. In fact, I think every word she said was true—especially when you consider the context of where she said it.

But Hannity, of course, never bothered to point out that Sotomayor was addressing a seminar on the contribution of Latinos to America's judiciary system. And, specifically, she was speaking about ruling on cases of discrimination based on race or gender. She never said, as she was widely quoted, that "a Latina woman is better than a white man" or "would make a better judge than a white man."

Sotomayor, in fact, spoke very carefully. She merely said that (1) *in those kinds of cases* (2) *she would hope* (3) that a Latina woman, based on her experiences, would *more often than not* reach a better conclusion than a white male. Frankly, I believe it was her use of the future conditional tense that confounded Hannity. He didn't understand that the conditional is not a statement of the way things are, but of the way we would hope them to be. But, of course, that may be expecting too much from someone whose brain has turned to mush after years of regurgitating GOP agitprop.

At the same time, neither Hannity nor his right-wing compadres bothered to point out that, in the very next paragraph of her speech, Sotomayor added that she believed that white males were also capable of reaching solid decisions in cases involving racial or sexual discrimination, citing as an example the Supreme Court's historic *Brown v. Board of Education* ruling—by nine white men.

In the end, Hannity's nightly rants against Sonia Sotomayor had zero effect. She was confirmed by a 68–31 bipartisan vote. But Hannity had nevertheless done his job, as he'd been instructed, carrying water for the Republican opposition.

HANNITY FOR TORTURE

In fact, no matter how reprehensible the position, you can bet that Sean Hannity is ready and willing to be the GOP waterboy. Even on torture.

On only the second full day of his presidency, President Obama banned the use of torture, closed the network of CIA "Black Site" prisons around the world and announced his goal to shut down the military prison at Guantánamo Bay within a year.

Judging by the howls of outrage from Hannity and others, you'd think he'd turned over the keys to the White House to Osama bin Laden. Didn't the president realize, Hannity wanted to know, that torture is what kept America safe from another terrorist attack? "That is what protected American citizens. That is what protected American towns. That is what has protected American cities."

By singing the praises of torture, Hannity was of course repeating the official Republican Party line, best and most often expressed by former Vice President Dick Cheney, who actually joined CIA officials in briefing members of Congress on the efficacy of "enhanced interrogation techniques." But, curiously enough, he directly contradicted the views of 2008 Republican Party candidate John McCain, who was himself tortured for six years in the Hanoi Hilton. In his book, *Faith of My Fathers*, McCain admits signing a fake confession and telling his torturers anything they wanted to hear, in order to stop the pain. Later, as a senator, he introduced legislation making torture illegal.

Speaking of carrying water, Hannity seems to have a special fondness for waterboarding, the simulated-drowning technique ostensibly reserved by the CIA for its top-tier al Qaeda suspects. He excoriated President Obama for ending the use of waterboarding: "Clearly, this president has not done his homework, and it is putting each and every American at risk."

On a roll, he denounced foes of the practice as "moral fools." In fact, Hannity became so enthusiastic about the virtues of waterboarding that he got carried away. On April 22, he actually volunteered to be waterboarded himself as a fund-raiser "for the troops' families."

As they say, be careful what you ask for, because you just might get it. The next night, MSNBC rival talk show host Keith Olbermann took Hannity up on his offer and agreed to pay $1,000 for every second Hannity remained underwater. As Olbermann told his audience, the point was not to do Hannity any harm, but to help prove, once and for all, that waterboarding was, indeed, cruel and inhuman torture, or "slow-motion suffocation." So much so, in fact, that the CIA's own practices manual required that agency officials have a tracheotomy kit on hand to revive a detainee who had effectively drowned.

You will not be surprised to learn that, following Olbermann's challenge, Hannity never mentioned his personal waterboarding plans again.

That idiotic stunt was instead taken up by another talk show host, Matthew Erich Muller of Chicago, who goes by the name of "Mancow." On Friday, May 22, 2009, he arranged to be waterboarded live on his radio show, with Chicago Fire Department paramedics standing by. He lasted all of six or seven seconds. His verdict? It was definitely torture!

"It is way worse than I thought it would be," Mancow told assembled TV cameras. "It is such an odd feeling to have water poured down your nose with your head back. . . . It was instantaneous. . . . And I don't want to say this: absolutely torture."

Of course, what neither Hannity nor Mancow would admit is: There's a big difference between waterboarding when you can stop it anytime you want and waterboarding when you're handcuffed and at the mercy of your sadistic handlers.

Professional cynic Christopher Hitchens also decided to challenge those who condemned waterboarding as torture by arranging to have himself secretly waterboarded by American Special Forces somewhere in the mountains of North Carolina. After nearly drowning—twice!—he made it clear to readers of *Vanity Fair* what waterboarding was all about: "If waterboarding does not constitute torture, then there is no such thing as torture."

MISINFORMER OF THE YEAR

Throughout his broadcasting career, Sean Hannity has never been what you'd call a truth teller. From his earliest days as Ollie North's defender, he's always been a purveyor of misinformation. It's his bread-and-butter. Still, he outdid himself during the long campaign of 2008, where he proudly devoted three hours of national radio and one hour of national television a day—first, to the "Stop Hillary Express," and then to the "Stop Obama Express."

As a so-called electronic journalist, Hannity made no excuses for the blatantly partisan nature of his daily shows, explaining simply: "It's my job."

Every day for twelve months, he told so many lies, engaged in such repeated deception, and spread so much obvious propaganda that he was singled out on December 17, 2008, for special recognition:

> Because of the unending stream of falsehoods and character attacks that fueled the "Stop Obama Express," and the countless other distortions he promoted throughout 2008, Sean Hannity is Media Matters for America's Misinformer of the Year.

Among the countless falsehoods and attacks that Hannity broadcast, Media Matters identified those he repeated the most often.

OBAMA PLANS TO INVADE PAKISTAN

On many occasions, Hannity chided Obama's "rookie mistake" of announcing his plans to invade Pakistan, one of our allies. Actually, what Obama said—in a speech on August 7, 2007—was that we had made a mistake by invading Iraq instead of continuing to track down al Qaeda in the mountains of Afghanistan and Pakistan. His administration, he vowed, would resume the hunt for al Qaeda. As for Pakistan: "If we have actionable intelligence about high-value terrorist targets [in Pakistan] and President Musharraf won't act, we will."

Imagine, by the way, the conservative outcry had Obama said that, even if we knew for sure where al Qaeda terrorists were hiding out, we would *not* go after them unless Musharraf first gave his permission. We would never hear the end of it. Every sunshine patriot in the GOP, starting with Hannity, would be pounding the airwaves to tell us how soft on terrorism Obama turned out to be.

KILLING CIVILIANS

Hannity also charged that Obama was "not fit to be commander-in-chief" because of his August 2007 statement that we needed to send more ground troops to Afghanistan "so that we're not just air-raiding villages and killing civilians, which is creating enormous pressure over there." For Hannity and, later, vice presidential candidate Sarah Palin, that statement amounted to a direct attack on our troops.

Another misrepresentation. In fact, several villages had recently been accidentally or indiscriminately bombed, resulting in numerous civilian deaths and provoking angry protest from President Hamid Karzai. Secretary of Defense Robert Gates was even forced to issue a statement apologizing for the bombings.

In any case, in direct defiance of Hannity's comments, one of President Obama's first acts as commander-in-chief was to send 17,000 additional ground troops to Afghanistan—followed by another 30,000 in December 2009.

NO VISIT TO LANDSTUHL

More right-wing blathering about Obama's lack of support for American troops came during the candidate's European trip in July 2008. After addressing a record-breaking crowd of 200,000 in downtown Berlin, the Democratic candidate had planned a visit to wounded soldiers from Iraq and Afghanistan undergoing medical treatment at the Landstuhl Regional Medical Center. But the Bush Pentagon had other plans.

At the last minute, the Defense Department informed Obama he could visit Landstuhl as a senator, but not as a presidential candidate. Obama offered to leave his presidential plane and traveling press corps behind, but that was still unacceptable. Military officials even vetoed Obama's bringing along retired Air Force General Scott Gration. Finally, the frustrated candidate, realizing that both the Bush White House and the McCain campaign were pulling the strings here, dropped the visit.

Playing his part in the great charade to a tee, Hannity immediately jumped to misinform the public that Obama had canceled his visit to Landstuhl because "the Pentagon wouldn't allow him to bring cameras." McCain ran campaign commercials repeating the same charge—a charge immediately debunked by NBC chief foreign affairs correspondent Andrea Mitchell, who accompanied Obama on the trip. She told MSNBC: "There was never any intention—let me be absolutely clear about this. The press was never going to go. The entourage was never going to go. There was never an intention to make this political. . . . And the McCain commercial on this subject is completely wrong, factually wrong." But that didn't stop Hannity from repeating the claim to this day.

Obama, in fact, was very sensitive to the temptation of politicians to use wounded soldiers as political props—a common practice of George W. Bush, who never visited troops at Bethesda Naval Hospital without dragging TV cameras along. Obama resisted the temptation, both as candidate and later as president.

On June 1, 2009, I stood with reporters on the White House driveway to watch President Obama walk out of the Oval Office, cross the South Lawn, and climb aboard Marine One. We were told only that the president was headed to Bethesda. We were given no reason for his trip. I wondered, in fact, if the president was going out for a medical checkup.

No press accompanied the president to Bethesda Naval Hospital. No press were waiting for him once he arrived. Later, we were informed that the president had visited with wounded troops and awarded two Purple Hearts—all in private.

PUBLIC PRAYER

Just days before the Landstuhl bait-and-switch, Hannity had leveled a similar charge against Obama on his visit to Jerusalem. Before dawn on his last day there, the candidate donned a white yarmulke and visited the Western Wall. After a rabbi had read Psalm 22, Obama followed tradition by placing a handwritten note of prayer into a crack in the wall.

When Obama's private prayer later appeared in the press, Hannity accused him of blatant showmanship: "Everything was well orchestrated, all the timing—you know, for example, even the release of the note that he put at the Western Wall, that was all leaked to the press, and that was a big deal as well."

Yes, Obama's prayer did make its way into the press: "Lord—Protect my family and me. Forgive me my sins, and help me guard against pride and despair. Give me the wisdom to do what is right and just. And make me an instrument of your will."

But, as Richard Wolffe reports in his landmark book *Renegade*, the prayer was *not* leaked by the Obama campaign. No sooner had Obama departed the site than a yeshiva student leaped on the wall, extracted the note, and handed it to reporters.

"MOST LIBERAL SENATOR"

In January 2008, the prestigious *National Journal* issued its congressional ratings for 2007. Based on only 99 out of 388 nonunanimous votes, the *Journal* ranked Barack Obama number one among liberals.

Hannity and others immediately branded Obama the nation's "most liberal senator" and repeated the charge throughout the campaign, even though, in a more accurate analysis, based on all 388 votes, Obama scored in tenth place, behind Teddy Kennedy, Tom Harkin, Barbara Boxer, and others.

Even "most liberal" wasn't enough for Hannity. He graduated to branding Obama "the No. 1 radical liberal in the Senate." Apparently, just plain old "liberal" doesn't cut it as a scare tactic in GOP circles anymore. Which is why Hannity and his conservative sidekicks have gone back to the well to dig up the pejorative "socialist." Pretty soon they'll be calling Democrats "Bolsheviks" or "Trotskyites." Actually, Lou Dobbs already called me that.

CUTTING DEFENSE SPENDING

In October 2007, Obama spoke of the need to practice fiscal responsibility and cut wasteful spending, even in the Pentagon. In doing so, he weighed his words carefully: "I will cut tens of billions of dollars in wasteful spending. I will cut investments in unproven missile defense systems. I will not weaponize space. I will slow our development of Future Combat systems. And I will institute an independent Defense priorities board to ensure that the quadrennial defense review is not used to justify unnecessary spending."

The key words, of course, are *wasteful* and *unnecessary* spending. But, of course, that's too fine a distinction for Hannity. He just reads what they put in front of him. In typical partisan fashion, he repeatedly accused Obama of promising to cut "tens of millions of dollars in defense spending." Somehow the words "wasteful" and "unnecessary" got lost.

LIPSTICK ON A PIG

One of the most ridiculous back-and-forths of the 2008 presidential campaign was triggered by the Republicans' feigned outrage over Obama's quip that John McCain's policies were no different from those of George W. Bush: "But, you know, you can—you can put lipstick on a pig; it's still a pig. You can wrap an old fish in a piece of paper called change. It's still going to stink after eight years."

Serving his Republican handlers as always, Hannity took the lead, accusing Obama of sexism and a deliberate personal attack against Sarah Palin, who had earlier joked to delegates at the Republican National Convention that the only difference between a hockey mom and a bulldog was: lipstick! There's no doubt, Hannity told his listeners, that

Obama "was talking about Sarah Palin." McCain rushed out an ad, claiming Obama was personally attacking Palin. And McCain supporter and former Massachusetts governor Jane Swift said Obama "called a very prominent female governor of one of our states a pig" and demanded an apology.

It is true that Obama used the "lipstick on a pig" analogy in ridiculing McCain's economic policies. It's also true that he'd used it before, in talking about Iraq. "George Bush has given a mission to General [David] Petraeus, and he has done his best to try to figure out how to put lipstick on a pig," he told *The Washington Post* in 2007. But Obama's not the only one. John McCain is fond of the phrase, using it to dismiss the merits of Senator Hillary Clinton's health reform plan: "I think they put some lipstick on a pig, but it's still a pig."

It's pretty clear, as former Arkansas governor and 2008 presidential candidate Mike Huckabee told Hannity, that this was a totally manufactured political issue. "It's an old expression, and I'm going to have to cut Obama some slack on that one," said Huckabee. But not Hannity.

OBAMA AND FARRAKHAN

Guilt by association is a favorite Hannity trick. If he couldn't attack Barack Obama directly, he smeared him indirectly by attempting to link him to various controversial figures—starting with Nation of Islam leader Louis Farrakhan.

Indeed, Hannity claimed that Obama, as a community organizer in Chicago, had closely "associated" himself with Farrakhan. His proof? That Obama's former church, Trinity United, had given an award to Farrakhan through its magazine *Trumpet Newsmagazine.*

The truth is that Obama issued a statement at the time disagreeing with the award and criticizing Farrakhan. In his statement, then-Senator Obama described himself as "a consistent denunciator of Louis Farrakhan." But of course Mr. Hannity, the consistent denunciator of Barack Obama, ignored that important bit of information.

OBAMA AND TONY REZKO

Even Obama himself admitted it was a "boneheaded" mistake to get involved in any real estate deal with Chicago businessman, now convicted felon, Tony Rezko.

During the heat of the campaign, the facts of their business transaction became well known. In June 2005, Obama and Rezko bought adjacent properties on Chicago's South Side: Rezko paying $625,000 for a vacant lot, Obama paying $1.65 million for the house next door—$300,000 less than the asking price. Seven months later, wanting to enlarge his own yard, Obama bought a slice of the next-door property from Rezko for $104,500.

But for Hannity it was a lot more sinister than that. The whole deal smelled of political payoffs, bribes, and kickbacks. He demanded an answer to the question: "Did Obama know at the time that Rezko was saving him three hundred grand on the purchase of his home?" Actually, the sellers of the house told Bloomberg News that the only reason they sold Obama the house for $300 grand less than the asking price was because Obama had made the best offer of any they received. Mystery solved . . . for most everybody but Sean Hannity, who consistently tried thereafter to imbue the word "Rezko" with the same talismanic power of "Watergate" or "Whitewater." It didn't take.

OBAMA AND JEREMIAH WRIGHT

As soon as the 2008 campaign was over, Sean Hannity should have sent Pastor Jeremiah Wright a check. He got more mileage, more exposure, and more airtime out of denouncing Obama's connection with Pastor Wright than any other aspect of the Obama campaign. True, Wright provided Hannity and others plenty of ammunition. In early March 2008, after mining years of Wright's sermons, ABC's Brian Ross broke the now infamous story. He played clips of the preacher's most controversial and indefensible statements from the pulpit, including his condemnation of the United States for its treatment of African-Americans:

"The government gives them the drugs, builds bigger prisons, passes the three-strike law and then wants us to sing God Bless America. No, no, no. Not God Bless America. God Damn America. That's in the Bible. For killing innocent people. God Damn America for treating tis citizens as less than human."

Most shocking of all, perhaps, was Wright's sermon following the terrorist attacks of September 11. He said in part:

"We bombed Hiroshima. We bombed Nagasaki. And we nuked far more than the thousands in New York and the Pentagon, and we never batted an eye. We have supported state terrorism against the Palestinians and black South Africans and now we are indignant, because the stuff we have done overseas is now brought right back into our own front yards. America's chickens are coming home . . . to roost."

It was a disgusting, anti-American screed, for sure. But Obama's response was weak at first. He disassociated himself from Wright's remarks, and insisted he hadn't been present when those particularly offensive sermons were given. And then, on March 18, Obama gave a remarkable sermon on race relations in Philadelphia, in which he nevertheless admitted that, because of his long, close relationship with Wright, he could no more turn his back on him than he could his own white grandmother.

A month later, however, Wright gave an incendiary speech and news conference at the National Press Club in Washington in which, among other outrageous remarks, Wright elaborated on his earlier statement that, on September 11, America really got what it deserved. "You cannot do terrorism on other people and not expect it to come back on you," he told reporters. "Those are biblical principles, not Jeremiah Wright 'bombastic' principles." Obama had finally had enough. The next day, in Winston-Salem, North Carolina, he bitterly and publicly severed his relationship with Pastor Wright. "His comments were not only divisive and destructive," said Obama, "but I believe that they end up giving comfort to those who prey on hate and I believe that they do not portray accurately the perspective of the black church. They certainly don't portray accurately my values and beliefs."

For most observers, that was the end of the story. But not for Sean

Hannity and his GOP puppet masters. For them, Pastor Wright was the gift that kept on giving, the new convenient bogeyman for every excuse invented by Hannity to cast aspersions at Obama. He repeatedly reinvented Jeremiah Wright in order to question Obama's faith or patriotism, even after Obama was in the White House.

For example, Hannity immediately resurrected the Jeremiah Wright flap when Obama called out the Cambridge, Massachusetts, police department for their arrest of Harvard professor Henry Louis Gates. "He was supposed to be post-racial," Hannity said of Obama. "Now are people going to look a little more closely at this case? Are they going to look at the twenty years in Wright's church?"

Hannity even went on to claim that the Gates incident proved there was no difference between Obama and Wright. In fact, charged Hannity, "I think he *is* Reverend Wright. I think he hid it well, but I think he's now implementing and proving me right."

And in April 2009, when Obama spoke to a town meeting in Strasbourg, France, Hannity accused him of exporting Wright's "hate America" message. In his remarks, Obama acknowledged that there were times when Americans had "shown arrogance and been dismissive, even derisive" of the contributions of Europeans. To most people, that is nothing more than a statement of fact. To Hannity, it was proof that "the liberal tradition of blame America first, well, that's still alive. But should we really be surprised from a man who sat in Reverend Wright's church?" Of course, Hannity didn't point out that Obama went on to chastise those Europeans who stereotype Americans and "choose to blame America for much of what's bad."

You have the feeling that Sean Hannity will continue to hang Jeremiah Wright around Obama's neck as long as he's in the White House.

OBAMA AND FRANKLIN RAINES

When the sputtering Bush economy finally collapsed in the fall of 2008, everybody on the Republican side of the aisle went looking for one. Sean Hannity found another target in Franklin Raines, who'd been forced to resign in 2004 as head of the Federal National Mortgage Association, or "Fannie Mae," over accounting tricks that earned him and fellow executives huge bonuses, while individual investors lost their shirts. Based on one mention in *The Washington Post*, Hannity claimed that Raines was "a chief economic adviser" of Obama's.

Once again, Hannity and the Republican Party were marching in lockstep. McCain picked up Hannity's charge and made a TV commercial out of it:

"Obama has no background in economics. Who advises him? *The Post* says it's Franklin Raines, for 'advice on mortgage and housing policy.' Shocking. Under Raines, Fannie Mae committed 'extensive financial fraud.' Raines made millions. Fannie Mae collapsed. Taxpayers? Stuck with the bill."

Shocking, indeed. Except, once again, the part about Raines serving as Obama's economic guru just wasn't true. *The Washington Post* even said so itself. On September 19, 2008, its "Fact Checker" column reported that the Hannity-McCain attack was based on a casual conversation *Post* reporter Anita Huslin had had with Raines, after running into him at some Washington event. When she asked if he was involved in the presidential campaign, he shrugged and said he'd twice talked to "someone" in the Obama campaign about economic issues in general. He couldn't even remember whom he'd talked to. Which is a long, long way from his being Obama's "chief economic adviser." In making that charge, said the *Post*, John McCain was "clearly exaggerating wildly." And so was Sean Hannity.

OBAMA THE MUSLIM

Where Hannity and Fox News really went wild was in their repeated efforts to brand Barack Obama as a card-carrying, Mecca-praying, Koran-reading, America-hating Muslim. Which is not to imply, as Colin Powell pointed out when he endorsed Obama, that there's anything wrong with being a Muslim. But Hannity and fellow Foxers knew that, after September 11, just the word "Muslim" was enough to send chills up the spine and suspicions to the brain of many Americans. And they deliberately, repeatedly, played on that primal fear.

When some of the accusations became too unfounded for even Hannity himself to make, he invited highly dubious Obama haters like Andy Martin and Jerome Corsi on his program to spread the smears: Obama was not born in the United States; he attended a madrassa in Indonesia; he took the oath of office on the Koran; he was, in fact, a practicing Muslim. Martin even labeled Obama's work as a community organizer, working for a coalition of Christian churches, as "training for a radical overthrow of the government."

Even after many media reports discounted the rumors, Hannity continued to repeat them or invite others to do so, frequently reminding listeners and viewers that John McCain's opponent was Barack *Hussein* Obama.

Ironically, Hannity unwittingly ended up helping Obama shoot down the Muslim rumor. By making such a federal issue over Obama's close ties with Pastor Jeremiah Wright, Hannity, in effect, conceded the obvious point: Obama was a practicing Christian and had been a member of Trinity United Church for twenty years.

In the end, of course, Obama's close ties with Islam—the fact that his father and grandfather were Muslims and that he had lived in a Muslim country—have proven invaluable to him as president. Unlike any president before him, he has been able to reach out to other nations in his efforts to rebuild a supportive, mutually advantageous relationship between the United States and the Muslim world.

THE MIGHTY ACORN

We all learned in grade school that "mighty oaks from little acorns grow." But only when Barack Obama came along did we learn that mighty scandals grow from little acorns, too. While Glenn Beck took up the standard once Obama was in the White House, Sean Hannity in particular, and Fox News in general, probably spent more time fanning the flames of the so-called ACORN scandal than any other aspect of the Obama-McCain campaign.

And no wonder. Hannity and friends at Fox constantly referred to ACORN as a "domestic terrorist group."

In the *National Review*, Stanley Kurtz called ACORN "the most politi-cally radical large-scale activist group in the country."

And on the Internet, *Yahoo! News* actually asked readers the question: "Is the Obama/ACORN scandal the biggest threat to democracy the U.S. has faced?" Holy cow! Who is ACORN? And what is their connection to Barack Obama? The truth is: far less than meets the eye—and even that's not much.

ACORN, or the Association of Community Organizations for Re-form Now, got its start in the 1970s, in Little Rock, where it began as an offshoot of the National Welfare Rights Organization. Its acronym, in fact, originally stood for Arkansas Community Organizations for Reform Now.

From Little Rock, ACORN's work expanded to fight for low- and moderate-income families nationwide. Today, it has 850 chapters in over one hundred cities across the United States. It focuses on a range of issues affecting inner city neighborhoods, including welfare reform, better hous-ing and schools, neighborhood safety, and stronger regulation of banks. It has led campaigns for a "living wage" targeted at big-box stores like Walmart. It has also organized voter registration and get-out-the-vote drives in several states. And it was its voter registration project that got ACORN in hot water in 2008.

When I was active in Democratic Party politics in California, I ran sev-eral voter registration drives. And I can tell you from my own experience that voter registration programs are notoriously inefficient and ripe for abuse. What happens is you send a lot of volunteers out to prime locations to sign up new voters, and you trust they'll come back with valid signa-tures. But that's not always the case. During my term as Democratic state chair of California, for example, workers for the California Republican Party were actually caught in a Ventura County cemetery, filling out voter registration forms from names on the tombstones. Where did they think they were? Chicago?

Apparently, ACORN's voter registration efforts were similarly sloppily organized and poorly supervised. By the end of 2008, fourteen states were conducting investigations into alleged irregularities in ACORN-run voter registration drives. Charges of voter fraud have been filed against ACORN workers in at least four states: Pennsylvania, Ohio, Nevada, and Washington. And Congress cut off all federal funding to ACORN, a move that was later declared unconstitutional. So what's Barack Obama got to do with that? Well, if you believe Sean Hannity, EVERYTHING!

Hannity, in fact, devoted an entire Fox broadcast special to *Obama and Friends* in which he called ACORN a "shady organization," guilty of practicing "shady tactics and intimidation." And it wasn't just their voter registration problems that we should be concerned about. Because their "strong-arm tactics" forced banks into making bad loans, Hannity even insisted that ACORN was directly responsible for the Wall Street collapse in October 2008.

Yes, according to Hannity, ACORN is basically like S.P.E.C.T.R.E. from the James Bond books, and is probably also responsible for the death of Jimmy Hoffa and the spread of brain cancer.

And, of course, he charged that the sinister power behind ACORN was none other than Barack Obama himself—whom Hannity dubbed "The Senator from ACORN." Actually, Obama's real-world connections to ACORN were either distant or fleeting.

As a community organizer on Chicago's South Side, Obama inevitably ended up working with ACORN members on several community projects. On at least one occasion, he was invited to conduct a training session for ACORN staffers. Later, working for a public interest law firm, Obama joined a team of lawyers who defended ACORN in their efforts to force the state of Illinois to enforce the federal Motor Voter Act, hardly a subversive plot. As a board member of the Woods Fund and Joyce Foundation, he voted with other members to award grants to many community organizations, including ACORN. And, when he ran for state senator, U.S. senator, and president, Obama was endorsed by ACORN's political wing and several ACORN volunteers worked on his campaigns.

And that's it. It's not true to say Obama had no connection to ACORN, but it's even less true—in fact, it's preposterous—to claim Obama is "The Senator from ACORN." How could such a limited relationship between Barack Obama and ACORN be painted as the biggest scandal of any presidential campaign in American history? Only through the political bias of Fox News and the warped mind of Sean Hannity.

OUT OF MANY, FIFTEEN DISTORTIONS

Sean Hannity loves to dish it out. But, like so many other media bullies, he can't stand it when others dish on him. He is incredibly thin-skinned, as he proved in June 2004, when John Podesta, president of the Center for American Progress, accused him of not always telling the truth.

Speaking to the annual "Take Back America" conference, Podesta suggested: "I think when you get so distant from the facts as—as guys like Rush Limbaugh and Sean Hannity do, yeah, I think that tends to—it kind of—it tends to corrupt the dialogue."

Podesta obviously struck a nerve with Hannity, who denied ever making a false statement in his life and challenged President Clinton's former chief of staff to "defend and explain one example where I—where I said something that was so false."

Podesta was more than happy to oblige, and shortly thereafter the center released a paper that documented not one, but fifteen Hannity distortions. And here they are:

HANNITY DISTORTION NO. 1

Responding to a listener who called to dispute his enthusiastic support for George W. Bush's war in Iraq, Hannity asserted (for the 2,633rd time): "You've got to learn something. He had weapons of mass destruction. He promised to disclose them. And he didn't do it." (4/13/04)

The Truth

Six months earlier, David Kay, Bush's own envoy to Iraq, told Congress that he and his team of investigators had "not uncovered evidence that Iraq undertook significant post-1998 steps to actually build nuclear weapons or produce fissile material" and, no matter where they looked in Iraq, Kay and company had not discovered "any chemical or biological weapons."

HANNITY DISTORTION NO. 2

Looking to buttress his own gung ho support for the war in Iraq, Hannity cited Secretary of State Colin Powell, who actually argued privately against the war, as his ally: "Colin Powell just had a great piece that he had in the paper today. He was there [in Iraq]. He said things couldn't have been better." (9/19/03)

The Truth

Here's what Colin Powell actually wrote: "Iraq has come very far, but serious problems remain, starting with security. American commanders and troops told me of the many problems they face—from leftover loyalists, who want to return Iraq to the dark days of Saddam, from criminals who were set loose on Iraqi society when Saddam emptied the jails and, increasingly, from outside terrorists who have come to Iraq to open a new front in their campaign against the civilized world."

HANNITY DISTORTION NO. 3

It wasn't until he was out of office that Vice President Dick Cheney finally admitted there was no known link between al Qaeda and Saddam Hussein, even though that was one of Bush-Cheney's main justifications for the invasion of Iraq. And, of course, that evil connection was relentlessly asserted by Sean Hannity.

For example, on December 9, 2002, in typical, fractured Hannity-speak, he told his listeners: "And in northern Iraq today, this very day, al Qaeda is operating camps there, and they are attacking the Kurds in the north, and this has been well documented and well chronicled. Now, if you're going to go after al Qaeda in every aspect, and obviously they have the support of Saddam, or we're not."

The Truth

Again, David Kay, who was head of the U.N. inspectors and later went back to Iraq as George Bush's personal envoy, knew the lay of the land better than anyone. He concluded: "We simply did not find any extensive evidence of links with al Qaeda, or for that matter any evidence at all."

HANNITY DISTORTION NO. 4

The work of the 9/11 Commission, headed by Republican Tom Kean and Democrat Lee Hamilton, is one of the best examples of valuable, effective government action in modern times. Who gets credit for its establishment? According to Hannity, all credit goes to the visionary George W. Bush, and all blame goes to those obstructionist congressional Democrats.

In his book *Let Freedom Ring*, Hannity writes: "After 9/11, liberal Democrats at first showed little interest in the investigation of the roots of this massive intelligence failure." Meanwhile, he claimed, Bush and his national security team "made it clear that determining the causes of America's security failures, and finding and remedying its weak points would be central to their mission."

The Truth

Immediately after the 9/11 attacks, top Democrats in Congress, led by Congresswoman Jane Harman of California, then ranking Democrat on the House Intelligence Committee, began calling for creation of an independent commission to investigate the apparent lapses in intelligence that enabled al Qaeda to carry out their terrorist plot. President Bush ignored their pleas for over a year. In May 2002, for example, CBS News reported: "President Bush took a few minutes during his trip to Europe Thursday to voice his opposition to establishing a special commission to probe how the government dealt with terror warnings before September 11." Clearly,

Bush was worried that any such commission might focus on the CIA warning he received on August 6, 2001, while on vacation on his ranch in Crawford, Texas. After being briefed on a document with the headline "Bin Laden Determined to Strike in U.S.," he decided to go fishing for the rest of the day. It was only in September 2002 that Bush relented and authorized creation of the 9/11 Commission.

HANNITY DISTORTION NO. 5

Hannity is master of the Big Lie theory: that if you repeat a lie often enough and with enough certitude, most suckers will eventually believe you. God knows, he tried hard to convince people that the recession Americans suffered in George Bush's first year in office should actually be blamed on Bill Clinton.

"Now here's where we are. The inherited Clinton-Gore recession. That's a fact," he said on May 6, 2003.

And again on July 10: "The president inherited a recession."

"They did inherit the recession. They did inherit the recession. We got out of the recession," he proclaimed again on December 12.

It was a claim he repeated over and over again in 2004.

"He did inherit a recession and we're out of the recession." February 2.

"The president inherited a recession." February 23.

"The president inherited a recession." March 3.

And so on and so on. Yet, early in the Obama administration, when a guest noted that he had inherited a horrible economic situation from George W. Bush, Hannity interrupted her: "Blah, blah, blah. I don't want to hear this anymore."

The Truth

As any objective student of history knows, George W. Bush actually inherited a healthy economy and a $128 billion surplus from President Clinton— the only president since Jimmy Carter who not only delivered on his promise to balance the budget, but built up a budget surplus. According to the

National Bureau of Economic Research, the last word on such matters, the Bush-Cheney recession did not begin until March 2001, two months after Bush had taken office.

HANNITY DISTORTION NO. 6

George W. Bush was a Texan (actually, he was a transplanted Connecticut Yankee). Therefore he spoke fluent Spanish (actually, he mangled Spanish as much as he mangled English). Therefore Hispanics rushed out to vote for him. So says Sean Hannity: "The Hispanic community got to know him in Texas. They went almost overwhelming for him. He more than quadrupled the Hispanic vote that he got in that state." (9/16/03)

The Truth

Wrong again! In the 1998 Texas gubernatorial race, George W. Bush did, indeed, dramatically increase his standing among Latino voters: from 24 to 49 percent. However, that's a doubling, not a quadrupling. And that love affair didn't last long. In the 2000 presidential election, Bush lost Texas Hispanics to Al Gore, 54 to 43 percent.

HANNITY DISTORTION NO. 7

Some of the most repeated and most inaccurate political reporting ever seen occurred when Bill and Hillary Clinton left the White House. Remember? With zero evidence to support it, word spread like wildfire that the Clintons and their cohorts had trashed the West Wing and left it in disgraceful condition—just what you'd expect from trailer-trash hillbillies from Arkansas. It was a rumor Sean Hannity was more than happy to spread: "Look, we've had these reports, very disturbing reports—and I have actually spoken to people that have confirmed a lot of the reports— about the trashing of the White House. Pornographic materials left in the printers. They cut the phone lines. Lewd and crude messages on phone machines . . . $200,000 in furniture taken out." (1/26/01)

The Truth

The federal government's official landlord, the General Services Administration, reported that, contrary to the outlandish claims made by Hannity
and others, little if anything out of the ordinary occurred during the
Clinton-Bush transition and that, in fact, "the condition of the real prop-
erty was consistent with what we would expect to encounter when tenants
vacate office space after an extended occupancy."

HANNITY DISTORTION NO. 8

"I never questioned anyone's patriotism."

The Truth

He does so almost daily. Guests appearing on Hannity's radio or TV show
have come to expect that they will either agree with Hannity's right-wing
political views or they will be accused of hating America. Typically, on
April 30, 2003, he asked the Center for Constitutional Rights' Stanley
Cohen: "Is it you hate this president or you hate America?"

Earlier, he had pounced on Sara Flounders, co-director of the International Action Center, an antiwar organization founded by former Attorney
General Ramsey Clark. "You don't like this country, do you?" he demanded
of Flounders. "You don't—you think this is an evil country. By your descrip-
tion of it right here, you think it's a bad country." And we already saw what
Hannity had to say about Barack Obama in the patriotism department.

HANNITY DISTORTION NO. 9

In trying to force their brand of extreme Christianity on every American
and make this a Christian nation, religious right leaders James Dobson,
Pat Robertson, and Gary Bauer often fall back on the meaningless argument that the words "separation of church and state" do not appear in the

Constitution. Like the right-wing parrot he is, so does Sean Hannity: "It doesn't say anything in the Constitution [about] this idea of the separation of church and state."

The Truth

Nonsense. In fact, I wrote a whole book on this question, *How the Republicans Stole Religion* (still available in paperback).

While it is true that the exact phrase "separation of church and state" is not written in the Constitution, its spirit is clearly contained in the wording of the First Amendment: "Congress shall make no law respecting the establishment of religion, or prohibiting the free exercise thereof." And it is reaffirmed by the Sixth Amendment: "no religious Test shall ever be required as a Qualification to any Office or public Trust under the United States."

Thomas Jefferson and James Madison spent much of their political lives fighting for the strict separation of church and state, first as Virginia state legislators, later as presidents. And the bedrock principle of separation has been repeatedly affirmed by the U.S. Supreme Court. It is one of the proud pillars on which this nation was built and, over the two centuries since, it has helped both our country and our churches to flourish.

HANNITY DISTORTION NO. 10

To buttress his religious argument, Hannity even reinvented history. He flatly asserted: "The author of the Bill of Rights [James Madison] hired the first chaplain in 1789, and I gotta tell ya somethin', I think the author of the Bill of Rights knows more about the original intent—no offense to you and your liberal atheist activism—knows more about it than you do." (9/4/02)

The Truth

Say what? Poor Madison must still be rolling over in his grave. The first chaplains for the House and Senate were, in fact, hired by congressional committees even before the First Amendment was adopted. But let Madison speak for himself: "Is the appointment of Chaplains to the two Houses of Congress consistent with the Constitution, and with the pure principle of religious freedom? In strictness the answer on both points must be in the negative."

HANNITY DISTORTION NO. 11

Among deniers of the separation of church and state, few were nuttier than Alabama's so-called Ten Amendments judge, Roy Moore, who lost his job as chief justice for refusing to remove a 2.6-ton monument of the Ten Commandments from the lobby of the State Supreme Court building. Naturally, Sean Hannity rushed to defend him, claiming on August 21, 2003 that the Alabama constitution "clearly it says, as a matter of fact that the recognition of God is the foundation of that state's constitution."

The Truth

Forget for a moment the illogic of his statement. One can recognize the existence of God, yet still honor the separation of church and state. But, once again, Hannity is simply wrong in his facts. While the Alabama constitution does, indeed, reference "the Almighty," it echoes the U.S. Constitution in building a wall of separation between the two realms of church and state: "That no religion shall be established by law; that no preference shall be given by law to any religious sect, society, denomination, or mode of worship; that no one shall be compelled by law to attend any place of worship; nor to pay any tithes, taxes, or other rate for building or repairing any place of worship, or for maintaining any minister or ministry; that no religious test shall be required as a qualification to any office or public trust under this state; and that the civil rights, privileges, and capacities of any citizen shall not be in any manner affected by his religious principles." Roy Moore was dead wrong, and so was Sean Hannity.

HANNITY DISTORTION NO. 12

Okay, let's be honest. You wouldn't expect anyone who just signed a five-year radio contract worth $100 million (not nearly as generous as Rush Limbaugh's $400 million deal, true, but still pretty sweet) to understand anything about public housing. But Sean Hannity doesn't stop pretending he does.

While discussing the issue with former New York lieutenant governor, now sometimes health care pundit, Betsy McCaughey, Hannity claimed that those living in public housing projects were actually getting "free housing." He ridiculed McCaughey's assurances that "Most people in public housing are not receiving free housing. Many of them are paying almost market rates." (October 23, 2003)

The Truth

According to the Department of Housing and Urban Development, HUD, residents of public housing pay rent scaled to their household's anticipated gross annual income, less deductions for dependents and disabilities. The basic formula for rent is 30 percent of adjusted monthly income. There are exceptions for extremely low incomes, but nobody lives in public housing for free.

HANNITY DISTORTION NO. 13

As we've seen before, facts never get in the way of Hannity's political attacks. On May 12, 2004, he accused John Kerry of promising tax cuts for the rich: "The Kerry campaign wants to cut taxes on people who make $200,000."

The Truth

The exact opposite. Is Hannity dyslexic? Kerry actually proposed restoring the capital gains and dividend rates for families making over $200,000 to their levels under President Clinton. Of course, when President George W. Bush had earlier given the wealthiest Americans a huge tax cut, Hannity did nothing but praise him.

HANNITY DISTORTION NO. 14

Up against a genuine war hero in 2004, Republicans adopted the diabolical, and ultimately successful, strategy of undermining John Kerry's personal military credentials and questioning his support for military spending in general. And so the Swift Boat campaign was launched.

Hannity took the Republican Party playbook and ran with it. He regularly invited John O'Neill, Jerome Corsi, and other leaders of the so-called Swift Boat Veterans for Truth on his program to attack Kerry's record. And he accused Kerry of trying unilaterally to disarm the Pentagon: "He wanted to cancel every major weapons system. Specific votes that he would have canceled the weapons systems that we now use." (2/26/04)

The Truth

Again, the exact opposite of what Hannity claims. Is there blanket permission for Fox News hosts to lie?

Particularly for a liberal, John Kerry was unusually supportive of military spending. In fact, you might say he gave the generals everything they asked for. His pro-Pentagon spending record was documented by *Slate*: "In 1991, Kerry opposed an amendment to impose an arbitrary 2 percent cut in the military budget. In 1992, he opposed an amendment to cut Pentagon intelligence programs by $1 billion. In 1994, he voted against a motion to cut $30.5 billion from the defense budget over the next five years and to redistribute the money to programs for education and the disabled. That same year, he opposed an amendment to postpone construction of a new aircraft carrier. In 1996, he opposed a motion to cut six F-18 jet fighters from the budget. In 1999, he voted against a motion to terminate the Trident II missile."

HANNITY DISTORTION NO. 15

For Republicans, the 2004 presidential campaign was merely a chance to keep fanning the flames of September 11 and to paint Democrats as being soft on terror. They held their convention in New York City, not far from Ground Zero. They repeatedly invoked September 11. And even though George W. Bush had ignored intelligence warnings about possible terrorist attacks on U.S. soil, they accused John Kerry of wanting to dismantle American intelligence agencies. Fellow traveler Sean Hannity dutifully read the script that was handed him: "If he had his way . . . the CIA would almost be nonexistent." (1/30/04)

The Truth

According to official Senate voting records, John Kerry had voted for a total $200 billion in intelligence funding from 1997 to 2004—an increase of over 50 percent. Case closed.

FINDING THAT SPECIAL HANNITY IN YOUR LIFE

Give Hannity credit for this: He has taken conservatism where no other talk show host dares to go.

On his Web site, hannity.com, listeners can not only join the Hannity Book Club (Jim DeMint, Mark Levin) or buy tickets to his latest Freedom Concert (Charlie Daniels, Billy Ray Cyrus), they can also join "Hannidate"— and hook up with a like-minded conservative. Yes, Hannity has created his own dating service to help lonely conservatives in the same Zip Code find each other, tell each other how much they love Sean Hannity, and maybe even fall in love themselves.

Don't tell Pat Robertson, but one remarkable thing about "Hannidate" is that it's not limited to male-female relationships. Even though the religious right still condemns homosexuality as evil, "Hannidate" actually provides the option of "male seeking male" or "female seeking female."

Hannity insists he is still against gay marriage, but he has no problem with gay relationships. It's okay for gays and lesbians to have sex with each other, in other words, as long as they do it outside of marriage. Which, more power to him, is about as enlightened as conservatives ever get on the question of gay and lesbian rights.

But I suspect there's another motive behind Hannity's gay-friendly stance: He doesn't want to offend gays because they're a potential source of revenue. Who cares if they're gay? As long as they're also conservative, they might also listen to his radio show, support his sponsors, purchase a book, buy a ticket to one of his concerts, or buy a T-shirt. Hannity's never going to turn anyone away, as long as there's a chance to make a buck. God bless America.

In the end, that's what sets Hannity apart and above all other conservative talk show hosts. He is a brilliant self-promoter. He is the ultimate huckster. He will never be known for his ideas, but he will always stand head and shoulders above the rest for his financial acumen.

Today, in addition to the nation's second-most-popular political talk radio and cable TV shows, Hannity Inc. includes a conservative book club, a song club, Hannity's own books for sale, an annual string of freedom concerts, a dating service, a newsletter, and frequent personal appearances around the country. Can a restaurant chain or line of designer clothing be far behind?

Above all else, Hannity is a hugely successful businessman—and that, not the power of his conservative message—is the key to his success. He may be the most listened to political talk show host after Rush, but he's still relatively harmless. Because even his loyal fans see him for what he is: a trustworthy and faithful mouthpiece for the Republican National Committee—nothing more or less.

Hannity may offend, but he will never alienate.

He may pontificate, but he will never come up with an idea of his own.

On the marketing side of talk radio, Hannity has no peers.

On the ideas side, perhaps Al Franken said it best: "I love Hannity, because he's just dumb."

4

THE SAVAGE MICHAEL SAVAGE

After Glenn Beck and Sean Hannity, the next biggest conservative talk radio show host Rush Limbaugh has "spawned" is Michael Savage.

Limbaugh and Savage have some things in common. They are both big-time conservative talkers. They are both extremely popular. And both are heard by millions of Americans every day. But there are also big differences between them.

For all his outrageous comments, you can still imagine Rush turning his mike off once in a while, and laughing at his own irreverence. Not so with Michael Savage. You know he means every word of it. Rush can sometimes be funny. Savage is always deadly serious. And, of course, Rush has not yet been banned from entering any country. Not so Michael Savage.

In May 2009, British home secretary Jacqui Smith published the names of sixteen people banned from the U.K. for hate speech. "I am determined to stop those who want to spread extremism, hatred, and violent messages in our communities from coming to our country," she said.

Michael Savage made the list, joining, among others: former KKK grand wizard Stephen Black, antigay preacher Fred Phelps, militant leaders of

Hamas and Hezbollah, two leaders of a Russian skinhead gang, and six Islamic fundamentalists who advocate terrorist violence—many of the same people Savage regularly rails against.

It was a move that civil libertarians everywhere deplored, even those who despise what Savage stands for. But, for Savage, who couldn't seem to understand why he would be grouped with such people, it was just one more chance to play the victim. "This lunatic is linking me up with Nazi skinheads who are killing people in Russia, she's putting me in a league with Hamas murderers who kill Jews on buses," he whined to his listeners. "My views may be inflammatory, but they're not violent in any way."

At first, Savage blamed his critics at Media Matters for his banishment. Then he pointed the finger at an unnamed official in the Obama White House. And later he shifted blame to Saudi Arabia: "The U.K. banned Savage for oil. We think the Saudis pulled the strings on this one, my friend. That's why they can't let go. It was a straight out, get Savage for the Dubai ports deal." Savage's biggest disappointment was that Limbaugh wasn't in such a rush to support him.

Evidently, Savage's savagery even turns off the conservative king of talk. And that gave Savage an inclination for regicide. "Limbaugh has turned out to be the biggest phony of all of them, all of them," he declared on May 19, 2009. "Amongst all of them he is the biggest fraud. Rush Limbaugh is a fraud. When he was accused of drug usage, I supported him. But that man is a one-way street. It's all about him. He's in it for nobody but himself."

So there you have it: Rush is a fraud and Savage is for real—at least in his own mind. Well, at least he's half right.

Two months later, Britain's new home secretary reversed his predecessor's position and dropped the so-called enemies list. Yet for Savage, being banned from Britain proved to be a blessing. He used it as a shameless excuse to beg his listeners to send checks for his defense, claiming his "very life may be in danger because of this McCarthy-like witch hunt." And it gave him one more opportunity to reinvent himself, which he had already done several times.

Who is the real Michael Savage?

Once upon a time, there was a young Jewish kid named Michael Weiner who grew up in Brooklyn, then moved to the San Francisco Bay Area, where he became interested in herbal medicine. He went to Hawaii, got a degree from the University of Hawaii as an ethnobotanist, and then relocated to Fiji to study herbs with native experts. While there, he got married in the rain forest, and met and went skinny-dipping in the ocean with beat poet Allen Ginsberg. Back in the Bay Area, Weiner hooked up again with Ginsberg and his liberal friends, hung out in San Francisco's North Beach, taught and practiced herbal medicine, and wrote eighteen books on natural cures. Frequenting City Lights Books and nearby Café Trieste, he became a popular figure in Northern California's literary and hippie scene.

Now meet another prominent resident of the Bay Area. His name is Michael Savage. He calls himself an "independent-minded individualist," but he's among the ugliest voices, by far, on talk radio. He's an extreme right-wing conservative. He regularly and viciously attacks blacks, Latinos, liberals, women, and, especially, gays and lesbians.

On the radio for three hours every afternoon, Savage lashes out at enemies real and perceived. He suggests launching missile strikes against Arab countries in the Middle East. He argues that the answer to illegal immigration is simply to gun them all down. He calls for locking up anti-war activists for treason. And he dismisses attempts to eliminate discrimination against homosexuality as nothing but a crusade for "anal rights."

Two totally different personalities. Except for the fact, as you might have guessed, that Michael Weiner and Michael Savage are one and the same person. And the combination of those dueling personalities in one mind and body makes for very scary results.

CLOSE ENCOUNTERS

Like most Americans, I know Savage best as a disturbing personality on the radio. Actually, I find him very hard to listen to. Even notwithstanding all the hate he spews, he's so intense that I'm always afraid he's simply going to blow up and have a stroke right on the air. Meeting him once, briefly, and speaking to several associates of his in the San Francisco Bay Area, only confirmed that fear. For a while, Savage appeared on conservative station KSFO-AM, the sister station of more moderate KGO-AM, both under the stewardship of the legendary radio genius Jack Swanson.

Savage was assigned a cubicle in the same workplace occupied by other talk show hosts, which soon became a problem. He was so loud, his language was so abusive, and he was so offensive to fellow hosts that one of them told me he petitioned station managers to raise the walls around Savage's cubicle all the way to the ceiling—in effect, cutting him off from everyone else in the newsroom. Needless to say, no tears were shed when Savage left KSFO and moved across town to KNEW-AM 910.

Which is where I ran into Michael Savage again . . . or should have. Actually, when visiting the Bay Area, I have used his studio several times to broadcast my morning show on KNEW's sister station, San Francisco's progressive talk, 960 AM, "The Green." It's a great studio—absolutely state-of-the art, very comfortable, very user-friendly.

The new studio was built to Savage's specifications, as part of his deal with KNEW. But it's never difficult to schedule time in this studio because he seldom, if ever, uses it. I've been told by several staffers that Savage is so paranoid he never broadcasts from the same studio two days in a row, never tells anyone where he's broadcasting from, and seldom, if ever, takes advantage of the studio built for him at KNEW. In his case, as they say, "just because you're paranoid doesn't mean they're not out to get you."

MADNESS AT MSNBC

Of course, Savage thinks everyone is out to get him. That probably includes me, given what happened the one time I interviewed him.

In February 2003, Savage was inexplicably hired by Erik Sorenson to host a one-hour show on MSNBC. I have great affection and respect for Sorenson (after all, he also hired me), but adding Savage to the lineup was a big mistake.

In fact, once I heard rumors of a possible Savage show, I urged Sorenson not to put him on the air. This was, after all, the man who had once ridiculed the network by claiming its initials MSNBC actually stood for "More Snotty Nonsense by Creeps"—later, "More Snotty Nonsense by Chicks." And, besides, I warned, it was only a matter of time before Savage would self-destruct. NBC News anchor Tom Brokaw also weighed in, asking network executives: "Is this the sort of man who embodies the values of NBC?"

But Sorenson, ignoring my advice and that of Brokaw and others, launched Savage with great fanfare, praising him as "brash, passionate, and smart" and promising that he would deliver "compelling opinion and analysis with an edge." Well, he got the "brash" part right. As I had warned, Savage soon blew himself up—even sooner than I thought.

At the time, Pat Buchanan and I were hosting our own daily show, *Buchanan and Press,* from 2–4 P.M., out of the MSNBC Washington bureau at 400 North Capitol Street. One day, we got word from headquarters in Secaucus, New Jersey, that we had to invite Michael Savage as a guest that afternoon in order to promote his new show, which would premiere the following weekend.

Ever the good soldiers, Pat and I agreed. Actually, we had no choice. But I didn't think we had to go soft on him. After all, he was a talk show host, not exactly known for being nice to people. The way he dishes it out, I figured he'd be able to handle anything.

Savage had recently published his hate-filled screed *The Savage Nation: Saving America from the Liberal Assault on Our Borders, Language, and Culture.* In it, he was highly critical of MSNBC's war coverage, especially the work of reporter Ashleigh Banfield, whom he called "the mind slut with a big pair of glasses that they sent to Afghanistan." Savage didn't like the questions she raised about the Afghan war, and he didn't like her appearance. "She looks like she went from porno into reporting," he sniffed, with his usual lack of class.

Now, I had never met Ashleigh, but I admired her work. And I was certainly loyal to my own network. So I decided to challenge Savage on both points. After Pat threw him a couple of softballs about when the show would start and what kind of topics he would talk about ("liberals and immigrants" . . . duh!), I asked Savage why he'd agreed to work at MSNBC, after he'd so roundly trashed the network in his book. I followed up by expressing my appreciation for Ashleigh Banfield's work and offering him, now that he was joining her at MSNBC, an opportunity to apologize to her.

Of course, Savage would not apologize. Apparently, he even called her a slut again. Frankly, I don't know because I never heard his response. At this point, all I could hear was the voice of MSNBC management, screaming in my ear from the control room in Secaucus: "NO, NO, NO! YOU CAN'T ASK HIM ABOUT THAT! END THIS INTERVIEW NOW!"

Which I did. After the broadcast, I was ripped a new one for challenging Savage on this issue. Somewhat stunned by this reaction, I pointed out that we had not been warned ahead of time that any issues were out of bounds. And, besides, I argued, as a talk show host, Savage was more than capable of tackling tough questions. Nice try, but no cigar. I remained in the doghouse for weeks.

What I didn't realize at the time, but learned later, was that Ashleigh Banfield had been pressuring her bosses at MSNBC not to hire Savage because of his calling her a slut in print. Having rejected her pleas for some reason, management's case was made even weaker after I inadvertently gave Savage the opportunity to call her a slut again—on her very network.

In the end, as I predicted, Savage didn't last long. Only four months, in fact. His first show was March 8, 2003. His last was July 7, 2003. On that day, Savage took a call from a man—later identified as prank caller Bob Foster—who made an unflattering remark about Savage's teeth. Savage took the bait. "Are you a sodomite?" he asked. Foster said yes. And Savage went nuts.

"Oh, so you're one of those sodomites," he screamed. "You should only get AIDS and die, you pig. How's that? Why don't you see if you can sue me, you pig? You got nothing better to do than to put me down, you piece of garbage? You got nothing to do today? Go eat a sausage, and choke on it. Get trichinosis."

Savage was finished with that caller, but not finished with his diatribe. He continued: "Now do we have another nice caller here who's busy because he didn't have a nice night in the bathhouse, who's angry at me today? Put another, put another sodomite on . . . No more calls? . . . I don't care about these bums; they mean nothing to me. They're all sausages."

The next day, Savage—beginning to understand the hot water he was in—apologized for his remarks on his radio show, explaining that he thought MSNBC had gone to a commercial break as soon as they determined it was a crank caller. Which, of course, is nonsense. Every radio and TV host knows you don't continue ranting and raving during commercial breaks— because, one, your mike is never really turned off; and, two, there is always *somebody* listening! At any rate, it was too late for Savage. MSNBC had already shown him the door. Then again, they should never have hired him in the first place.

MICHAEL SAVAGE HATES—OBAMA!

For Michael Savage, 2008 was the perfect storm. Almost everything he feared—a liberal; a person of color; a man whose father was from Kenya and whose grandfather, father, and stepfather were practicing Muslims; the product of a mixed-race marriage; and, did I mention, a liberal?—all came together in the person of Barack Obama.

If possible, Savage hated Obama even more than he hated Bill and Hillary Clinton (at least they were white), and he did everything he could to destroy him. He even insulted Obama's long-dead mother, calling her a "quasi-revolutionary Patty Hearst wannabe who had a baby with this African just to piss her parents off."

As Obama emerged as the favorite to win the Democratic nomination and, later, the general election, Savage's daily attacks against him intensified. Depending on his mood, he accused Obama of being:

- "An Afro-Leninist, and I know he's dangerous."
- A Muslim. "How could he not be a Muslim if he has a Muslim name? How could he not be a Muslim if his father and grandfather were Muslims?"

- "An unknown stealth candidate who went to a madrassa in Indonesia and, in fact, was a Muslim."
- "America's first affirmative action candidate, about to become president."

And Savage joined the ranks of those right-wing critics who questioned whether Obama was even a citizen of the United States and was, therefore, ineligible to be president. Even after the Obama campaign posted on its Web site a copy of his birth certificate provided by the state of Hawaii, Savage continued to insist that his birth certificate "does not exist, they can't find it in the Hawaiian government. It's never been produced. The one that was produced is a forgery." Not surprisingly, in October 2008, when Obama interrupted his campaign to visit his dying grandmother in Honolulu, Savage smelled a rat. He accused Obama of using his grandmother as an excuse "to fudge the birth certificate in question."

Once he was in the White House, Savage's attacks on Obama didn't end. If anything, they became more severe. You follow the news. Surely, you must know that Obama is:

- "The biggest liar in the history of the presidency." (3/3/09)
- "A dictator." (3/4/09)
- "Even more of a terrorist than Hugo Chávez is." (3/5/09)
- "A neo-Marxist fascist dictator in the making." (3/6/09)
- "Chairman Mao Tse-Obama." (9/3/09)

Wait! It's even worse than that:

- "Obama has a plan to force children into a paramilitary army." (3/23/09)
- "Obama appointees actually have almost the same exact policies as the Nazi Party did." (3/13/09)
- "Obama hates and is raping America." (4/21/09)
- "He may as well be an illegal alien from Mars for the way he's running America." (7/23/09)

And God only knows what Barack and Michelle Obama are doing to the interior of the White House. "I pray to God," says Savage, "that the Obamas don't take down the pictures of Lincoln and such and replace them with, you know, Malcolm X."

(Note to Michael Savage: As a member of the White House Press Corps, I'm in the White House two or three times a week. I promise you, the same presidential portraits that were hanging there when Barack Obama moved into the executive mansion are still on the walls. Malcolm X is nowhere to be seen. Relax!)

Of course, if you agree that President Obama is as dangerous as Michael Savage paints him to be, then you must leap to the same conclusion—the conclusion Savage reached as early as March 10, 2009: "I think it is time to start talking about impeachment."

Hyperbole and paranoia, thy names are Michael Savage.

For President Obama, there is one consolation: He's not alone. Michael Savage hates most of the rest of humanity, too.

MICHAEL SAVAGE HATES–*YOU!*

Actually, when you hear Michael Savage's show, you wonder why anybody would hire him for any radio or TV job—unless you personally get your rocks off listening to a demented, nonstop litany of hatred. Because Savage really does hate everybody, with the possible exception of white, male, paranoid, repressed heterosexuals who are as crazy as he is. Everybody else is on notice, starting with . . .

IMMIGRANTS

Among conservatives, on the issue of immigration reform, there are wide differences: from the moderate views of George W. Bush or John McCain, to the hard-line conservatives of talk radio who strongly oppose illegal immigration. But Michael Savage simply hates *immigrants,* and doesn't mind saying so.

For Savage, illegal immigrants are such a serious national threat that we need to deploy the military against them. On his radio broadcast of August 8, 2008, he praised the Italian government for sending troops into the streets to combat street crime and illegal immigration. "So they've done what we need to here," Savage concluded. "We need to get our troops out of Iraq and put them on the streets of America to protect us from the scourge of illegal immigrants who are running rampant across America, killing our police for sport, raping, murdering like a scythe across America while the liberal psychos tell us they come here to work." Defying evidence of the millions of immigrants working in fields and orchards, restaurants, construction projects, hotels, car washes, landscaping, and a host of other jobs, Savage insists: "They do not all come here to work. They come here to work the system, sell drugs, rape, and kill on contract."

Liberty herself has been defiled by illegal immigrants, insists Savage. "The Statue of Liberty is crying, she's been raped and disheveled . . . raped and disheveled by illegal aliens." Yes, that's the same Statue of Liberty which once welcomed to America Savage's father, an immigrant from Russia.

On several occasions, Savage has told his listeners how best to show their disgust with immigrants: "That's right, burn the Mexican flag on your street corner, show what you care about, show that you won't take it anymore, show that you're sick of everybody pushing us around like we are a pitiful, helpless giant of a nation that is out of control because we have nothing but rot and corruption at the highest level. Do that, burn a Mexican flag for America, burn a Mexican flag for those who died that you should have a nationality and a sovereignty, go out in the street and show you're a man, burn ten Mexican flags if I could recommend it." Not the type of guy you'd want at your Cinco de Mayo party. (For the record, in response to Savage's rant, there was no recorded wave of massive burnings of the Mexican flag.)

But, for Savage, the stakes are high. We have to fight back because our very existence as a nation is at stake: "We, the people, are being displaced by the people of Mexico. This is an invasion by any other name. Everybody with a brain understands that. Everybody who understands reality understands we are being pushed out of our own country."

Again, do you detect, maybe, a touch of paranoia here?

And what about those organizations fighting for immigration reform, like La Raza? Usually, Savage equates all political opponents with Nazis, carrying out another Holocaust. This time, he picked an enemy closer to home: "In my opinion, La Raza is the equivalent of the Ku Klux Klan for the Hispanic people. It's true they haven't hung anybody, but they certainly stand only for one race. That's the name of their group: La Raza—'The Race.' They didn't say 'all races.' They said, 'the race,' so they're saying their race is *the* race, and that means all the other races, who are not Hispanic, are to be subjugated to their race—*the* race—which is superior and supreme."

Do you detect, just maybe, a little ignorance here?

The phrase "La Raza" was originally coined by Mexican scholar José Vasconcelos as "La Raza Cósmica," to indicate that the people of Latin America are a mixture of many of the world's cultures, races, and religions. From the beginning, it was an inclusive term meant to celebrate all the world's races, not to assert the superiority of any one race. But the paranoid Savage can't seem to wrap his mind around the whole inclusion thing.

LIBERALS

No doubt, immigrants rank pretty low on Savage's totem pole of hate. But they're still probably a notch or two above—liberals!

In addition to scorching liberals daily on his radio show, Savage has written three books attacking them: the aforementioned *The Savage Nation: Saving America from the Liberal Assault on Our Borders, Language, and Culture*; a companion screed, *The Enemy Within: Saving America from the Liberal Assault on Our Schools, Faith, and Military*; and, summing it all up, *Liberalism Is a Mental Disorder: Savage Solutions*.

Nobody but Michael Savage has ever talked seriously about his running for president. But were he ever elected—now there's a scary thought!—there's little doubt who his first target would be. He's already warned liberals: "I can guarantee you, you wouldn't be in business too long. I can guarantee you you'd be arrested for sedition within six months of my taking power. I'd have you people licking lead paint, for what you did to this country."

Meanwhile, there's not a liberal walking, including yours truly, who's been spared Savage's wrath, but at least I'm in good company. Barney Frank, Barbara Boxer, Hillary Clinton, Ted Kennedy, Nancy Pelosi, John Kerry, Bill Clinton, Joe Biden, and Jimmy Carter ("an anti-Semitic bastard!") are just a few of today's leading liberals Savage regularly singles out for vitriol.

Not even Ted Kennedy's ultimately fatal bout with cancer spared him Savage's venomous wrath. "Does a man who spent his entire political life destroying the fundamental tenets of American morality become miraculously rehabilitated, simply because he entered the hospital?" Savage asked his listeners the day after Kennedy was diagnosed with a brain tumor. "Do so-called conservatives stop being conservative because of a medical diagnosis?"

Savage answered his own question: Hell, no! He then listed Kennedy's career sins: "We cannot forget that he opened the borders as early as 1965, lying to the American people saying it would not change the demographics of America. We cannot forget that the lion of the left voted to destroy the flag and destroy traditional marriage. . . . We cannot forget that he voted no on a constitutional ban on flag desecration; that Kennedy voted no on a constitutional ban on same-sex marriage; that Kennedy voted yes on adding sexual orientation to the definition of hate crimes; that Kennedy voted no on banning affirmative action hiring with federal funds . . ." Duh! Of course he voted that way. Kennedy was a liberal.

Still, Savage wasn't as cruel to Kennedy as he was to Madeleine Albright. When the former secretary of state urged the Bush administration to resume direct talks with North Korea, Savage pounced: "I want to direct you to a traitor. In my opinion, she should be tried for treason, and when she's found guilty, she should be hung."

It doesn't help if liberals call themselves progressives, either. Michael Savage has their number. "A progressive is basically a pervert covering it up with liberal politics," he contends. And, in his sick worldview, liberals are public enemy number one: just as dangerous as those who attacked this country on September 11 and just as important to exterminate: "To fight only the al Qaeda scum is to miss the terrorist network operating within our own borders. . . . Who are these traitors? Every rotten radical left-winger in this country, that's who."

Just in case his listeners find the al Qaeda analogy too mild, Savage has his favorite old standby up his sleeve. In vintage Savage-speak, liberals are not just acolytes of Osama bin Laden, they worship at the altar of Adolf Hitler: "So, in fact, they are the Brown Shirts of today—only today, they wear green shirts and they cloak themselves in environmentalism and peace. But no mistake about it, it's the same rabble that brought Hitler to power, and we have them today—and they're all on the left."

A little over-the-top? Not for Savage. There's always another Nazi conspiracy waiting in the wings.

Not even the Democratic Party's historic support for Israel could persuade Savage, himself a Jew, that liberals/Democrats/progressives have the best interests of the United States, and Israel, in mind. When four Israeli naval officers were killed by a terrorist rocket, Savage blamed it on liberals: "Now I realize that the American left is cheering today. They'll probably break open the jug wine and cheer that Jews are dying, and that they're living and cowering in bomb shelters. One day, the 'Deutschland Uber Alles' may be played in Jerusalem, and the American left can tear off their masks once and for all and show themselves to be what they really are—which is the Nazis of our time."

Mein Gott!

For liberal politicians, there is one consolation. No matter how brutally treated in Savage land, they usually fare better than the leaders of the ACLU. For them, even Abu Ghraib is treatment too mild. "Cops are getting knocked off all over the country because of the rules of engagement, written primarily by the scummiest class in America, the vermin of vermin, which are the left-wing lawyers who should be put in Abu Ghraib with hoods over their head, as far as I'm concerned," decreed Savage. If not Abu Ghraib, then he has another destination in mind: "If I had the power by executive order, I would round up every member of the ACLU and of the National Lawyers Guild, and I'd put them in a prison in Guantánamo and I'd throw the key away."

Good thing he didn't. When Savage was banned from Britain, who were the first people to rush to his defense? Of course! That vermin of vermin, the left-wing lawyers of the ACLU. They defended him. And they won.

MUSLIMS

No doubt about it. If white Christian males were imprisoned at Guantánamo or Abu Ghraib, Savage would have a different opinion. But in his warped mind, no punishment is too harsh for Muslims.

Arabs? Muslims? It makes no difference. Each and every one of them—man, woman, and child—is a terrorist. They are the enemy and must be dealt with accordingly, no matter how numerous they are. "They say, 'Oh, there's a billion of them.' I said, 'So, kill 100 million of them, then there'll be 900 million of them.' I mean, would you rather die—would you rather us die than them?"

Men? Women? It makes no difference to Savage. They are equally evil, and equally dangerous. "When I see a woman walking around in a burqa, I see a Nazi. " (There's that Hitler analogy again.) "That's what I see, how do you like that? A hateful Nazi who would like to cut your throat and kill your children."

After September 11, George W. Bush went out of his way—some unfortunate "crusader" rhetoric notwithstanding—to reassure the world that the United States had no beef with the religion of Islam, nor did we consider every Muslim an enemy of the United States. No such mealy-mouthed distinctions for Michael Savage. As far as he's concerned, they're all guilty. "When you're dealing with Arabs, there are no friends. They're old rug traders going back a thousand years in that part of the world. Right now, one side is your friend; the other side is your enemy. The next day, they're both stabbing you in the back and picking your pockets."

The only answer in dealing with the Muslim world, says Savage, is to re-create what, according to his sick mind, most Americans want: another Hiroshima. To drop the "Big Boy" on a major Arab capital. And if Arab leaders don't think we'd do it, argues Savage, they're mistaken. "They haven't seen the white male. They don't understand the white male dropped two atomic bombs on Japan. They don't remember what the white male is capable of, because he's been awfully subdued for a long period of time. But if push comes to shove, I can guarantee you all the turbaned folks are going to find out all over again just how vicious the white male can really be. They keep provoking this nation, they're going to wind up with a nuclear cloud over their country."

In other words, says Savage, "We need to do the same thing to Muslims that the good Germans did to the Christ killers." (Isn't it strange, hearing a Jew refer to "good Germans" and "Christ killers"? Is this guy sick, or what?)

Even a second Holocaust is not enough punishment for Muslims, however. Savage insists he would couple nuclear devastation of their homeland with "an outright ban on Muslim immigration, laws making the dissemination of enemy propaganda illegal, and the uncoupling of the liberal ACLU. . . . I would also make the construction of mosques illegal in the United States, and the speaking of English only in the streets of the United States the law." Tourists, you have been warned!

And if that still doesn't do the trick, Savage has one more card up his sleeve: "I think these people need to be forcibly converted to Christianity."

Ah, yes, because converting people to Christianity at gunpoint has worked so well in the past.

GAYS AND LESBIANS

As we have already seen from his virulent response to a supposedly gay caller on MSNBC, Michael Savage has what appears to be a pathological problem with gays and lesbians. Which is strange, coming from a man who used to embrace Allen Ginsberg as one of his best friends.

Today, Savage doesn't just hate individual gays and lesbians, he honestly believes in a great gay conspiracy: "When you hear 'human rights,' think gays. When you hear 'human rights,' think only one thing: someone who wants to rape your son."

Not only that, Savage worries that homosexuals are destroying Western civilization as we know it—or, at least, destroying the United States. Little did you realize the dangerous threat posed by that gay couple living down the street or the nice lesbian who works in the next cubicle. "The homosexual dance of death is the seminal issue of our time," Savage warns.

Over the years, Savage has lashed out on every related issue, from gay adoption, to gays in the Boy Scouts, to attempts to ban discrimination against gays in the workplace. But the one issue that really drives him over the top is same-sex marriage. "I don't like a woman married to a woman," he told his radio listeners on February 26, 2007. "It makes me want to puke . . . I want to vomit when I hear it. It's child abuse."

Of course, he heard a lot about it in 2008, when the California ballot featured Proposition 8, a measure to overturn the State Supreme Court's recent decision recognizing the legitimacy of same-sex marriage. Savage became one of the initiative's most passionate supporters. "You must vote 'yes,' if you're sane," he lectured his audience. "If you're insane, hate the family, hate man and woman, hate your mother and father, hate the Bible, hate the church, and hate the synagogue, of course, you're in favor of 'no' on Proposition 8."

When Prop 8 won, Savage's joy was short-lived because of the widespread national outrage that followed its passage. To many around the country, and I was one of them, Prop 8 was a giant and embarrassing step backward for California. Savage, of course, saw it as just the opposite. And, as always, when Savage encounters something he doesn't like, he reaches into his bag of this-is-the-most-evil-thing-that-ever-happened-in-the-world analogies and pulls out—Hitler! "Socially, we're far worse—more degenerate than Weimar Germany," Savage complained in November 2008. "At least in Weimar Germany, men couldn't marry men and women couldn't marry women. So we're probably ten leagues below the degeneracy that brought about Hitler. We're probably *fifty* leagues below the degeneracy that brought about Hitler. We are the sickest, most disgusting country on the earth, and we are psychotically—we are psychotic as a nation."

Hey, love it or leave it. And you have to admit, there is something ironic about Michael Savage's calling someone else "psychotic."

Look, let's be honest. There's also something fishy about Michael Savage's hatred for those who welcome a sexual attraction that he's come close to admitting he feels himself. "I choose to override my desires for men when they swell in me," the forty-something, Jewish male protagonist in his 1983 novel *Vital Signs* muses, "waiting out the passions like a storm, below decks." Note the interesting, and deliberate, use of the phrase "swell in me." Could Michael Savage's hatred of gays be an expression of poorly disguised self-hatred? Just asking.

In any case, in Savage's twisted mind, there are not just symbolic, but two very real reasons why same-sex marriage is wrong. First, Savage mourns for all the potential future radio talk show hosts we are missing. "One of the reasons America is suffering right now is because so many people who are gay have not had children. . . . Some of the most wonderful genetic material is going to waste."

And, second, gays and lesbians are, according to Savage, clearly responsible for the country's economic collapse in 2008. Don't blame the bankers, hedge fund operators, or investment fund managers. Blame it on the gays! Says Savage: "Why should we care about homosexuals trying to destroy families through the mock marriage that they perform in order to mock God, the church, the family, children, the fetus, the DNA of the human species? Why should we care about it while we have a financial meltdown? Because the spiritual side of the downturn on Wall Street is directly related to the moral downturn in the United States of America."

Whatever you do, don't make the mistake of thinking the debate over same-sex marriage is the end of the story. According to Savage, gay activists have a much broader goal. They've launched the Second American Revolution, and they aim to seize control. "They will not stop until they force their agenda down your throats," warns Savage. "Gay marriage is just the tip of the iceberg. They want full and total subjugation of this society to their agenda." In other words, start looking for a same-sex partner now, because soon the sinister homosexual conspiracy will force us all into gay marriages.

In the 1950s, Senator Joseph McCarthy saw a communist under every bed. Today, Michael Savage sees a gay or lesbian under every bed—or, worse yet, *in* every bed. You, dear reader, may be among those millions of Americans who have mellowed on the issue of sexual orientation. You may simply accept the fact that some Americans are different, in terms of their sexual orientation, and are willing to live with it. You may even have been lulled by the mainstream media into accepting the coexistence of gays and lesbians in your own community, workplace, church, book club—yes, even in your own family.

What a fool you are! Don't you recognize the danger? Listen to Michael Savage. Barney Frank and his friends are more dangerous than Osama bin Laden and al Qaeda: "The radical, homosexual agenda threatens your very survival."

When gays and lesbians take over the entire country and make heterosexuality illegal, don't say Michael Savage didn't warn you.

WOMEN AND BLACKS

Alas, women, in Savage's world, can't win for losing. He hates them if they're gay, and hates them if they're straight. And, lesbian or straight, he blames them for placing Barack Obama in the White House: "Patchouli oil, hair under the arms, no brassieres, and the next thing you know Obama is president."

Some of his most deplorable comments have been directed against some of America's most successful women. We've already noted his personal criticism of former MSNBC reporter Ashleigh Banfield, now with Tru TV. Other women in the media have been just as brutally burned. Savage described CNN's Susan Roesgen as a "self-hating white woman who couldn't get a job as a hooker." After her interview with Iranian president Mahmoud Ahmadinejad, he denounced ABC's Diane Sawyer as a "hag," a "low-life witch," and a "lying whore." But that was just for starters. Then, addressing Sawyer directly, Savage really got down and dirty: "You're lower than Anna Nicole Smith on her worst day. You're dumber than Paris Hilton. You're more shallow than Lindsay Lohan."

Savage is equally cruel to women in public office, particularly Democrats. In his vocabulary, for example, Speaker Nancy Pelosi is "Nancy Mussolini," or sometimes "Mussolini in a skirt." Senator Barbara Boxer is nothing but "a loud-mouthed, foul-tempered woman bossing men around." Boxer, of course, is, according to Savage, one of the seventeen reasons the U.S. Senate is "more vicious and more histrionic than ever: because women have been injected into it." And Madeleine Albright is nothing but a "fat moron who looks like she would have been comfortable just cooking in a kitchen. Somehow she wound up secretary of state."

Mature women usually get the brunt of Savage's attacks: "Any heterosexual woman today over the age of twenty-five who grew up in America is basically a dominatrix." But he doesn't stop there. Even high school girls merit his scorn.

Located in the Marin County town of Ross, Branson School has long been one of the highest-rated private schools in the San Francisco Bay Area. It started as an all-girls high school, but has been coed since 1985. Like many other private schools, Branson encourages its students to volunteer their time for local charities—which, includes, for Branson students, helping serve meals to San Francisco's homeless population every Thanksgiving.

Most talk show hosts, liberal or conservative, would applaud such a display of altruism, especially on a national holiday. But not Savage. To his sick mind, those high schools girls are just looking for what every woman secretly wants: "the girls from Branson can go in and maybe get raped . . . because they seem to like the excitement of it. There's always the thrill and possibility they'll be raped in a Dumpster while giving out a turkey sandwich."

Now, yes, I believe in free speech. But you go ahead and defend Michael Savage for depraved remarks like that. Please be my guest. I can't do it. Nor can I understand why stations continue to broadcast his filth.

Blacks don't fare much better in the savage's demented universe. He seems to regards all African-Americans as mentally inferior to white males. And he chose Martin Luther King Day 2007 to dismiss the entire civil rights movement as a giant con job. "It's a whole industry, it's a racket," he warned listeners. "It's a racket that is used to exploit primarily heterosexual, Christian, white males' birthright and steal from them what is their birthright and give it to people who didn't qualify for it."

So much for the life work of Martin Luther King Jr. According to Savage, it's too bad King wasted so much time on so frivolous a project as civil rights.

But that does raise the question: Is there *anybody* Michael Savage likes? Of course. Take away blacks, Latinos, women, Muslims, Jews (even though he is one)—and you've got the answer:

WHITE CHRISTIAN MALES

For many believers, Armageddon is the eagerly awaited battle between good and evil that will usher in the Second Coming of Christ. But not for Michael Savage. He believes Armageddon is already here: It's the battle between beleaguered white Christian males—and everybody else.

If there's an underlying theme to his program, the same thread that weaves its way through his daily diatribes against a wide variety of targets, it's his conviction that the whole world is out to get, and that life itself is stacked against, male Caucasians. White males, in Savage's warped worldview, are the only endangered species—and our only salvation: "The white Christian heterosexual married male is the epitome of everything right with America."

That argument underlies his beef with illegal immigrants. The problem is not that they came here illegally, it's that they're the wrong color—and, therefore, will eventually dilute the supremacy and cultural values of white Americans. In fact, he claims, they're already doing so. "We, the people, are being displaced by the people of Mexico," Savage says flatly.

He dismisses the idea that America is a land of immigrants, who come here from different lands and cultures and blend together to form a new country. That was only true, Savage asserts, when all our ancestors came from Europe.

"When you bring immigrants in from Europe," he explains, "whether they be Irish, whether they be Italian, whether they be English, whether they be Romanian, whether they be Czechoslovakian, whether they be Yugoslavian, whether they be German—they're from Europe, and there is a melting pot possibility. . . . When you start bringing in masses of immigrants from everywhere on earth, you don't have a melting pot; they cannot be melted into an American, and that's what's going on in the country today. We're bringing in millions of people from countries that have no compatibility with the values of Europe, not any values whatsoever."

Of course, for Savage the phrase "bringing in masses of immigrants from everywhere on earth" is just code for bringing in too many people of color—as he makes clear in denouncing the very idea of a multicultural society. "Multiculturalism has completely failed America. It is a disaster, an unmitigated disaster. Multiculturalism—as a premise that all cultures are equal and all cultures have an equal amount to contribute to the world—that's utter hogwash! The reason my ancestors came to this country as immigrants, and the reason your ancestors came to this country as immigrants, is because of the great enterprise created by white, Anglo-Saxon Protestants. It is the greatest country ever created in the world. It is built upon the best—the best of the white, Anglo-Saxon world."

And Savage therefore rejects as anti-white-male any movement to win equal rights for women, gays, or people of color. To his very bizarre way of thinking, the only way to grant them equal rights is to take those rights away from someone else. Guess who?

"Take a guess out of whose hide all of these rights are coming. They're not coming out of women's hides, are they? No, there's only one group that's targeted, and that group are white, heterosexual males. They are the new witches being hunted by the illiberal left using the guise of civil rights and fairness to women and whatnot."

Poor white males. They've already had to move over and let an African-American occupy the Oval Office. Someday, they may have to make room for a woman.

SAVAGE ON THE ISSUES

Occasionally, Savage abandons his personal attacks in order to talk about the issues of the day. Although to this discussion, too, he brings a morbid level of bile.

There are countless examples of how Savage seizes on issues, not to enlighten or inform his audience, but only to fan the flames of hatred against certain groups or individuals. For the purposes of this book, three examples will suffice. Any more, and you may start to feel queasy.

ABU GHRAIB

At first, nobody could believe they were real. Photographs of a nude, black-hooded prisoner with wires attached to his genitals. Other photos of nude prisoners piled on top of each other, like a pyramid; prisoners being attacked by dogs; prisoners being sodomized; prisoners forced to masturbate or commit homosexual acts.

Yet, we soon learned, the photographs were indeed real. These shocking photographs had captured evidence of the abuse and torture of Iraqi prisoners held at the U.S. military prison of Abu Ghraib.

Once the authenticity of the photos had been determined, everybody from President Bush on down condemned the inhumane treatment of prisoners at Abu Ghraib.

Well, almost everybody. Everybody except—Michael Savage and Rush Limbaugh. Not only did Savage not condemn what happened at what he called "Grab-an-Arab" prison, he said, "I commend" the abuse of prisoners, and insisted "we need more of the humiliation tactics, not less."

Echoing Limbaugh's comments that those who conducted the torture of prisoners were just a bunch of boys "having a good time," Savage argued that the acts he saw being performed in the photos were "mild in comparison to what goes on in South of Market clubs in San Francisco."

For Savage, the only problem with sodomizing prisoners was that it didn't go far enough. "Instead of joysticks, I would have liked to have seen dynamite put in their orifices and they should be dropped from air-planes. . . . They should put dynamite in their behinds and drop them from 35,000 feet, the whole pack of scum out of that jail."

Indeed, according to Savage, there was only one way to solve the prob-lems at Abu Ghraib: simply kill all the prisoners. "I believe that a thou-sand of them should be killed tomorrow," he told his listeners, oblivious of the reaction this action might have around the world. "I think a thousand of them held in the Iraqi prison should be given twenty-four hours—a trial and executed. I think they need to be shown that we are not going to roll over to them."

If Democrats in Congress interfered with operations at Abu Ghraib, warned Savage, there would be hell to pay in the form of another terrorist attack on U.S. soil before the November 2004 general election: "What's gonna happen is terrible. What's gonna happen now is even worse than you can imagine. Because these interrogation tactics which were working, by everything I can read, are no longer permissible, you are gonna have an event in this country before the election, and you can thank your friends [Senator Carl] Levin and Kennedy for that, you can thank all the phonies on the Democrat [sic] side for that."

Well, Savage got that wrong. But he did get one thing right. He didn't buy the White House line that the torture carried out at Abu Ghraib was just the work of a few, out-of-control rednecks from West Virginia. He knew they were the merely the bottom links in a chain of command that stretched all the way back to Washington—for which, he believed, Bush and Cheney should have been congratulated.

"These are not a few individuals who made this up. That's crap. That's crap in my opinion. This came from the top. And how high up it goes I don't know but frankly I commend them for it. It's wise intelligence tech-niques, to break the enemy where he's vulnerable, not try to get him where he's strong."

Savage, in fact, grew so fond of "enhanced interrogation techniques," he wanted to use them against a group of his own political opponents.

SAVAGE V. CAIR

As noted above, Michael Savage has a special hatred for Islam and Muslims. In 2004, he stated: "I think Muslims need to be forcibly converted to Christianity. . . . It's the only thing that can probably turn them into human beings." In 2006, as we've seen, he called for a ban on Muslim immigration and recommended making "the construction of mosques illegal in this country."

Still, Savage's hatred of Muslims kept growing. And on October 27, 2007, it boiled over. In a long tirade, extraordinarily ugly even for him, he lashed out against Muslims, Islam, and the Council on American-Islamic Relations, or CAIR, which he had earlier accused of being linked to terrorist organizations.

Imagine you're a peaceful, practicing Muslim. How'd you like to hear this shouted at you over the radio?

"I'm not gonna put my wife in a hijab. And I'm not gonna put my daughter in a burqa. And I'm not gettin' on my all-fours and braying to Mecca. And you could drop dead if you don't like it. You can shove it up your pipe. I don't want to hear any more about Islam. I don't wanna hear one more word about Islam. Take your religion and shove it up your behind. I'm sick of you." He wasn't done yet.

"What kind of religion is this? What kind of world are you living in when you let them in here with that throwback document in their hand, which is a book of hate. Don't tell me I need reeducation. They need deportation. I don't need reeducation. Deportation, not reeducation. You can take C-A-I-R and throw 'em out of my country. I'd raise the American flag and I'd get out my trumpet if you did it. Without due process. You can take your due process and shove it."

But wait. There's more!

"What sane nation that worships the U.S. Constitution, which is the greatest document of freedom ever written, would bring in people who worship a book that tells them the exact opposite. Make no mistake about it, the Koran is not a document of freedom. The Koran is a document of slavery and chattel. It teaches you that you are a slave."

Whew!

The leaders of CAIR had had enough. In early November 2007, they took action. While acknowledging Savage's right to say whatever he wanted, they also borrowed a page from the conservative playbook and asked their followers to boycott companies that advertised their products on Savage's radio show and inform sponsors they were doing so.

The response was immediate. Citrix Systems pulled its advertisements from the show. So did OfficeMax and TrustedID.

At which point, Savage sued CAIR for posting audio excerpts from his show on their Web site, alleging copyright infringement, and accusing them of using selective sound bites to deliberately distort his message.

As expected, the U.S. District Court dismissed Savage's lawsuit, upholding CAIR's rights under the First Amendment and the fair use policy to publish the talk show host's actual comments. Savage was invited to file an amended complaint, but declined to do so. Even he knew he didn't have a legal leg to stand on.

Lesson learned: You can't use free speech against others, without expecting free speech to be used against you. God bless America!

Having lost his case against America's Muslims, schoolyard bully Michael Savage turned to an easier target: children with autism. And it turned into one of the few times Savage got in trouble for comments having nothing to do with race, gender, or sexuality.

AUTISM

In his career as radio talk show host, as we've seen, Michael Savage has said some pretty ugly things. He's targeted a lot of people for abuse. But not even his mockery of Ted Kennedy's brain cancer, nor his suggesting that Abu Ghraib prisoners be dropped from an airplane at thirty thousand feet, nor his demand that Madeleine Albright be hanged for treason, match his cruel attacks on autistic children.

He fired his first salvo on the July 16, 2008, broadcast of *The Savage Nation,* dismissing autism as a "fraud" and a "racket." Today's concern over autism, he insisted, is as phony as yesterday's concern over asthma.

"For a long while, we were hearing that every minority child had asthma. Why did they sudden— why was there an asthma epidemic amongst minority children? Because I'll tell you why: The children got extra welfare if they were disabled, and they got extra help in school. It was a money racket."

So with asthma, same with autism. "Now the illness du jour is autism. You know what autism is? I'll tell you what autism is. In 99 percent of the cases, it's a brat who hasn't been told to cut the act out. That's what autism is. What do you mean they scream and they're silent? They don't have a father around to tell them, 'Don't act like a moron. You'll get nowhere in life. Stop acting like a putz. Straighten up. Act like a man. Don't sit there crying and screaming, idiot.'"

This time, Savage's comments stirred up a storm of criticism. Parents of children with autism and their supporters held protests outside radio stations that carried his program, demanding that Savage be fired. One major sponsor, the insurance company Aflac, pulled all its advertising. Nervous radio executives rushed to insist that Savage's comments were his opinion alone, and did not reflect that of station management.

Meanwhile, medical experts pointed out that Savage was badly misinformed about autism and simply repeating myths dating back to the nineteenth century that autistic children were nothing but children lacking parental discipline. Catherine Lord of New York University's Child Study Center explained, "Any tendency to blame the children or to think they're just being bratty if they misbehave perpetuates the myth that autism isn't a learning disability. It's a neurobiological condition, just like epilepsy or another medical condition like diabetes or a heart condition. It would be like blaming the child with a heart condition for not being able to exercise."

Still, Savage refused to apologize. After all, he knows more about anything than anybody else, even medical science. "My point remains true," he told *The New York Times* in a telephone interview. "It is an over-diagnosed medical condition. In my readings, there is no confirmed medical diagnosis for autism."

Later, Savage appeared on CNN's *Larry King Live,* with fellow talk show host Glenn Beck hosting (before he moved to Fox News). Unable to defend his indefensible remarks, he chose instead to reinvent himself and attack his critics. After replaying Savage's statements from July 16 about autism's being a fraud, Beck noted: "It seems pretty clear that you don't really believe autism exists."

"Who, me?" responded an incredulous Savage. "No, no, no, no, no. Again, you took what they gave you. But you didn't take the entire preceding material. . . . This was in the broader context of the over-medicalization, the over-diagnosis of disease, using our children as profit centers."

And then—the man has no shame!—Savage actually insisted that he doesn't attack children, he *defends* them. In fact, he said, "There's no one in the media who's done more for the defenseless than Michael Savage, particularly children." He goes on: "I've spent all day saying what a shame it is that I—as a man who has spent his entire life defending the defenseless, mainly children—should have to defend myself from charges leveled at me from men who specialize in hating families and children, namely Media Matters—who probably come after you as well—by ripping things out of context and making me look like the monster that they are." So now we know who's to blame for Savage's comments that autism is nothing but a fraud and racket. It's not his fault for saying it, it's Media Matters' fault for reporting it. Savage even threatened to post names and photos of Media Matters staffers on his Web site.

Notice that Savage never explains in what context it *is* okay to label children with autism as brats, and part of a huge money racket. And that, of course, is because he can't.

LEAVING "THE SAVAGE NATION"

By now, you probably feel like you want to stop, put the book down, and wash your hands. I know. I feel the same way, every time I listen to Michael Savage.

And we're not alone. Even some of those who broadcast Savage's program find him too obnoxious. In September 2009, Savage was forced to scramble for a new home when his flagship station, San Francisco's mighty KNEW-AM 910, dropped his show. "We have decided to go in a different philosophical and ideological direction," managers of the Clear Channel–owned station said in a statement. Which is spin for: We simply couldn't stand that guy anymore.

Yet, in national syndication, Savage still shows up on the air, three hours a day, spewing his bile and exorcising his inner demons.

Unlike Rush Limbaugh or Sean Hannity, the problem with Michael Savage is not that he's a conservative or takes an extreme right-wing position on every issue. It's that he's so ugly, so mean, and so inflammatory. For Savage, it's not enough to disagree with someone, he must try to obliterate them with the most vicious personal attacks. And, let's face it, Savage is also paranoid. Mega-paranoid, even. He takes everything, and everyone, personally. If you're not white, male, Christian, and conservative, you're out to get him. You're his enemy. And his mission is to destroy you before you can destroy him.

I've often wondered what a miserable, unhappy life Michael Savage must lead. Unfortunately, given his platform, he has the capacity to make at least part of our lives miserable and unhappy, too.

But, in the end, what's most sad about Michael Savage is not the fact that he broadcasts three hours of hate every day. It's that 6 million people a week tune in to listen to it. And that, I'm afraid, says more about us than it says about him.

5

TOXIC TV

So where did all these radio talk show hosts come from, anyway?

Well, a lot of them came from a little radio factory called cable television. And, more and more, as cable TV became less objective and more opinionated, radio personalities have migrated the other way, from radio to television.

The TV–radio feeder relationship began long before cable news for one simple reason: owners of many local television stations also owned a talk radio station in the same market, with hours of airtime to fill and talent needed to fill them.

Take it from me. I began my broadcasting career at KABC-TV in Los Angeles in September 1980. I'd only been there a couple of months before I received a call from the program director of KABC Radio, asking me if I'd be interested in filling in for Michael Jackson and Ray Bream, two of the station's top-rated hosts. Naturally I said yes, even though I'd had no radio experience or training whatsoever. My only qualification to take over the microphone was that I appeared every night on the Channel 7 local news—and, of course, had an opinion on just about everything.

Congratulations, Bill Press! You are now a radio talk show host!

MAKING THE LEAP

Since even many people in radio still, erroneously, consider their medium the ugly stepsister of television, every radio talk show host yearns to have his or her own television show. Some make it, but more don't. That's because there's a big difference between the two mediums. Being comfortable talking into a radio microphone doesn't mean you're automatically comfortable in front of a television camera.

It's a lesson I learned up close. On L.A.'s KABC, where I co-hosted an early version of *Crossfire* called *The Dueling Bills* with conservative Bill Pearl, one of the most popular hosts was psychologist David Viscott. For two hours, Viscott simply took phone calls and doled out advice. It may not sound like much, but the variety of personal or family problems people called in about, and the insightful advice he offered, made for compelling broadcasts.

Indeed, Viscott's program was so successful he was offered his own TV show. Which made the rest of us insanely jealous. Until the first show aired. No matter how weird the problems people called in about, a doctor sitting at a desk talking into a telephone or microphone for two hours— magic on radio—was obviously not going to work on television. It didn't work for him, and it didn't work for *Loveline,* either. That colorful medical/ relationship show, a huge hit on radio since 1983, had a brief, four-year run on MTV, but ultimately failed despite efforts to "sex" it up for the screen by adding various female co-hosts. Radio doesn't always work on television, not even music TV.

In his time, Rush Limbaugh learned the same lesson.

For a television debut, no one was predicted to make a bigger splash than Limbaugh. And few have laid bigger eggs. His TV show lacked the spontaneity that made his radio show so successful. He was clearly faking it, by playing to the camera so much. He looked uncomfortable in front of his studio audience. He was so overweight at the time he looked like a beached whale—even before the camera added ten pounds. His jokes fell flat. He just wasn't the same old Rush that people loved on the radio dial. Nevertheless, his TV show—produced by Roger Ailes, who later created Fox News—dragged on for four years.

Which, as we saw in the last chapter, was forty-four months longer than Michael Savage lasted. Despite the wide popularity of media theorist Marshall McLuhan's teachings (he even made it into *Annie Hall*), many people still don't understand that television is a "cool" medium. Savage was way too hot. The vicious language that turned people on to his radio show turned them off on TV. And television managers were less tolerant of ugly, personal attacks than radio programmers. Or at least they used to be—until, as we saw, Fox News producers got their claws on Glenn Beck.

And then there was *Dr. Laura*, whom I knew back in the days when she was still a flaming liberal. Laura Schlessinger and I worked out of adjacent studios at KFI in Los Angeles, which I had joined after leaving KABC. Schlessinger created one of radio's first successful "ask the doctor" shows, even though she has a Ph.D., not an M.D. degree. Her doctorate is in early childhood education.

Back then, she was a hugely successful local radio host, dispensing personal, family, and lifestyle advice in a very friendly, chatty, personable style. I broadcast only on weekends, but Laura would often call my show from her car to agree with me on some liberal argument I was making, especially when I was taking on members of the religious right for their extreme positions on homosexuality and other social issues.

In 1994, Laura jumped from KFI to national syndication—and somehow morphed into a conservative shrew. She no longer gave advice to callers. Instead, she attacked them personally, reserving particular venom for single moms, unmarried couples who lived together, anybody who dared have sex before they were married, and, in a total reversal of opinion, for gays and lesbians—about whom she now said she had earlier been misinformed.

Whoever this person was, she wasn't the same Laura Schlessinger those of us who worked with her at KFI knew and loved. In fact, about a year after moving to Washington, while driving to a radio station to fill in for a local host, I was shocked when I tuned into *Dr. Laura* and heard her repeatedly humiliating callers with extreme, ugly, judgmental criticism. Walking into the studio, I told the producer I'd decided to devote my first hour to the topic: "When did Dr. Laura become such a bitch?"

Nonetheless, conservatives loved the new Dr. Laura. So, naturally, some brain-dead producer figured: What the hell, if she makes good talk radio, she'll make great TV. And, once again, the experiment failed. For one thing, the judgmental radio personality didn't translate well to television. For another, Schlesinger faced the same problem as Dr. Viscott and *Loveline*— dispensing advice rarely makes for compelling television. And finally, the gay and lesbian community, offended by her constant, hateful, anti-homosexual tirades, successfully persuaded several major sponsors not to advertise on her show. The TV version of *Dr. Laura* lasted exactly one year.

Two liberal talk radio hosts, however, have defied the odds.

Rachel Maddow was barely making a living on a local talk show in Holyoke, Massachusetts, doing stand-up comedy on the side, when she landed a job on a new, start-up, progressive radio network called Air America, perhaps most famous for launching the radio career of another stand-up comic, now U.S. Senator Al Franken. Rachel started out as one of three co-hosts of the zany morning show *Unfiltered*, appearing with comedy writer Lizz Winstead and rapper Chuck D. It was a fun show. I actually filled in a couple of times for Lizz, and loved working with Rachel. Chuck D, as I recall, spent most of his time looking at his BlackBerry, while contributing little to the program.

But Rachel had too much talent to bury in a three-person show. She soon had her own evening gig on Air America. Frequent guest appearances on cable TV also landed her a television job on MSNBC, appearing on Tucker Carlson's new nightly program as the liberal voice in a nightly left-right encounter with conservative talk show host Jay Severin, whom we'll meet later on.

When the 2008 campaign started gearing up, Rachel was made an MSNBC political contributor and given a regular slot on the highly popular, and much more highly rated, *Countdown with Keith Olbermann*. She occasionally filled in as guest host for Olbermann. From there, given her talent and ease with television, it was only a matter of time before she was given her own prime-time MSNBC slot, following Keith. *The Rachel Maddow Show* was an instant ratings hit, and has remained so. Once she settled into MSNBC, Rachel gave up her radio gig.

Her television show was such a huge success, however, that MSNBC went searching for another progressive talk radio host. They didn't have to look far.

In 2003, Ed Schultz was the biggest name in radio—in Fargo, North Dakota. But nobody outside of that godforsaken town—apologies to all Fargoans!—had ever heard of him. Six years later, Ed is not only America's most successful progressive talk radio host, he also has his own nightly political show on MSNBC.

Ed's big break came when he was discovered by Amy Bolton, who was then vice president of Jones Radio Networks, the country's fifth largest radio station owner and largest syndicator of radio programming. Soon afterward, Clear Channel, the largest radio network, with over four thousand stations, made an important business decision. They had so saturated the airwaves with conservative talk radio, as we shall see in Chapter 8, that they decided the only way to grow their business was to offer counterprogramming with progressive talk stations in the same markets.

Bolton remembered Schultz, saw him as the perfect candidate for Clear Channel, and convinced her boss, Glenn Jones, to make him their first nationally syndicated progressive host. In January 2004, Jones Radio (purchased in 2008 by Triton Media, owner of Dial Global Radio Networks) launched *The Ed Schultz Show.* He was soon heard on over one hundred stations nationwide—only one fifth of the number that carry Rush Limbaugh, but still the most stations booked by any progressive host. But Fargo soon proved too small to contain the media-savvy Schultz, even with his own nationally syndicated radio show. He began making regular trips to Washington, where he was able to get himself booked as a guest on cable television's political shows: CNN's *Situation Room* and *Larry King Live,* and MSNBC's *Hardball, Tucker,* and *1600 Pennsylvania Avenue,* hosted by David Shuster.

After Barack Obama's inauguration, when MSNBC managers decided to expand their lineup, they turned to Ed Schultz, who launched *The Ed Show* in March 2009, while continuing to do three hours of radio every afternoon.

For a few years, I co-hosted *Buchanan and Press* on MSNBC, while appearing on WMAL Radio four hours each morning. But Maddow and Schultz remain the two rare liberal exceptions in the list of those who maintain successful programs on both radio and television today. Once again, the field is dominated by conservatives.

The reality is, you can no longer escape the poison of right-wing talk by turning off the radio and turning on the television. The toxic talkers infest television, too—repeating at night on television the same lies they tell during the day on the radio.

In the galaxy of successful radio and TV stars, as we saw in Chapter 3, one name stands out above all others: Sean Hannity. Give him credit for this. He is the undisputed king of the straddle: the number-two man in talk radio and the number-two man in cable television, year after year. Close behind Hannity is Glenn Beck, longtime radio host and sudden rising star on Fox News, who may someday overtake both Limbaugh and Hannity as the undisputed champion of right-wing media.

After Hannity and Beck, two other conservative talkers have demonstrated considerable success in both radio and television, to the detriment of truth, justice, and the American way: Bill O'Reilly and Lou Dobbs.

THE O'REILLY FACTOR

Pompous. Arrogant. Mean. Condescending. Not the kind of personal attributes that would normally win you a lot of friends. But, surprisingly enough, they have certainly worked to win Bill O'Reilly a lot of viewers.

As unbelievable as it seems, *The O'Reilly Factor,* which premiered with the birth of Fox in 1996, is the highest-rated show on cable television—

and has been so since 2000. Which is quite a feat. No other television show, not even *The Ed Sullivan Show* or *60 Minutes,* has dominated its time slot on network or cable TV for that long.

In the TV rating wars, Fox News is the kingdom and Bill O'Reilly is the king. And although bloggers make great sport of the running feud between O'Reilly and Keith Olbermann—which network presidents once tried but failed to suppress—*The Factor* nightly clobbers *Countdown* in the ratings, usually by a commanding margin of three to one.

What accounts for O'Reilly's success? It didn't come automatically. For years, he toiled in relative obscurity as the ho-hum host of CBS-TV's *Inside Edition.* And even his first couple of years as host of *The Factor* scored so low in the ratings it looked like legendary Fox president Roger Ailes was going to have to admit a rare hiring mistake and fire O'Reilly. But O'Reilly persevered, improved his technique, refined his on-air presence, sharpened his program's focus—and *The Factor* took off. O'Reilly succeeds because he is a larger-than-life personality. He exudes self-confidence (even when he's dead wrong), and he brings a laserlike intensity to the events of the day, all from a conservative point of view. He also never allows himself to be put in a position where he might be overshadowed. He either surrounds himself with sycophants, like radio talk show host Dennis Miller, or people he can easily beat up on. Unlike other cable shows, which scramble to book as guests the biggest newsmakers of the day, O'Reilly generally looks for people who've never been on TV before and are therefore guaranteed to be nervous or ill-prepared. Said the spider to the fly . . .

Once in a while, however, he makes a mistake in sizing up his opposition—which I was able to take advantage of.

My first book, *Spin This!,* published in November 2001, was an outgrowth of *The Spin Room,* which I was then co-hosting on CNN with Tucker Carlson. In it, I examined the many forms of spin—in politics, law, business, sports, religion, and personal relationships—and poked fun at those who, like Bill O'Reilly and his "No Spin Zone," insisted they were never guilty of the practice. On November 29, Big Bill's producers took the bait and invited me on the program. O'Reilly began by accusing me of being "none too friendly to your humble correspondent" and reading a couple of lines from the book: "In the aftermath of the Marc Rich pardon, the ever so pompous Bill O'Reilly blasted President Bush for suggesting there were more important issues facing the country than continuing to talk about Bill Clinton.

"What Mr. O'Reilly was really saying, of course, is don't try to stop me from talking about Bill Clinton because that's all I know how to talk about. Actually, O'Reilly deserves a special spin award for opening his ever so predictable nightly TV program with the warning caution, 'You're about to enter a no-spin zone.' He's just published a book called *The No-Spin Zone*. It should be called *The Nothing but Spin Zone*."

Now, having watched O'Reilly often enough, I knew what he would do next. The man is a one-trick pony in that regard. And, sure enough, he demanded one example of where he was guilty of spin—which I had prepared ahead of time and immediately provided. "When you had [Gore campaign manager] Donna Brazile on last June, you told her that if Al Gore had only appeared on *The Factor*, *The Factor* has so many viewers in Florida, that Al Gore would be president of the United States today. Now, Mr. O'Reilly, you have to agree that's just—it's not a lie, it's not the truth, either. It's just spin."

O'Reilly insisted that was merely his opinion, not spin. He also denied he was a conservative. And then he demanded one more example of where he had spun the news in a conservative direction. Again, I was ready. "Here's how you opened your show on March 3, 2001: 'Tonight, violent demonstrations on the rise all over the world as capitalism comes under assault and America's college campuses are being besieged with socialistic messages. We'll have a report. The first hundred days of Hillary Clinton in the Senate. Did she actually do anything? We'll find out. And was Al Gore antagonistic toward some of his students at Columbia? That's the word. Caution: You're about to enter a no-spin zone.'

"Now I just find that very funny," I concluded. "That's full of spin." At which point, O'Reilly blew up, insisted that his show clobbered *Crossfire* in the ratings (even though the two shows did not air at the same time), accused me of being jealous of him, then huffed "Baloney!" and summarily ended the segment.*

Once I was safely gone, O'Reilly started off the next segment denouncing me, while claiming that the very fact he invited a well-known liberal on his show proved how fair and balanced he was. The next night, he piled on again, devoting his entire "Talking Points" segment to an attack on me personally—while, of course, I was not there to defend myself.

On his radio show, O'Reilly seldom entertained guests, but he developed an even more intimidating way to make sure that callers were friendly. In March 2006, when caller "Mike" from Orlando mentioned the name of Keith Olbermann, with whom O'Reilly was then having a public feud (more on that later), Big Brother immediately cut him off and issued this warning: "Mike is—he's a gone guy. You know, we have his—we have your phone numbers, by the way. So, if you're listening, Mike, we have your phone number, and we're going to turn it over to Fox security, and you'll be getting a little visit."

And Mike wasn't the only one. "When you call us, ladies and gentlemen, just so you know, we do have your phone number, and if you say anything untoward, obscene, or anything like that, Fox security then will contact your local authorities, and you will be held accountable." Yes, in O'Reilly's ego-warped mind and in the best traditions of Soviet-style broadcasting, it's a criminal offense to utter an unkind word about him on his program.

---

* It wasn't long before I got even for O'Reilly's rude treatment of me. We all remember how, in the buildup to the Iraq War, conservatives went berserk over the refusal of France to send troops to Iraq. Right-wingers demanded that Americans boycott French wines and French restaurants. Congress changed their cafeteria menu from "French fries" to "Freedom fries." From his perch at Fox News, Bill O'Reilly led the boycott-anything-French campaign. In the middle of this craziness, I was having lunch in one of my favorite restaurants, La Colline (no longer in business), located on the first floor of 400 North Capitol Street in Washington: a building that also housed MSNBC, CNBC, Fox News, and C-Span. And guess who walked in to have lunch? None other than Mr. Factor himself. In a French restaurant!

I quickly finished my lunch, stopped by his table to say a quick hello, rushed upstairs to my office and called Lloyd Grove, who was then editor of "Reliable Sources," the daily gossip column of *The Washington Post*. The next morning, the *Post* not only duly noted O'Reilly's hypocritical presence in a French restaurant, but reported what he ordered for lunch, how much it cost, and what he tipped the waiter. Just call it Press's Revenge.

But, again, my one and only appearance on *The Factor* was a rare exception for any bona fide liberal. At least 99.9 percent of the time, O'Reilly reserves his nightly platform all to himself or guests who agree with him, earning his stripes as cable television's top conservative—and, for a while, also as one of the top conservatives on radio.

Indeed, O'Reilly appeared unfettered on his radio show, often making more outrageous comments over the radio than he ever uttered on television.

RADIO FACTOR

O'Reilly walked away from his *Radio Factor* on February 26, 2009, but only after a good run. It lasted almost seven years, was heard on over four hundred stations, plus Sirius XM, and was rated by *Talkers Magazine* number twelve in listenership of all news-talk shows.

At the time, O'Reilly said he was giving up radio in order to devote more time to prepare for his TV show. He also claimed to have hosted a program that was totally objective. "I knew my show couldn't be ideological," he said with a straight face. "So I was doing a show that was fact-based."

Which may be the biggest whopper O'Reilly's ever told. His show wasn't fact-based. It was fact-free! It often seems that there's a restraining order out there, keeping Bill O'Reilly at least fifty feet away from the truth at all times.

Thanks again to Media Matters for America for documenting many of the countless falsehoods made by O'Reilly from his radio chair. Among the issues that he has consistently distorted are:

* *Gay Marriage.* Explaining his support for California's Proposition 8, which banned same-sex marriage, O'Reilly asserted that states which recognize gay marriage are required under "the equal protection clause" to legalize polygamy. Not true. He went further to claim that, without Prop 8, people would be free to

marry a goat, duck, dolphin, or turtle. Definitely not true. And, frankly, kinda weird.

- *The War on Christmas.* As part of his perennial "War on Christmas" crusade, O'Reilly claimed that Best Buy forbade its employees from saying "Merry Christmas" to customers. The store has no such policy.
- *Jack Abramoff.* You can't blame Republicans alone for taking money from the corrupt lobbyist, O'Reilly charged, because he also made contributions to Democrats. In fact, this top Republican lobbyist gave money to Republicans only.
- *Viewership.* O'Reilly implied he didn't really need his radio show because "I already got the 6 million people watching me every night." Actually, his nightly TV audience is about 3.5 million viewers. Making him the number-one cable television host by far, but still with a nightly audience far short of 6 million.
- *Drug Wars.* Attempting to fan anti-Mexican sentiment, O'Reilly accused former President Vicente Fox of stationing "his troops on the northern border helping the drug traffickers bring the loads across." In fact, Fox was using the army to track down drug traffickers.
- *Torture.* In the wake of reports of prisoner abuse at Guantánamo Bay and Abu Ghraib, O'Reilly insisted he had seen no evidence of the use of "electric shock" on detainees. Yet, in releasing photos from Abu Ghraib, the Pentagon itself acknowledged the use of electric shock interrogation techniques.
- *John McCain.* During the 2008 campaign, O'Reilly denied any connection between McCain and convicted Watergate conspirator G. Gordon Liddy. "McCain has nothing to do with G. Gordon Liddy—nothing," he asserted. The truth is, Liddy once held a fund-raiser for McCain in his home, made a 2008 contribution to McCain, and frequently hosted McCain on his radio show. Which, by the way, is more of a connection than any link, often asserted by Bill O'Reilly and his ilk, between candidate

Barack Obama and former Weather Underground member William Ayers.

- *Paul Krugman.* In March 2006, O'Reilly accused *New York Times* columnist Krugman of writing a column about illegal immigration but refusing to "put the word 'illegal' in there." Did he read the column? In it, Krugman actually used the phrases "illegal immigrants," "illegal immigration," and "an illegal immigrant." This isn't even spin on O'Reilly's part. It's just a flat-out lie.

And the list goes on and on.

Falsehoods were not the only hallmark of *The Radio Factor.* O'Reilly also frequently let loose on the radio with a string of especially ridiculous charges—again, even more outrageous claims than he would dare make on television. Not even on Fox News.

It was on his radio show, for example, that he dismissed the controversy over the government's sluggish response to Hurricane Katrina. O'Reilly's only problem was that the hurricane struck the wrong location: "I just wish that Katrina had only hit the United Nations building, nothing else, just had flooded them out, and I wouldn't have rescued them."

Some of O'Reilly's most notorious comments came in September 2007, after he'd joined Rev. Al Sharpton for dinner at the famous Sylvia's restaurant in Harlem. Sounding every bit like a Southern white plantation owner, a stunned O'Reilly told his radio listeners the next afternoon that he "couldn't get over the fact that there was no difference between Sylvia's restaurant and any other restaurant in New York City. I mean, it was exactly the same, even though it's run by blacks, primarily black patronship."

I'm surprised Willie Boy didn't add: "They even used knives and forks!" But, in fact, he did add something even worse: "There wasn't one person in Sylvia's who was screaming 'M-F'er, I want more iced tea!'" Imagine! A roomful of black people and not one of them is hollering "Motherfucker." Haven't we come a long way?

Well, maybe the rest of us have, but not Bill O'Reilly. He didn't appear much more enlightened in his reaction to Michelle Obama's offhand

statement that "for the first time in my life, I am proud of my country because it feels like hope is finally making a comeback." It was clear to any
fair-minded observer that she was expressing pride in her husband's campaign, and not any deep-seated hatred for America, but O'Reilly wasn't
about to cut her any slack. With just a little more evidence, he was ready
to suggest the ultimate punishment whites have always held out for uppity
blacks: "I don't want to go on a lynching party against Michelle Obama
unless there's evidence, hard facts, that say this is how the woman really
feels. If that's how she really feels—that America is a bad country, or
flawed nation, whatever—then that's legit." Hang her from the nearest
tree.

Think that was cruel? Maybe O'Reilly just has a problem with women.
He was equally harsh with eighteen-year-old Jennifer Moore, raped and
murdered on the streets of New York in summer 2006. But O'Reilly shed no
tears. He called her "moronic." After all, he sneered, she was walking the
streets alone at night while "five foot two, 105 pounds, wearing a miniskirt
and a halter top with a bare midriff." In other words, O'Reilly seemed to say,
she was asking for it. "Now, again, there you go. So every predator in the
world is going to pick that up at two in the morning."

HOLD THE FALAFEL

Speaking of predatory behavior, if O'Reilly does have a problem relating to
women, Exhibit A may well be his embarrassing relationship with a female producer. You know, the "falafel" lady.

In October 2004, hours after he had sued her for extortion, claiming
she tried to shake him down for $60 million, former Fox producer Andrea
Mackris countersued O'Reilly for repeated instances of sexual harassment,
including phone calls in which he explicitly discussed vibrators, three-
somes, masturbation, the loss of his virginity, and sexual fantasies. The text
of her complaint, quoting him directly, reads like a cheap, sordid, dirty
novel.

Mackris had obviously recorded several of O'Reilly's phone calls, one
of which—known as the "Caribbean shower fantasy"—became instantly

famous because of his mistakenly suggesting use of a "falafel" as a sex toy. He told Mackris he wanted to take her on a Caribbean vacation because: "Once people get into that hot weather they shed their inhibitions, you know they drink during the day, they lay there and lazy, they have dinner and then they come back and fool around . . . that's basically the modus operandi."

But O'Reilly doesn't stop there. He describes in detail what fun they would have in the shower, with the help of a loofa, which he ends up confusing with a falafel. Back to the phone: "Well, if I took you down there then I'd want to take a shower with you right away, that would be the first thing I'd do . . . yeah, we'd check into the room, and we would order up some room service and, uh, and you'd definitely get two glasses of wine into you as quickly as I could get into you I would get 'em into you . . . maybe intravenously get those glasses of wine into you . . . You would basically be in the shower and then I would come in and I'd join you and you would have your back to me and I would take that little loofa thing and kinda soap up your back . . . rub it all over you, get you to relax, hot water . . . and, um . . . you know, you'd feel the tension drain out of you . . . and, uh, you still would be with your back to me then I would kinda put my arm—it's one of those mitts, those loofa mitts you know, so I got my hands in it . . . and I would put it around front, kinda rub your tummy a little bit with it, and then with my other hand I would start to massage your boobs, get your nipples really hard . . . cuz I like that and you have really spectacular boobs . . .

"So anyway I'd be rubbing your big boobs and getting your nipples really hard, kinda kissing your neck from behind . . . and then I would take the other hand with the falafel [!] thing and I'd put it on your pussy but you'd have to do it really light, just kind of a tease business . . ."

Eew! Now imagine that creepy passage delivered with O'Reilly's trademark sonority.

After reading the complaint, O'Reilly's archrival, Keith Olbermann, offered Mackris $99,000 for releasing the tape. But, alas, we never got to hear it. After sixteen days of legal proceedings, O'Reilly and Mackris agreed to an out-of-court settlement, under terms of which he reportedly paid her millions of dollars, and the tapes were never made public. Never-theless, O'Reilly will always be known as "Falafel Bill"—except, of course, to his hard-core, right-wing followers, who will forgive any of his sins, in-cluding cheating on his wife, as long as O'Reilly continues to preach the conservative gospel. In September 2009, O'Reilly was even presented the Media Courage Award by the Family Research Council at its annual Value Voters Summit.

Note to all those wondering about Bill O'Reilly's qualifications to speak on "family values": Please reread the above transcript.

And, yes, may I remind you, this sex-starved, food-challenged oddball is the most popular host on cable television.

Indeed, O'Reilly's radio adventure was just a sideline to his long-running and remarkably successful TV show, which has generated more than its own share of controversy—not just because of the outrageous things he says but because of the fights he's constantly picking with his critics or people in the news.

BULLY ON THE PROWL

O'Reilly's such a schoolyard bully, it's impossible to keep track of all his targets. He's always on the prowl for someone or some organization he can beat up on verbally. But we do remember a few of the more colorful ones.

Senator Al

O'Reilly's long feud with the freshman senator from Minnesota began in 2003 when Franken published his book *Lies and the Lying Liars Who Tell Them: A Fair and Balanced Look at the Right*—with O'Reilly's picture on the cover and a whole chapter devoted to him inside. No doubt provoked into it by O'Reilly, Fox sued Franken over his use of the phrase "fair and balanced," but later dropped the suit when a judge refused to grant them injunctive relief.

Their spat famously escalated when Franken and O'Reilly, both tout-ing new books, appeared together on a luncheon panel at BookExpo

America in Los Angeles. Franken spoke first, ending by accusing O'Reilly of lying when he claimed that his previous television show, *Inside Edition*, had won a Peabody Award.

When O'Reilly began by admitting he had misspoken—it was a Polk Award, not a Peabody Award—Franken chided: "Don't you think it's odd you got it wrong about a *journalism* award?" At which point O'Reilly exploded: "This guy accuses me of being a liar, ladies and gentlemen, on national television. He's vicious, and that's with a capital V, a person who's blinded by ideology." As Franken tried to respond, O'Reilly stunned the luncheon crowd by roaring: "Shut up! You had your thirty-five minutes. Shut up!"

O'Reilly later carried his feud with Franken into the Minnesota Senate race. He cheered on the reelection of Norm Coleman over challenger Al Franken—later insisting, incorrectly, that Coleman led throughout the long recount. On July 7, 2009, when the Minnesota Supreme Court declared Franken the winner, Coleman delivered a gracious concession statement. O'Reilly proved he was the real loser in the race with one last smear at his rival. He told his television audience that night: "In a sad day for America, Al Franken is now a U.S. senator. The Minnesota Supreme Court ruled he won the election by about three hundred votes. Franken is a blatantly dishonest individual, a far-left zealot who is not qualified to hold any office, a man who trafficked in hate on his failed Air America radio program. . . . With people like Franken on the Hill, this country is in deep trouble."

Well, if "blatantly dishonest" people who "traffic in hate" on radio programs are not permitted to serve in Congress, thank God Bill O'Reilly never ran for public office!

Sweden or Switzerland?

One of O'Reilly's most embarrassing dust-ups was a fight he picked with actress Jessica Alba the night of Barack Obama's inauguration.

On January 20, 2009, a Fox News crew spotted Alba at an inaugural party in Washington and asked her to give a shout-out to O'Reilly. She declined, explaining to reporters off camera, "He's kind of an asshole." She then tried to turn the tables, asking reporters what they liked best about Obama. When they wouldn't answer, she told them: "That's right. Be neutral. Be Sweden."

Upon hearing the story, O'Reilly pounced. The next night on his TV show he called Alba a "pinhead" for mixing up Sweden with neutral country Switzerland. Several conservative bloggers piled on, agreeing with O'Reilly.

But Alba had the last word. A few days later, she posted this retort on *MySpace Celebrity*: "I want to clear some things up that have been bothering me lately. Last week, Mr. Bill O'Reilly and some really classy sites (e.g. TMZ) insinuated I was dumb by claiming Sweden was a neutral country. I appreciate the fact that he is a news anchor and that gossip sites are inundated with intelligent reporting, but seriously people . . . It's so sad to me that you think the only neutral country during World War II was Switzerland."

And, of course, she's right. Switzerland remained neutral in World War II, but so did Sweden. On history, the score reads: Jessica Alba—1; Bill O'Reilly—0.

The ACLU

For right-wingers, hating the American Civil Liberties Union is like a saliva test—which O'Reilly passes with flying colors.

The ACLU argues that, since its only client is the Bill of Rights, it has no choice but to defend in the interest of free speech the expression of what are often unpopular causes. But that doesn't wash with O'Reilly. For their defense of groups as disparate as the KKK and NAMBLA, O'Reilly has called the ACLU "the most dangerous organization in the United States of America."

Using that favorite shorthand of contemporary conservatives, he's even compared them to Nazis: "Now the ACLU is free to come to your town and sue the heck out of it. And, believe me, that organization will. The ACLU doesn't care about the law or the Constitution or what the people want. It's a fascist organization that uses lawyers instead of panzers. It'll find a way to inflict financial damage on any concern that opposes its secular agenda and it's growing in power."

Yet you can count on it: If Bill O'Reilly ever gets in legal trouble for something he says, the ACLU will be the first to defend him, as they did Michael Savage. With enemies like these, who needs friends?

Media Matters

As founder David Brock and the good people at Media Matters for America have learned, Bill O'Reilly is not just thin-skinned. He's so sensitive to criticism, he barely has any skin at all. Like any schoolyard bully, he loves to dish it out . . . but he just can't take it.

Naturally, as host of the most popular program on cable television, and one of the most popular on radio, Bill O'Reilly is frequently under the microscope of Media Matters. On their Web site, almost daily, they call attention to his latest outrageous remarks and publish the truth in response to O'Reilly's lies. When O'Reilly dropped *The Radio Factor*, they compiled a list of falsehoods that he'd told on his radio show.

Without ever once denying the accuracy of what Media Matters has reported, O'Reilly routinely denounces them as a subversive, leftist organization that's just out to get him. He's attacked Media Matters as nothing but "smear merchants" and "guttersnipes" and calls the people who work there "the most vile, despicable human beings on the planet." Which is really saying something, given that—thanks, Dubya!—Osama bin Laden and the leaders of al Qaeda are still at large.

Countdown v. Factor

For a talk show host, and for political candidates, one of the oldest games in the business is saying something unkind about your most well-known rival—in the hope that you can con them into responding, and therefore put you on the map.

It's a cheap trick of which I plead guilty as charged. When starting out at KFI-AM in Los Angeles, I used to poke fun mercilessly at Rush Limbaugh on every show, mainly because the man is wrong about so many things, but also just to see if he'd respond. Most of the time, Rush did the smart thing and ignored me. When it came to Keith Olbermann, O'Reilly wasn't as smart or as disciplined.

The O'Reilly Factor was already a big hit on Fox when Keith Olbermann's *Countdown* bounced Phil Donahue off the air and took over the competing 8 P.M. slot on MSNBC. Knowing how pompous his competitor was, Olbermann saw an opportunity to get O'Reilly's goat—and took it.

As documented by media critic Jack Shafer on *Slate*, it all started on May 5, 2003, when Olbermann concluded a piece on red-baiter Senator Joseph McCarthy with the comment: "So it was all programmed to look for fish to shoot in the barrel. Oddly, that's also how they program Bill O'Reilly's show."

Zing! Smelling blood, Olbermann followed up by frequently naming O'Reilly "Today's Worst Person in the World." All of which O'Reilly could have ignored, but didn't. Instead, he opened up one program by whining about NBC's continuing attacks on him (he makes a silly point of never mentioning Olbermann by name). Which, of course, simply encouraged Olbermann to taunt him more often.

By February 2004, O'Reilly had had enough. So he actually drew up a petition demanding that MSNBC cancel *Countdown* and bring back Phil Donahue. A gleeful Keith Olbermann signed the petition on the air! And, of course, six months later, Olbermann took full advantage of the opportunities for ridicule afforded by the sexual harassment lawsuit against O'Reilly and the falafel tape.

You might think a professional broadcaster, on top of his game, would sooner or later realize that this feud was doing him no good—and stop paying attention to it. But you'd be wrong. The sniping continued back and forth until . . . an off-the-record Microsoft forum in May 2009, when PBS interviewer Charlie Rose asked News Corporation Rupert Murdoch and GE chairman Jeffrey Immelt how they felt about the feud. Both agreed it was not healthy for either network, and reportedly issued orders for a cease-fire.

If so, it didn't last long. Even though a spokesman for GE told *The New York Times,* "we all recognize that a certain level of civility needed to be introduced into the public discussion," Olbermann insisted "I am party to no deal." Within a week of the reported truce, both Olbermann and O'Reilly were back at it: with Olbermann continuing to taunt O'Reilly as the "Worst Person in the World," and O'Reilly, still refusing to mention Olbermann by name, accusing his parent company, GE, of supplying parts for bombs that terrorists use to kill American soldiers in Iraq. As of this writing, they're still sniping. And why not? It's good for both networks. Some media purists may wring their hands over the lack of civility, but ratings for both shows continue to climb—thanks, in part, to the "Bill O-Keith" running feud.

And at least, when Bill attacks Keith, there are no real victims. That was not so when O'Reilly went after the doctor from Wichita.

"Tiller the Killer"

When Dr. George Tiller was assassinated in his Wichita church on Sunday, May 31, 2009, Fox News executives went on immediate alert. For years, they feared Bill O'Reilly had made such incendiary comments about Tiller he had practically invited the doctor's murder.

Tiller was one of a handful of doctors in the country who performed late-term abortions. As such, he was frequently the named target of O'Reilly's venom. He was first mentioned by O'Reilly on February 25, 2005—and was the subject of twenty-eight subsequent episodes on *The Factor,* the last one on April 27, less than a week before his death. In most of them, O'Reilly smeared the Kansas doctor as "Tiller the Killer."

He attacked Tiller as a man who "destroys fetuses for just about any reason right up to the birth date for $5,000." He accused him of being guilty of "Nazi stuff." He described him as "executing babies" and "operating a death mill." Of Tiller's family planning clinic, O'Reilly said, "This is the kind of stuff happened in Mao's China, Hitler's Germany, Stalin's Soviet Union." Without suggesting anyone pull the trigger, O'Reilly did repeatedly put Tiller (who'd already been shot once) in the public eye, condemned anyone, like then-Governor Kathleen Sebelius, who supported him, and made it clear that, in his opinion, Kansas and the world would be better off without him. On June 15, 2007, he said: "No question Dr. Tiller has blood on his hands. But now so does Governor Sebelius. She is not fit to serve. Nor is any Kansas politician who supports Tiller's business of destruction. I wouldn't want to be these people if there is a Judgment Day. I just—you know . . . Kansas is a great state, but this is a disgrace upon everyone who lives in Kansas. Is it not?"

True to form, on his first broadcast following Tiller's murder, O'Reilly did not express any remorse for stirring the pot of hatred against the murdered doctor. Instead, he painted himself as the victim of left-wing blogs, which were accusing him of contributing to the doctor's murder by his inflammatory language.

Which, of course, had a ring of truth to it. Violent words do, indeed, have violent consequences. Clearly, Bill O'Reilly never learned that lesson, either before or after George Tiller's murder.

The War in Iraq

Remember: Even a broken clock is right twice a day. So, it's not surprising that, once in a while, Bill O'Reilly makes sense or shows some sign of intelligence—as he did, belatedly and almost involuntarily, on the war in Iraq.

Marching lockstep with other conservatives, O'Reilly began as a cheerleader for the war, supporting George Bush and Dick Cheney, and impugning the patriotism of any who dared question their often dubious case for war.

However, two days before the invasion began, O'Reilly appeared on ABC's *Good Morning America* and declared: "If the Americans go in and overthrow Saddam Hussein and it's clean, he has nothing, I will apologize to the nation, and I will not trust the Bush administration again." Oops!

Of course, we did go in, we did overthrow Saddam Hussein, and we did not find any weapons of mass destruction. Eleven months later, back on *GMA*, O'Reilly apologized . . . kind of. "My analysis was wrong and I'm sorry. I was wrong. I'm not pleased about it at all. . . . What do you want me to do, go over and kiss the camera? . . . I am much more skeptical of the Bush administration now than I was at that time."

Yet O'Reilly continued to insist the United States "did a good thing by trying to liberate a country," accused antiwar activists of rooting against the United States, and refused to say the invasion of Iraq was a mistake. Some apology.

Still, his eleventh-hour ambivalence on the war rattled some of his most conservative loyalists, though not half as much as his later love letter to Barack Obama.

America's Role Model

On August 9, 2009, the millions of readers of *Parade* magazine started their day with a bang. There in the pages of their favorite Sunday morning wake-up call, written by Bill O'Reilly, was a glowing tribute to the country's leading role model for children today: none other than Barack Obama himself.

O'Reilly's essay was titled "What President Obama Can Teach America's Kids." In it, he outlined five lessons kids today can learn from Obama's own life story: forgiveness, respect, persistence, hard work, and the knowledge that in America anything is possible.

Acknowledging that these are tough times for America's kids, O'Reilly noted that children today need to learn life's lessons quickly in order to succeed. Then, in a question bound to strike fear into the heart of any red-blooded conservative, he asked: "Who better to teach them than the President of the United States?"

Isn't it ironic that, only a month later, conservatives would loudly complain of socialist indoctrination when President Obama scheduled a routine back-to-school, obey-your-teacher, and work-hard-at-your-studies address to America's schoolchildren? This despite the fact that Presidents Ronald Reagan and George H. W. Bush had made the same beginning-of-school-season speeches—and that Reagan had used his to push supply side economics.

I almost hate to say it, but in his comments of Obama's back-to-school remarks and in his *Parade* magazine essay, Bill O'Reilly proved a lot more reasonable than his television and radio audience.

We all believe that America is the land of unlimited opportunity, O'Reilly reminded *Parade* readers, but "never has it been more vividly illustrated," he argued, than in the life of the forty-fourth president. Whether you agreed with his policies or not, wrote O'Reilly, you had to admit: "Barack Obama, a youngster in Hawaii without his parents around, has toughed it out and become one of history's great stories, no matter what happens going forward. What he has achieved in his 48 years is simply astounding."

O'Reilly continued: "Consider the odds. The United States is a nation of more than 300 million citizens. Only one person is currently the Commander in Chief. That man had no fatherly guidance, is of mixed race, and had no family connections to guide him into the world of national politics.

"That adds up to one simple truth that every American child should be told: 'If Barack Obama can become the President of the United States, then whatever dream you may have can happen in your life.'"

That doesn't mean Bill O'Reilly went soft on President Obama. He has continued to oppose almost every program undertaken by the Obama administration (although he did support the public option as part of health care reform legislation). He remains one of Obama's fiercest critics. But for whatever reason, be it true admiration or an attempt to shore up his "independent" bona fides, he is at least willing to acknowledge Obama's unique and impressive life story. Give him credit for that.

Sadly, it's more than you can say for most other conservative talk show hosts. Nor did O'Reilly question the fact that Obama is, indeed, an American citizen. He left that up to the man who was then the scourge of CNN.

LOU DOBBS

CNN prides itself on being "the most trusted name in news." And, for the most part, it is. Its anchors deliver the news relatively straight. Its commentators are evenly balanced. And its talk show hosts lead lively discussions of the issues without revealing their own hand.

But then there was Lou Dobbs, an island of Fox in a sea of CNN. For some strange reason, Dobbs was the only CNN anchor allowed to give his opinions, no matter how ugly or demented they are. This was a radical departure for CNN, and one that did not please all the network's veteran reporters. As John King, who eventually replaced Dobbs, put it: "Lou clearly has strongly held beliefs, and he's decided to share those beliefs. In doing that, does it sometimes cause concern in the company? Yes."

It wasn't always that way. Dobbs was part of Ted Turner's starting lineup at CNN. By the time I joined CNN in 1996, he had long been host of *Money Line,* which immediately preceded *Crossfire.* At the time, Dobbs was such a cheerleader for big business that I always suspected he was a big-time Republican, but I never knew for sure. Because, for the most part, he simply reported the business news of the day, right down the middle, without commentary. While his ratings were never that good compared to *Crossfire* or *Larry King Live,* we were told that Dobbs made more money for CNN than any program on the network. So he enjoyed an unusual amount of autonomy. Or at least he did—until he ran into a brick wall named Rick Kaplan.

Kaplan is a big man in television, in more ways than one. He has a long and distinguished résumé, having served as executive producer of ABC's *Nightline, Prime Time Live* and *World News Tonight with Peter Jennings* before becoming president of CNN in 1997. At six foot four, he's also a big bear of a man physically. Legend inside the company has it that when he first went to Atlanta to interview for the job, the outspoken Ted Turner asked him: "Are you really a Jew?" When Kaplan said yes, Turner replied: "You're the biggest goddamned Jew I ever met!"

He was also the biggest roadblock Dobbs ever encountered at CNN. Once Kaplan took over, everybody knew the two huge egos would eventually clash. And they did, in May 1999, shortly after the massacre at Columbine High School.

President Clinton had gone to Littleton, Colorado, to deliver a speech about school violence, which just happened to hit the same time *Money Line* would normally be on the air. Naturally, CNN, like MSNBC and Fox, carried the president's remarks live. So Kaplan, watching at home, was shocked when, in the middle of the speech, just as Clinton was saying "There is something you all can do . . ." CNN switched back to *Money Line*. Kaplan jumped on the phone, only to find out it was Dobbs himself who had demanded the network cut Clinton off. He overruled Dobbs and ordered producers to resume coverage of the president's speech—a decision Dobbs immediately derided by telling viewers: "CNN President Rick Kaplan wants us to return to Littleton."

A few days later, Dobbs announced he was leaving CNN—no one believed it was voluntary—to start up a new Web site called space.com, dedicated to collecting and reporting news about space exploration. Ironically, the new business venture launched by business expert Lou Dobbs turned out to be a big business flop. But by April 2001, Rick Kaplan had left CNN and Dobbs was invited back to take another shot at anchoring *Money Line*. This time, however, with a big difference. The first half of his program would be devoted, as before, to straight business reporting. But Dobbs insisted—and CNN agreed—that he would be free to offer his own opinions on issues of the day during the second half of the program.

And, for CNN's bottom line, one must admit, the experiment was a big success. Dobbs got some of the highest ratings on the network: snaring over 70 percent higher ratings as a nightly scold than he did in his previous incarnation as a cheerleader for big business. As for CNN's reputation as a legitimate news organization, that's another story.

Reflecting the new reality, the name of the program was changed from *Money Line* to *Lou Dobbs Tonight*. It could have been more accurately be called *Lou Dobbs Unchained*. Now, unlike Glenn Beck, not everything Dobbs says on radio or television is crazy. More often than not, as on immigration, he veers far to the right. And he admits that, for most of his life, he's been a conservative Republican. But sometimes, as on global trade, he veers far to the populist left. He can be hard to pin down. As some have noted, he comes across as a bizarre combination of Ralph Nader and Pat Buchanan.

SAVING AMERICAN JOBS

Indeed, on trade issues, it's hard to tell Nader and Buchanan apart. On *Crossfire,* I used to joke that Ralph was so far to the left, and Pat so far to the right, that they met themselves coming back the other way. Add Lou Dobbs to the mix. A self-described "economic populist," he's a strong opponent of globalization, free trade deals like NAFTA, offshore tax loopholes, and other measures that encourage the export of American jobs and threaten the middle class.

To his credit, Dobbs has emerged as a strong advocate for American workers. Here's Dobbs in an interview with Bill Moyers: "Corporate America will not tell us how many jobs they're shipping overseas to cheap foreign labor markets. We're not talking about an economic judgment, but a political judgment, a social judgment. . . . What kind of country do we want? Do we want to destroy the middle class? Because if we do let's continue outsourcing jobs."

Needless to say, that blast at big business from the man they had long considered their best friend on television sent shivers up the spine of every American CEO. But it warmed the hearts of millions of working men and women, as well as many union leaders. Dobbs won even more labor hearts by opposing the Bush tax cuts as welfare for the wealthy, condemning the Bush administration's attempted sale of management of six U.S. ports to a Dubai-owned company, and supporting a hike in the minimum wage: positions that certainly defy the definition of a cookie-cutter conservative.

In 2004, Dobbs collected his nightly fulminations about disappearing jobs, corporate greed, and foreign outsourcing in a book, *Exporting America: Why Corporate Greed Is Shipping Jobs Overseas.* As a result of free trade deals with the United States, he points out, "Germany, Japan, Russia, Canada, Brazil, and China have enormous trade surpluses and are the clear winners," while "the United States, Australia, and other deficit countries are the clear losers." The benefits of such deals, he asserts, are limited to "helping consumers save a few cents on trinkets and tee shirts"—made in China.

It was also concern for American jobs that first awakened Dobbs's interest in the twin issues of immigration and border control. Unfortunately, once so engaged, he went off the deep end.

SEAL THE BORDER!

Either because he believes it's a serious problem, or because he knows it's good for ratings, immigration has become an obsession with Lou Dobbs. As documented by Media Matters, in 2007 fully 70 percent of broadcasts of *Lou Dobbs Tonight* contained at least one segment on the topic.

In standing up against illegal immigration, Dobbs insists, he is simply standing up for American workers. And, to a certain extent, that is true. Some undocumented workers, especially in the construction industry, do indeed, for lower wages, move into nonunion jobs that might normally go to American workers at higher wages. Although for the most part, as has been proven by many studies, undocumenteds are far more likely to take jobs—picking crops, washing cars, cleaning homes, changing sheets, clearing brush—that Americans don't want or won't do.

If Dobbs stopped there—demanding enforcement of existing immigration laws on employers, for example—he'd be making a positive contribution to the debate over illegal immigration. But, oh no. Instead, Lou insists on attacking the immigrants themselves, spreading lies about why they come here and what they do once they get here. In so doing, he bought into, and therefore legitimized, every ugly rumor spread by the anti-immigrant crowd and delegitimized every effort made by CNN to appeal to Hispanic viewers, including a four-hour documentary, *Latino in America*, broadcast in October 2009. At best, Dobbs made CNN look schizophrenic; at worst, hypocritical.

ILLEGAL CRIME WAVE

Were you to believe Lou Dobbs, immigrants come to the United States for one reason only. Not to get jobs or seek a better life. But to commit crimes. As in the case of the 2006 murder of a Houston police officer by an illegal immigrant, he seizes on every isolated incident to drive home the point that criminal activity is the core of our illegal immigration problem. "When we have borders that are unprotected," he told Houston's police chief then, "when criminal illegal aliens are sent across the border, deported, and are returning and murdering police officers. You're talking about an unfunded mandate. And that unfunded mandate is laying straightforwardly on the taxpayers' back in this country, U.S. citizens who are paying for it all, the high cost of medical care, social services, crime prevention and prosecution, of course as well."

To prove his point, Dobbs contends our prisons are overflowing with illegals. And, on countless broadcasts, he repeated his contention that "just about a third of the prison population in this country is estimated to be illegal aliens."

He is wrong on both counts. There is no "illegal alien crime wave" sweeping this country—unless you count every undocumented worker as a "criminal" because he or she is here illegally.

But in terms of the standard definition of crimes, there is no evidence to suggest that immigrants are more likely to commit crimes than American citizens. *Au contraire, mon cher.* In fact, there are studies that prove (and common sense tells you the same thing) immigrants are *less* likely to commit crimes, even getting a speeding ticket, for fear of being apprehended and deported.

As for the prison population . . . wrong again! True, some illegal immigrants commit serious crimes and end up in prison, but not in disproportionate numbers. A study by the Public Policy Institute of California, for example, found that even in California, which counts more immigrants than any other state, the foreign-born are incarcerated at a rate half as high as their presence in the population.

When Dobbs claims one third of prisoners are illegal immigrants, he may be referring to federal prisons only. If so, he is at best deliberately misleading his audience, because federal facilities account for less than 10 percent of the total prison population. Most prisoners are housed in state or local jails. According to the Justice Department, noncitizen foreigners make up only 5.9 percent of the combined federal, state, and local prison population, while they comprise 11.7 percent of the general population.

The real question is not why are there so many illegal immigrant prisoners, but why are there so few?

BEWARE OF LEPROSY

Phase two of the Lou Dobbs "Scare America to Death Campaign" against illegal immigration was to accuse immigrants of carrying leprosy across the border and spreading it among the general population. Which would be zombie-movie scary if it were true. Except it's not. Not even close.

It all started on April 14, 2005, when correspondent Christine Romans reported on "horrendous diseases being brought into America by illegal aliens," including Chagas' disease, leprosy (or Hansen's disease), and malaria. Romans quoted "medical lawyer" Dr. Madeleine Cosman as saying "there were about nine hundred cases of leprosy in the U.S. for forty years; there have been seven thousand in the last three years."

Wow! Where's Father Damien when we need him?

But the truth is far from what Romans reported, and Dobbs subsequently repeated. Two years later, in fact, in a *60 Minutes* profile, Lesley Stahl challenged Dobbs on the accuracy of his leprosy warning. She cited data from the National Hansen's Disease Program of the Department of Health and Human Services showing that "seven thousand is the number of leprosy cases over the last thirty years, not the past three, and nobody knows how many of those cases involve illegal immigrants."

In response, Dobbs simply sniffed: "If we reported it, it's a fact." Well, maybe in his mind. For the rest of us, he has yet to correct the record.

SUCKING ON THE PUBLIC TEAT?

Having lived in California for over thirty years, having debated the issue countless times, and having survived several anti-immigration ballot campaigns, I guarantee you, no matter how many times it's been proven wrong by official reports, the most common, and most pernicious, argument voiced against illegal immigrants is that they're a drain on public services—and therefore a heavy, unnecessary burden on taxpayers.

You've heard the rap: They're crowding emergency rooms, getting free health care through Medicaid, taking home welfare checks and food stamps, filling public school classrooms with their kids, and signing up for social services. And, because they pay no taxes, they are a drain on society: costing everything, and contributing nothing.

Don't believe it. Federal programs such as Medicaid, welfare, food stamps, and SCHIP are unavailable to undocumented workers. Anyone who applies for them must first provide proof of legal status. In fact, even legal immigrants are ineligible for most forms of public assistance for the first five years they reside in the United States, or until they become citizens.

There are some exceptions. Yes, living up to the ideals of their profession, emergency room physicians do treat people who show up with medical emergencies without demanding to see proof of citizenship. And, yes, resident children are accepted in public schools, even if their parents have entered the country illegally. But immigrants more than pay for those services through taxes.

I remember one study commissioned by the California Business Roundtable, hardly a left-wing group, way back in the seventies, when I was working for Governor Jerry Brown. It showed that illegal immigrants contribute more in tax revenue than they cost in public services. And many studies since, both in California and other states, have come to the same conclusion.

Undocumented workers do, in fact, pay all kinds of taxes. They pay sales taxes, just like all the rest of us. If, as many do, they get a paycheck using a fake Social Security number, they pay payroll taxes and the FICA tax—which, not being citizens, they will never get back. A December 2007 report of the nonpartisan Congressional Budget Office concluded: "Over the past two decades, most efforts to estimate the fiscal impact of immigration in the United States have concluded that, in aggregate and over the long term, tax revenues of all types generated by immigrants— both legal and unauthorized—exceed the cost of the services they use."

On this aspect of the immigration issue, too, the facts are clear. But you never heard them on *Lou Dobbs Tonight*.

NORTH AMERICAN UNION

In the end, why even worry about this supposed drain on public services? Because we're going to cease to exist as an independent nation, anyway—and may already have. At least, according to the wacky gospel of Lou Dobbs.

Dobbs may seem rational by the admittedly low standard of Glenn Beck, but don't be fooled. He actually believes, and frequently warns his listeners and viewers, that George W. Bush began the movement, which Barack Obama is also pursuing, to surrender America's autonomy—without an act of Congress or a vote of the people—by making us part of a new "North American Union" with Mexico and Canada.

When completed, it will be just like the European Union, Dobbs declares. Except, instead of the euro, we'd all be spending "ameros."

Now, having often traveled in the EU, I think the system actually has many advantages, especially for tourists. No matter. A North American Union is not in the cards. True, there's NAFTA. And there's the Security and Prosperity Partnership established by the United States, Mexico, and Canada in 2005. But these are strictly mutually beneficial trade and security arrangements, like we've formed with many other countries. For labor unions, they have proven to be bad deals. But they in no way undermine the independence of the United States or add up to what Dobbs describes as "straightforward an attack on national sovereignty as there could be, outside of war."

Even George W. Bush had to laugh at that one. "It's quite comical, actually," he told reporters during a summit meeting in Quebec, "when you realize the difference between reality and what some people are talking on TV about."

When George W. Bush is the voice of reason, look out!

It's worth noting that the source of Dobbs's assertions about the loss of U.S. sovereignty is a book, *The Late Great USA: NAFTA, the North*

American Union, and the Threat of a Coming Merger with Mexico and Canada, written by Jerome Corsi. You may remember Corsi. In 2004, he also wrote a book challenging the military record of John Kerry, which fueled the Swift Boat attacks against Kerry. He followed up in 2008 with a widely discredited book, *The Obama Nation*, describing Barack Obama as "seething with black rage"—which won him frequent guest spots on Fox with Sean Hannity. And this is the same Jerome Corsi who called Islam "a worthless, dangerous, Satanic religion," and claimed of Muslims "They are Boy-Bumpers as clearly as they are Women-Haters." And the very Jerome Corsi who joined G. Gordon Liddy in raising questions about the legitimacy of Barack Obama's birth certificate.

Now, you would think that if you're really accusing both George W. Bush and Barack Obama of committing treason against the United States by giving away our standing as an independent nation, you would want a more credible source than Jerome Corsi—and CNN should have demanded one. However, such was not the case.

But that's not the end of the story. Start counting your ameros, amigos. Because, as crazy as his fear of the North American Union is, Lou Dobbs has an even nuttier obsession.

RECONQUISTA MEXICANA

The Mexicans are coming! The Mexicans are coming!

If you believe Lou Dobbs, the Mexicans are, indeed, coming—to take back the American Southwest—which, they believe, rightfully belongs to them. That's why Latinos turned out in such great numbers in support of immigration reform. According to Dobbs, illegal immigrants are but the first wave of invasion forces, sent by Mexico to prepare the way for the actual *reconquista*.

I told you it was crazy, but it was a recurring theme of *Lou Dobbs Tonight*: that the Mexican government considers large portions of the Southwest, known as the "Aztlán," to still be Mexican territory, and there is a not-so-secret plan by Mexico to retake it all. Correspondent Christine Romans warned: "Long downplayed as a theory of the radical ethnic fringe, the *reconquista,* the reconquest, the reclamation, the return, it's resonating with some on the streets. . . . The growing street protests in favor of illegal immigration, Lou, are increasingly taking on the tone of that very radicalism."

To verify his beware-of-Aztlán fears, Dobbs invited fellow xenophobe Pat Buchanan on the show. Buchanan raises the same red flag in his book *State of Emergency: The Third World Invasion and Conquest of America,* and he duly repeated it for Lou Dobbs: "The ultimate goal of Vicente Fox is the erasure of the border between the United States and Mexico. *La reconquista* is the objective, Lou."

Talk about the blind leading the blind!

Too bad I wasn't invited to join Buchanan on his show that night, because I'd have a question for both of them: If, as they both assert, President Bush has, in effect, already surrendered American autonomy through the Security and Prosperity Partnership, why does Mexico have to bother invading the Southwest? Why don't they just raise the Mexican flag over Phoenix?

CNN FIRES LOU DOBBS!

Imagine my surprise—as former co-host of CNN's *Crossfire* and *The Spin Room*—when, in August 2009, CNN president Jon Klein decreed that radio talk show hosts would no longer be booked as guests on CNN news programs. The reason, Klein told producers, was that they were dealing with very complex issues that radio talk show hosts could not possibly understand. And, besides, radio talkers were all too "predictable."

No sooner did word of Klein's "fatwa" (as it became known among CNN staff) leak out than the proverbial you-know-what hit the fan.

Now, to be fair, a friend in CNN's top management reassured me that Klein didn't want to ban *all* talk show hosts, just certain more obnoxious ones who contributed nothing to the conversation. I know the type. Indeed, I wrote a book about them, which you now hold in your hands. Nonetheless, in painting all talk show hosts with the same broad brush, Klein made what I thought was a dumb mistake—and I couldn't resist having some fun with it.

On my radio show and in my weekly column, I pointed out that, while I might miss appearing on CNN, that dark cloud did have one big silver lining: If I could no longer appear on CNN, then neither could Lou Dobbs! Because we were *both* radio talk show hosts. And surely, to be consistent and true to his word, Jon Klein would not only have to ban me from his airwaves, he would have to fire Lou Dobbs. In fact, I argued, he should have done so long ago, for all the poison Dobbs had been spewing on the air. With tongue fully in cheek, I entitled my column: "CNN Finally Fires Lou Dobbs!"

While my immediate target was Klein, my real goal, of course, was to bait Lou Dobbs. And to my delight, as thin-skinned as he is, Dobbs swallowed the bait—hook, line, and sinker. The very next day, he devoted several minutes of his radio program to attacking me.

Responding directly to my column, he started out: "Bill Press, by the way, used to be a colleague at CNN. I kind of liked the fellow. But he obviously doesn't like me. He's having a fit because CNN's president Jon Klein, whom I like, I work with him all the time, won't fire me. He's just having a little fit about it. And he goes through and he's talking about the opportunities that Klein had to fire Dobbs, and going on. He said that Klein missed two excellent opportunities to fire Dobbs. First, when Dobbs assumed the role of chief executioner for undocumented workers. I mean, does anybody talk about inflammatory language on the left?"

Yes, I dared criticize Lou. So what does that make me? Dobbs has a word for it: "Interesting that Press is a, you know, he's a propagandist. I mean, that's all he is now. That's pitiful. That is truly, truly pitiful."

He then turned back to quoting my column: "Klein also should have dumped Dobbs for fanning the flames of the birther issue." And then tried again to defend himself: "Let's see, I say, I say that Barack Obama is a citizen, but why not produce your doggone birth certificate? And Bill Press and the left wing are completely nuts. I mean, you can't ask questions like that. You can't do that. What in the world are we doing?"

I must have struck a raw nerve. Because just a couple of days later, Dobbs noticed a tweet I'd sent from a White House briefing, expressing my frustration over the continued hopes of the Obama White House that they could achieve a bipartisan consensus on health care reform. "What are they smoking?" I asked. Which provided Dobbs another excuse to tee off on me. "Bill Press, I mean, you know, this is one of the legendary journalists, at least in his own mind. You probably don't know who he is. He's just one of my fleas that I have to deal with from time to time. But what a . . . he thinks he's some sort of . . . I don't know, he's more of a . . . What would you say? Is he a Trotskyite? Or is he a Stalinist? What is he? He's a little left of Stalin, I think. My God."

A little left of Stalin? Simply for suggesting that Obama realize that Republicans in Congress—after having voted en bloc against the stimulus package, the 2010 budget, Sonia Sotomayor, and the "cash for clunkers" program—were unlikely to agree to any compromise on health care reform? Coming from Mr. Dobbs, comrades, I guess I should wear that criticism as a badge of honor.

At least he didn't say of me what, just a couple of days earlier, he'd said of Howard Dean: "He's a bloodsucking leftist—I mean, you gotta put a stake through his heart to stop this guy." What was that about "inflammatory language" again, Lou?

WHERE'S THE BIRTH CERTIFICATE?

For months, the fact that Dobbs maintained his presence on CNN while other radio talk show hosts were banned, and the fact that he alone among CNN hosts was allowed to spout his own opinions, did make you wonder: Who's running the network, Jonathan Klein or Lou Dobbs?

And so did the way Dobbs kept making such an issue of President Obama's birth certificate.

This whole crazy business started during the 2008 campaign when some looney tunes put the ultimate conspiracy theory together: Wait! His name's Barack Obama? His father's from Kenya? His mother's from Kansas? He was born in Honolulu, before Hawaii was even a state? He may not be a U.S. citizen! He's not even qualified to run for president!

The whole thing was absolutely, bat-shit crazy—and easily refuted. Hawaii became a state in 1959, Obama was born in 1961. Regardless, his mother was clearly an American citizen. Which means, according to the Constitution, he could have been born on the moon—or, like John McCain, in the Panama Canal Zone. He would still be an American citizen at birth. But, weird as it may have seemed, the rumor spread, it was reported in the media, some gullible people actually believed it, and the story started to get legs. So much so that the Obama campaign contacted the state of Hawaii, retrieved an electronic copy of his birth certificate (the only kind available in Hawaii), and posted it on their Web site. At the same time, FactCheck.org looked into the question, verified the birth certificate, and also produced birth announcements that appeared in two different Honolulu newspapers within a week of the blessed event. End of story. Right? Wrong!

A lawsuit challenging Obama's citizenship, and filed by perennial candidate Alan Keyes (who lost the 2004 Senate race to Obama), was rejected by the U.S. Supreme Court. Nevertheless, the issue refused to go away and, indeed, flared back to life in the summer of 2009, after Obama had already been in the White House for six months. But this time it was even more weird.

The "birthers"—doubters in Obama's standing as a citizen—rejected all physical proof presented. They demanded that Obama produce the "long form" of his birth certificate, whatever the hell that is. With no evidence, they asserted he'd been born in Kenya, not Hawaii. Even more sinister, some insisted he'd actually been born in Iraq! Ten Republican members of Congress introduced legislation requiring any future candidate for president to produce his or her birth certificate when announcing for office.

Again, the charge was ludicrous, so much so that not even Rush Limbaugh, Bill O'Reilly, or the patently crazy Glenn Beck would touch it. And the whole flap might simply have disappeared—were it not picked up by Lou Dobbs.

Up to that point, Dobbs was still considered a serious anchor, despite his outspoken views on illegal immigration. But on July 15, 2009, he surprised media critics, and many of his audience, by embracing the cause of the birthers. While insisting he personally believed that Obama had been born in Hawaii, and was therefore a legitimate U.S. citizen, he invited

Alan Keyes and other birthers to spread their lies on both his radio and TV shows—and, daily, he repeated their demand that Obama produce the goods.

"I believe Barack Obama is a citizen of the United States, folks, don't you? But I do have a couple of little questions, like you. Why not just provide a copy of the birth certificate? That's entirely within the president's power to do so. Then all of this nonsense goes away." Given that, on its news shows, political reporters had long ago debunked the claims of the birthers, Dobbs's sudden rush to their cause proved an embarrassment to CNN. On the afternoon of July 24, Klein sent an e-mail to Dobbs and staff informing them that, according to CNN's own researchers, Hawaii had switched exclusively to electronic records, so the demand for a paper copy was mute. For Klein, that was the end of it—or so he thought.

"It seems this story is dead," Klein wrote, "because anyone who is still not convinced doesn't have a legitimate beef." He closed his e-mail by telling Dobbs's producers to be sure to have Dobbs mention this on that evening's show.

Maybe Klein should have checked with Rick Kaplan before believing that Dobbs would follow suit. Sure enough, that evening Dobbs announced: "The state of Hawaii says it can't release a paper copy of the president's original birth certificate because they say the state discarded the original document when the health department records went electronic some eight years ago. That explanation, however, has not satisfied some critics." He then proceeded to devote yet another segment of his TV show to the claims of the birthers!

And Dobbs continued to flog that dead horse, even after the director of the State Department of Health reported that she had gone into the archives and inspected the actual original copy of Obama's birth certificate (it was not true that they had destroyed all paper records when going electronic) and could verify its existence.

Questioned by the *Los Angeles Times* how he could possibly order Dobbs to drop the issue and yet allow Dobbs to continue devoting so much time to it on CNN, Klein backtracked—insisting it was a "legitimate" issue and covering it or not was up to Dobbs: It's "his editorial decision to make."

"We respect our viewers enough to present them the facts and let them make up their own minds," Klein told the *Times*. Or, as Roger Ailes, president of Fox News put it even better: "We report, you decide."

In effect, Klein was admitting that, during that one-hour of *Lou Dobbs Tonight,* there was no difference between CNN and Fox News.

CNN REALLY FIRES LOU DOBBS!

With Klein going in one direction, and Dobbs persisting in another, it was only a matter of time before the other shoe dropped—and it did on November 11, 2009. Finally forced to choose between giving his opinion or continuing his TV show, Dobbs chose opinion.

With no advance notice, Dobbs stunned his viewers by announcing he was quitting the network: "Some leaders in media, politics, and business have been urging me to go beyond the role here at CNN and to engage in constructive problem solving as well as to contribute positively to the great understanding of the issues of our day."

Leaving CNN for the second time, Dobbs gave no indication of where he might be heading next, other than to say he was considering "a number of options and directions." Rumors immediately swirled that he might move to the Fox Business Channel, but it seemed clear that Dobbs had a bigger platform in mind: "As for the important work of restoring inspiration to our great free society and our market economy, I will strive as well to be a leader in that national conversation."

A leader in that national conversation? Sure sounds like a future political candidate to me. What will it be? Dobbs for Senate? Dobbs for President? Don't be surprised by either.

For his part, a relieved Jonathan Klein said in a statement that "Lou has now decided to carry the banner of advocacy journalism elsewhere."

However, it was *The Onion* that best captured the irony of the moment with its news bulletin: "Acting on anonymous tips from within the Hispanic-American community, U.S. Customs and Border Protection officials on Wednesday deported Luis Miguel Salvador Aguila Dominguez, who for the last 48 years had been living illegally in the United States under the name Lou Dobbs." Conan O'Brien had a similar take: "Lou Dobbs quit at CNN today. He's being replaced by a guy named Juan who'll work for five dollars an hour."

In the end, on immigration, Lou Dobbs lived by the sword and died by the sword. *Vaya con dios.*

DOUBLING DOWN

We've taken a long look at Bill O'Reilly and Lou Dobbs for a good reason. As is the case with Sean Hannity and Glenn Beck, these commentators are particularly dangerous because they were able to fire with both barrels. By appearing every day on both national radio and national television, they didn't dilute their message, they reinforced it.

Their daytime radio shows provided them much more than a chance to increase their exposure or make more money. It gave them the opportunity to test their attacks, sharpen their message, and double down on the arguments.

The combined radio-TV presence gives conservative talkers an enormous advantage in shaping public opinion: an advantage enjoyed by no talk show host on the left, with the exception of liberal Ed Schultz. But even though he also appears daily on both radio and television, his show is carried on far fewer radio stations and his MSNBC broadcast trails the competition on Fox.

What's good news for right-wing hosts, however, is not such good news for their audience. Talkers get double the time. But listeners get double the poison.

Unfortunately, there's lots of poison to go around. And not just from the big guns. Before or after their broadcasts, the little guns take over the airwaves—with the same old right-wing nonsense. They may not be as talented, but they're just as extreme and just as loud.

MINOR LEAGUE TALK RADIO

et's face it: In radio and TV, everybody wants to be a big star.

But let's also face it: Not everybody makes it. No matter how hard they try, some people have to settle for being little stars. Meet Mark Levin, Laura Ingraham, and Neal Boortz: conservative talk radio's second string. You might call them "The Little Engines That Couldn't." They huff and they puff, but they can never quite make it up that hill, and never will.

Not that they're not successful. For a while, at least, Mark Levin had the fastest-growing talk radio show in the country. They are each heard on hundreds of stations every day. In fact, they each have more stations than any liberal talk radio host. But in the world of right-wing talk, they must live with the stigma of being, like Ronald Reagan, B-actors. Their egos are as big, but their audiences will never be as big, as those of Rush Limbaugh, Glenn Beck, Sean Hannity, Bill O'Reilly, Lou Dobbs, or Michael Savage.

Nor do they bring anything new to the equation. As we will see, their daily drill consists of more personal attacks, more right-wing cheap shots at the same old lefty targets, and more prostrating before the usual Repub-

lican Party idols. In a word, all they deliver is more toxic talk . . . for those listeners content with the minor leagues.

MARK LEVIN

Someday, somebody's going to write a book about how easy it is to become a big-time conservative talk radio host. And the star of the book will be Mark Levin. If he can do it, they'll say, *anybody* can do it. And they'll be right.

Levin is one of the most unlikely people on the planet to become a successful talk radio host. He has, first of all, a high-pitched, annoying voice that makes him sound like a cross-dresser from Brooklyn. He had no background in media. He got his own radio show only because he used to hang out with Sean Hannity.

A former low-level member of the Reagan administration, Levin knocked around Washington for a while, practicing law, running the Landmark Legal Foundation, and popping up on radio and television as a conservative legal commentator. That's where I met him. Levin was one of our regular go-to conservative guests on *Crossfire* during the days of the Monica Lewinsky scandal. Guaranteed to cut Bill Clinton no slack, he was also one of the most lugubrious, least cheerful guests we ever booked.

I'll never forget one broadcast. Again, the topic was whether Clinton's confessed fling with Monica Lewinsky was grounds for impeachment. Levin was our guest on the right, up against Clinton campaign manager James Carville on the left. Levin was his doleful self; Carville, his devil-may-care self. The late Bob Novak and I were the hosts. Levin had just finished making a serious anti-Clinton argument, with the mien and manner of a funeral director, when Carville leaned across the desk, got right in his face, and asked: "Man, don't you ever smile?" No, in fact, he didn't.

Even though we booked Levin frequently on *Crossfire,* we never liked him enough to give him a show nickname. But his fellow conservatives did. Rush Limbaugh, where Levin appeared frequently as a legal analyst, dubbed him "F. Lee Levin," a takeoff on the famous trial lawyer F. Lee Bailey. And Sean Hannity, who practically adopted Levin, stealing him from Rush, liked him so much he called him "The Great One."

With Hannity's help, Levin landed his own Sunday afternoon show on WABC, New York's conservative blowtorch, in 2002. A year later, he was nationally syndicated five days a week by Citadel Media Networks, following his mentor, Hannity, in most markets, and soon skyrocketed to number one in his time slot. He now appears on over 150 stations, in addition to Sirius XM satellite radio.

NAME-CALLING

Don't expect anything new from Mark Levin. He differs from fellow conservative talk show hosts only in terms of style. Where others, like Neal Boortz, whom we'll meet in a bit, may even appear thoughtful on occasion, Levin is just the opposite: loud, ugly, know-it-all, impatient, and intolerant— even, as we shall see, toward fellow conservatives who dare disagree with his take-no-prisoners approach. He is, without doubt, one of the most hateful voices on talk radio—and that's saying something.

Levin, in fact, is known less for his insights or intellect than for his insults and name-calling. The Mark Levin Fan Club even posts a lexicon of the twisted names he has given his favorite targets, including:

ACTUAL NAME	LEVIN SLUR
New York Times	*New York Slimes*
The Washington Post	*The Washington Compost*
MSNBC	MSLSD
Hardball with Chris Matthews	*Screwball with Screwball*
Senator Barbara Boxer	The Dwarf Senator
Senator Al Franken	The Spiteful Troll
Senator Russ Feingold	Foolsgold
Bill Clinton	BJ Bill Jefferson Clinton
Harry Belafonte	Harry Belacommie
Mike Huckabee	Huck-a-phony

| John McCain | John McLame |
| Arnold Schwarzenegger | Arnold Jerkinator |

He's also described Senators Barbara Boxer and John Kerry as "two complete morons who look like they come straight out of . . . *The Addams Family.*"

Now, all that would be very clever—if Levin were still in elementary school. But for any adults looking for intelligent political debate on the radio, Levin's name-calling falls egregiously short. Hey, I warned you not to expect too much intellectual analysis from this guy!

WHERE'S THE BEEF?

As the above list shows, Levin is a master at ridicule, but little else. If he does understand the important issues of the day, or if he has any insights on effective solutions to problems facing this country, you'd never know it from listening to his radio show. I know. To my utter disgust, while dutifully doing my homework for this book, I've listened to many hours of Mark Levin. I have never heard him explain, for example, how a Republican plan for economic recovery would work better than the plan Democrats put forward. Probably because there is no Republican plan for economic recovery, or anything else.

Believe me, there were a lot of legitimate questions about the economic recovery plan, or so-called stimulus package, President Obama sent to Congress in the spring of 2009. It cost $787 billion, which is less than economists like Paul Krugman thought was necessary to get the job done. Still, none of it went directly to taxpayers. "Shovel-ready" projects aside, a lot of it was targeted at saving existing jobs, not creating new ones. And there was always the risk that cities and states would use stimulus funds to bail out failed programs, not spur new economic growth. Yes, it was aimed at bringing America back from the brink. But even I, as a liberal, had a lot of doubts about the cost of the program and whether we could be sure the money would be well spent.

It was an issue, and a time, demanding good, strong, critical comment.

Instead, as first spotted by columnist Conor Friedersdorf of *The Atlantic*, here's what we heard from Mark Levin on May 18, 2009:

"Let me tell you what I think you're doing, Mr. President. You want this economy to crash. You want this currency to crash. Because what a magnificent opportunity to rearrange and remake society once its basic institutions have failed. That's what you're up to. I'm the only one with the guts to say it, because I know history. I know economics. I know your mentors. I know what you're doing. You have a huge chip on your shoulder. And a really sick philosophical point of view. That's where you're taking us."

Now, again, you might think the bailout of Detroit was a mistake. You might not buy the theory, first posited by the Bush administration and then adopted by President Obama, that certain banks are too big to fail. You might not believe that investment in renewable energy is something the government should be involved in. All legitimate points of view. But, as Friedersdorf points out, to assert that the president—who is, after all, a politician counting on being be reelected—actually wants the American economy to fail, that is just plain babble. Especially when Obama was doing little more than following the lead of his predecessor. In fact, many conservative economists agreed that, given the huge cliff we were about to go over, Obama had no choice but to pump massive amounts of government spending into the economy. As for thoughtful analysis, note that the only evidence Levin puts forth to prove his premise about Obama's nefarious motives is: "I know history. I know economics. I know your mentors." Such bombast sheds no light on the subject, nor offers any new ideas or alternative solutions. And for that reason, Friedersdorf argues in *The Atlantic*, Levin actually hurts the conservative cause. He was echoing a point made earlier by conservative commentator David Frum, but with much more gusto.

In response, Levin defenders scolded Friedersdorf for just not understanding talk radio. The role of the talk show host, he was lectured, is neither to enlighten nor inform, it's just to get good ratings. And showmanship is how they do so. As one critic told Friedersdorf: "Talk pioneer Willis Duff once said that talk radio is like bullfighting. People appreciate the cape work—but they come to see the bull get killed. And nobody kills the bull like Mark Levin."

More often than not, however, the bulls Levin tries to kill—are cows.

LADIES, BEWARE!

It's not just the economy. On any issue, instead of in-depth discussion or debate, what we hear on *The Mark Levin Show* is a repetitive string of biting comments about the same liberals targeted by every other conservative radio host in the country. That being said, however, Levin seems especially to relish attacks against women.

He was quick to join the chorus of critics who called Supreme Court nominee Sonia Sotomayor a "bigot" for her 2001 comment about the special qualities a Latina judge would bring to the bench. He warned Democratic senators: "These people need to understand that if they vote to confirm a radical leftist—and I will now say what I actually believe—who is a bigot— that's right, I said it—then they need to pay a political price for this."

Again, as to Sotomayor's judicial qualifications or ideology, Levin never rose above the personal attack, not even about her physical appearance: "We don't owe these people anything. They owe us. And I'm telling you right now, she's Ruth Bader Ginsburg, plus about fifty pounds. . . . Now I'll say what others won't say: She does not strike me as particularly intelligent. Intelligent enough, but she's no Miguel Estrada [nominated by George W. Bush to the Court of Appeals in 2001, but blocked by a Democratic filibuster]. So she has to go by ideology. She has to go by agenda. That's what she'll rely on."

Sotomayor was not the only prominent Democratic woman Levin slammed for her avoirdupois. He called Secretary of State Hillary Clinton "Her Thighness."

And for Speaker Nancy Pelosi, the same treatment: critical analysis of her legislative policies, totally lacking; cheap shots at her appearance, gleefully given. Of course, he has his own nickname for her: "Now, Nancy Pelosi, or as we call her, with all due respect, 'Stretch,' given her multiple face-lifts. . . . What do I mean? Do you think eyes bulge out like that? Do you think that's a natural look? No! She spent a fortune for that look. She loves it."

Levin repeated the slam against Pelosi while appearing as a guest on Sean Hannity's radio show: "You could bounce a dime off her cheeks. The woman has had so many face-lifts, isn't it obvious to everybody?" Later, with Hannity as his guest, Levin seized the opportunity to poke fun at then-Senator Joe Biden for his hair transplants before, once again, turning on the speaker: "And then, of course, we have Pelosi. One more face-lift and those eyes are going to pop right out, don't you think?"

The loyal Hannity volunteered that people who didn't laugh at his buddy Levin's personal attacks on politicians were "utterly humorless." At which point, Levin gave us all even more laughs by insisting that the only reason Pelosi gets reelected by wide margins in San Francisco has nothing to with her politics, but all to do with her physical appearance. She doesn't have to worry about losing her seat because, says the mad talker, San Franciscans will keep reelecting "shrill" Pelosi "as long as her makeup holds up." Funny guy, that Mark Levin . . . if you're as sick as he is.

For all the wrong reasons, Levin acknowledges that Pelosi's House seat is secure. However, for him and other right-wingers, how Pelosi managed to get to and from her West Coast district did become a major issue. It wasn't fair, they argued, that Speaker Dennis Hastert had a small military jet and Speaker Nancy Pelosi was assigned a bigger one. "Doesn't she have a big military jet? Why is it that these politicians can live like kings and queens, and nobody gives a damn? She fought like hell for an extra-big military jet so she can take her staff, and her staff's staff, and her relatives and her friends and have a grand old party on that jet."

The misogynistic Levin saw Pelosi's jet as just one more example of government giving in to pushy women. After senators suggested that auto executives travel to Washington by car caravan instead of corporate jet, he demanded to know why Pelosi shouldn't be required to do the same thing. (From the West Coast? Every weekend?) But, oh no. "She's gotta have a big military jet. I mean, she's the first woman speaker, she wants a really, really big one, and if she doesn't get it, well that's sexual discrimination."

Not letting the truth get in the way of an easy personal shot, Levin failed to inform his listeners of two pertinent facts. First, the requirement that the speaker of the house be assigned a military jet for official travel was decided by the Bush administration, for security purposes, immediately after September 11—when Dennis Hastert was speaker. Second, the only reason Pelosi has a bigger jet than Hastert is because he's from Illinois and she's from California—and, as any third-grader could tell you, it takes a bigger jet to get there nonstop.

Indeed, for anyone seriously interested in the issue, and not just trying to score a cheap political point, the new travel arrangements for speaker were explained in a February 8, 2007, statement by House Sergeant at Arms Wilson Livingood:

"As the Sergeant at Arms, I have the responsibility to ensure the security of the members of the House of Representatives, to include the Speaker of the House. The Speaker requires additional precautions due to her responsibilities as the leader of the House and her Constitutional position as second in the line of succession to the presidency.

"In a post 9/11 threat environment," Livingood continued, "it is reasonable and prudent to provide military aircraft to the Speaker for official travel between Washington and her district. The practice began with Speaker Dennis Hastert (R-Il) and I have recommended that it continue with Speaker Pelosi. The fact that Speaker Pelosi lives in California compelled me to request an aircraft that is capable of making non-stop flights for security purposes, unless such an aircraft is unavailable. This will ensure communications capabilities and also enhance security. I made the recommendation to use military aircraft based upon the need to provide necessary levels of security for ranking national leaders, such as the Speaker. I regret that an issue that is exclusively considered and decided in a security context has evolved into a political issue."

Pelosi and Sotomayor may take some grim relief in the fact that it's not just women in public life that are the victims of Levin's sharp tongue. He loathes them all. On his show, he routinely refers to the National Organization for Women as the "National Organization of Really Ugly Women." And he can turn on a female caller to his program, just as fast and mean.

Like the woman from Westchester, New York, who called to suggest that President Obama was smarter than Levin was giving him credit for. Levin exploded: "Why do you hate my country? Why do you hate my Constitution? Why do you hate my Declaration of Independence? Let me say this, are you a married woman, yes or no?" When she admitted she was, Levin screamed: "Well, I don't know why your husband doesn't put a gun to his temple. Get the hell out of here!" Nice talk. But you do have to ask: Is Levin helping his cause—or hurting it?

FRUM TO THE RESCUE

As we saw above, that question was considered by *Atlantic* magazine columnist Conor Friedersdorf. But the first one to dare raise it—and challenge Levin directly on it—was prominent conservative journalist, Canadian-born, now American citizen, David Frum.

A longtime contributor to the *National Review*, Frum now has his own blog, *NewMajority.com*. But he's best known as a former speechwriter for George W. Bush, where he penned the phrase "Axis of Evil."

I can't claim to know David Frum well. I've interviewed him, and debated him on *Crossfire*. But I know him well enough to know this: He's the opposite of Mark Levin. He's brilliant. He's thoughtful. He's a committed conservative, yet willing to listen and consider opposing points of view (and then decimate them). He's something no one ever accused Levin of being: a gentleman.

As a gentleman, Frum understands that insulting people may be the best way to get their attention, but it's not the best way to win their support. He first had the audacity to raise this point about Rush Limbaugh in a March 2, 2009, post on his blog—and repeated it in the March 9 cover story of *Newsweek*.

On March 1, White House Chief of Staff Rahm Emanuel had appeared on *Face the Nation* with Bob Schieffer and very cleverly anointed Limbaugh "the voice and energy behind the Republican Party." Frum noted that having Rush declared the de facto head of the GOP was great publicity for him, but not necessarily for the rest of the party.

As we saw in Chapter 1, Frum pointed out that Rush, as America's most popular talk radio show host, could rightfully brag that 20 million Americans loved him. But at the same time, another 100 million hated him. So what? As a talk show host, he can make a very good living off his 20 million fans. He doesn't have to worry about the other 100 million. But Republican Party leaders don't have that luxury. They have to worry about reaching out to the 100 million, because they vote. They don't vote for Rush, but they do vote for or against Republican candidates. It's great to have Rush on your side, in other words, but he's not the guy you can count on to lead the Republican Party back from the political wilderness.

This makes perfectly good sense to me. An intelligent analysis of the way things are in the real world, in fact.

But among conservatives, Frum was immediately branded a traitor. In questioning Limbaugh's supremacy, he was deemed to have committed the worst possible sin. Indeed, he would have been in less trouble had he claimed that Jesus Christ was an impostor. And leading the pack of critics, of course, was Mark Levin.

The next day, Levin opened his show with a bombastic attack on Frum: "There are people who have somehow claimed the conservative mantle . . . You don't even know who they are . . . They're so irrelevant . . . It's time to name names . . . ! The Canadian David Frum: Where did this a-hole come from? . . . In the foxhole with other conservatives, you know what this jerk does? He keeps shooting us in the back . . . Hey, Frum: you're a putz."

Frum wasn't listening that day, but his fifteen-year-old son was. He called in to defend his dad, but Levin wouldn't let him on the show. So, the next day, after listening to the tape, Frum called in to try to make his case: that, in order to win back the political majority, the Republican Party needed to modernize its message and put forward a more effective messenger. But Levin wouldn't let him speak. Whenever Frum tried to make a point, Levin told the producer to cut off his mike. Then, having just the day before called him an "a-hole," "jerk," and "putz," Levin accused Frum of engaging in personal attacks and name-calling, and dismissed him with the final comment: "You're annoying."

To this day, Frum, like David Brooks, remains a rare conservative voice, daring to say what many Republican elected leaders realize but are afraid to say: Bombastic talk show hosts like Rush Limbaugh, Mark Levin, Sean Hannity, and Michael Savage are great for keeping the base energized. But their ugly personal attacks turn off the very moderates and independents the party needs to win back if it ever hopes to regain political power.

DOG LOVER

However, before he accuses me of being a putz for engaging in name-calling, I want to say one positive thing about Mark Levin: He once wrote a beautiful book about his dog Sprite. Any man who loves a dog can't be all bad.

In fact, I happen to know firsthand that all three talk show hosts in this chapter are dog lovers. Which leaves me with some residual hope for humanity. Time to meet another one.

LAURA INGRAHAM

As you may have noticed by now, the world of nationally syndicated conservative talk radio is mainly a manly group. With two notable exceptions, both named Laura. But Laura Ingraham is the only serious one of the two.

If conservative credentials determine your place in the hierarchy of right-wing talk show hosts, then Laura Ingraham deserves to be on top of the pile. As an undergraduate, she was editor-in-chief of *The Dartmouth Review*. For the last two years of the Reagan administration, she worked as a speechwriter in the White House. After graduating from the University of Virginia School of Law, she clerked at the Supreme Court for Justice Clarence Thomas. Eat your heart out, Mark Levin.

Ingraham has something else going for her, too: She is quite attractive. I don't add that fact to demean her in any way. I add that only because it's true. And because it's a gift she doesn't hesitate to take advantage of. Check out her official publicity photos. No brainy, studious, serious look there. She could just as easily pass for the latest Hollywood sex kitten with that irresistible, come-hither look in her eyes. In 1995, her appearance even won her a cover photo—in a sexy leopard print miniskirt, no less—on *The New York Times Sunday Magazine*. Add beauty to brains and you have the lethal combination that has made Ingraham so successful. It may seem quaint now that Fox News is basically fully staffed with them, but long before the flavor of the month for right-wing media consisted of a black conservative (Armstrong Williams, Alan Keyes, J. C. Watts, Larry Elder), the search was on for a blond conservative. Enter Laura Ingraham, who rose to the top of the pile. She started popping up on radio and TV's political shows. We often invited her as a guest on *Crossfire*, where she routinely demolished her opponents. She is a forceful and effective debater.

Realizing it was more fun to pontificate on the air than in a courtroom, Ingraham decided to abandon the practice of law for a media career: first, on television, where she enjoyed immediate, sporadic, but never long-lasting success. In the late 1990s, she appeared on the *CBS Evening News*, up against former Senator Bill Bradley in a left-right debate segment, and also briefly hosted the program *Watch It!* on MSNBC. In 2008, she auditioned for a new program on Fox News, *Just In*, but that only lasted three weeks.

Even though she still appears frequently on Fox, and is Bill O'Reilly's regular guest host, it's on talk radio where Ingraham found her new home and hit her stride. She launched her show in April 2001 and now is ranked number six among all talk shows in audience size. *The Laura Ingraham Show* is carried by over three hundred stations, as well as on XM satellite radio, and reaches some 5.5 million listeners a week.

GOP ACOLYTE

So what awaits you when you tune into the program of a smart, former White House speechwriter and Supreme Court clerk? Sadly, not the intellectual depth or analysis you might expect (unless you remember she clerked for Clarence Thomas). Instead, she delivers many of the same political and personal cheap shots you hear from Mark Levin. And much of the same Republican Party cheerleading you get from Sean Hannity.

Like Fox News, *The Laura Ingraham Show* is really a platform for the Republican National Committee. I used to tune in regularly during the 2008 primaries, because I knew I could almost daily hear an interview with one of the Republican presidential candidates. And while she was originally no fan of John McCain's, she did her best to get him elected once he became the party nominee. She was especially enthusiastic over his choice of Sarah Palin as his running mate.

Meanwhile, true to form, she followed the lead of her fellow conservative talk show hosts in making a big deal over Barack Obama's associations with Pastor Jeremiah Wright, Bill Ayers, and ACORN. Even after he reached the White House, she found fault with everything Obama did. And not just on big policy issues. On small personal matters, too.

For example, when Obama took his wife to New York for dinner and a Broadway show—fulfilling a promise the ever-absent candidate had made to his wife during the campaign—Ingraham slammed him for an "egotistical" outing carefully orchestrated by the White House to drown out any coverage of the latest missile test by North Korea. Not only that, she charged Obama with being insensitive for his willingness to "inconvenience" everyone else in the restaurant and theater, just so he could show up and "wave to the adoring crowds." She closed her tirade by asking her audience, "Are we just being terribly uncharitable here?" Why, yes, Laura, you are. Uncharitable and petty.

She evidenced an equally petty worldview in May 2009 when Obama and Joe Biden took off from the White House for an unscheduled lunch break at Ray's Hell-Burger in Arlington, Virginia. Most Americans thought it was kind of cool for the president and vice president to pop out for a burger. Just like two regular guys, right? Not Laura Ingraham. To her, Obama didn't even know how to order a burger. How dare he, she demanded to know, how dare he eat a cheeseburger with mustard, and not ketchup? Horrors!

Echoing almost word for word the childish complaint of Sean Hannity, she demanded to know: "What kind of man orders a cheeseburger without ketchup, but Dijon mustard? The guy orders a cheeseburger without ketchup? What is that?" That, Laura, probably represents 40–50 percent of all cheeseburger orders. Take it from a real man who always orders mustard, Dijon if available, on my cheeseburger.

When it comes to Obama, Ingraham is so blindly partisan she even blasted him for his observance of September 11. In 2009, his first 9/11 anniversary as president, President Obama presided over a moment of silence at the White House, followed by a memorial service at the Pentagon—the exact same schedule of events followed by George W. Bush before him. Then he and the first lady put in a couple of hours of volunteer work with Habitat for Humanity, painting new houses—doing his own part to observe his earlier call for all Americans to make September 11 a national day of volunteerism.

Once again, without knowing her facts, Ingraham went ballistic. Making 9/11 a national volunteer day? What kind of pinko commie idea is that? "Some critics believe that marking 9/11 as a day for volunteerism demeans the memory of the thousands who were killed by Muslim extremists on that fateful September morning," she told her listeners.

Too bad. A little homework could have saved her a lot of embarrassment. The truth is, in March 2009 the U.S. Congress, with strong bipartisan support, had already passed a law authored by Senator Ted Kennedy making September 11 a "National Day of Service and Remembrance." Not only that, the whole idea originated, not with Barack Obama or Ted Kennedy, but with George W. Bush.

Four months after September 11, in his 2002 State of the Union address, President Bush announced formation of the USA Freedom Corps, a national service organization created "in the spirit of 9/11." And he followed through. On the first anniversary of September 11, Bush put out a statement through USA Freedom Corps that called on all Americans to observe the day by volunteering for some noble cause. "Many ask, 'What can I do to help in our fight,'" Bush told the nation. "And the answer is simple. All of us can become a September the 11th volunteer by making a commitment to service in our communities. You can serve your country by tutoring or mentoring a child, comforting the afflicted, housing those in need of shelter. Whatever your talent, whatever your background, each of you can do something."

It was a cause President Bush pursued right up until the time he left office. Quoting a press release from the Corporation for National and Community Service in September 2008, Bush's last anniversary commemoration as president: "President Bush today renewed the call he made for every American to give 4,000 hours or two years of their lives in service to others." So there you have the difference among conservatives between George Bush and Barack Obama on community service. When Bush calls for it, it ennobles us all. When Obama calls for it, it demeans those who died on September 11.

Either Laura Ingraham doesn't know the truth, or she insults us all.

PULL THE PLUG ON GRANDMA

Ol' leopardskin didn't come close to the truth on the battle over health care reform legislation, either. A breast cancer survivor herself, who should know something about the importance of having health insurance, she nevertheless repeatedly spread the lies and distortions put forth by congressional Republican opponents of the Obama plan, starting with the specter of "death panels" raised by Sarah Palin.

Anybody who had done the tiniest bit of research on the pending health care reform legislation at that time would know there was no mandatory "death counseling" called for. Yes, the draft legislation stipulated that Medicare would reimburse doctors or nurses for counseling on end of life options—but only for those families and patients who requested it.

A little more digging would reveal that, especially after the Terri Schiavo fiasco, most American families today do seek and value that compassionate advice. And that George W. Bush, as governor of Texas, had in fact signed legislation authorizing reimbursement for those same services in the Lone Star State.

But why should Laura Ingraham be bothered with knowing or telling the truth? Sitting in as guest host for Bill O'Reilly on *The Factor*, she sounded like a blond Sarah Palin: "The fact that a government bureaucrat will come to an old person's house as a mandatory counseling session—first of all, stay away from my father, who is eighty-three years old. I do not want any government bureaucrat telling him what kind of treatment he should consider to be a good citizen. That's frightening."

Yes, that is, indeed, frightening—that a radio talk show host should so deliberately mislead her audience.

Because maybe the threat of *mandatory* death counseling didn't scare people enough, Ingraham went even further on her radio show. She first asserted that Obama's "approach to health care reform" is "making sure people don't live as long."

One day later she painted the ultimate, absurd scenario: "Can you imagine—if I were doing *Saturday Night Live*, like, if I were producing it this weekend, and I was going to be fair about political humor, I would have a hospice chute—like a door, a trapdoor, that does into a chute where the elderly would just walk up—'Oh, my hip hurts'—And all of a sudden you see this leg kicking Granny down the chute, and that's Obamacare." After portraying several seniors getting "kicked down the chute into hospice," she concluded: "Some will call them death camps, but this is the way Obamacare is gonna go for America."

"Death camps"? And then she had the nerve to demand that Florida congressman Alan Grayson apologize after characterizing the Republican health care plan as "Don't Get Sick." And, if you do, "Die Quickly." Puhleeze.

Of course, we all know how this will end. Someday, even Laura Ingraham's gonna grow old. She'll no longer be on radio and TV, and everybody will have forgotten all about her. She'll realize she doesn't have that many more years to live. She'll want to make sure she's taken care of. She may even want to make sure she's not kept alive by artificial means. She'll no doubt want to get the good advice of her physician about these questions—and she'll want Medicare to pay for it.

At that point, do you think she'll regret that she so misinformed millions of Americans about what Obama's health care plan is really all about? Don't bet on it.

BATTLE OF THE BLONDES

Even conservative talk show hosts are usually more careful about picking their battles. One of the silliest Laura Ingraham engaged in was her vendetta against John McCain's daughter, Meghan.

Meghan McCain got a lot of points for her supporting role in her dad's 2008 run for president. She campaigned hard for him, across the country. She helped bring young people into the campaign. She published a daily blog. And, unlike Chelsea Clinton, she didn't hesitate to make herself available for on-the-record interviews, some of them very colorful. She came across as smart, politically savvy, and even somewhat reasonable. In fact, too reasonable for some conservatives, who started a whispering campaign that daughter McCain was a RINO, or Republican in name only.

Once the campaign was over, Meghan McCain fired back, writing in Tina Brown's then-new blog *The Daily Beast* that you don't have to be mean and nasty to be a Republican. In fact, she argued, that kind of language turns a lot of people off, especially young people. And, as an example, she cited Ann Coulter. "I consider myself a progressive Republican," McCain wrote, "but here is what I don't get about Coulter: Is she for real or not? Are some of her statements just gimmicks to gain publicity for her books, or does she actually believe the things she says?"

But then the blonde-on-blonde criticism got a little sharper and more personal. "More so than my ideological differences with Ann Coulter," McCain continued, "I don't like her demeanor. I have never been a person who was attracted to hate or negativity. . . . Everything about her is extreme: her voice, her interview tactics, and especially the public statements she makes about liberals. Maybe her popularity stems from the fact that watching her is sometimes like watching a train wreck."

Ouch! But Coulter's smart. She simply ignored McCain. Ingraham, however, couldn't resist. The next day, she went after McCain—and, of course, in the snarkiest possible way. "Okay, Meghan," she chirped. "Do you think that anyone would be talking to you if you weren't kind of cute and you weren't the daughter of John McCain? Or do you just think that they would just think that you were just another Valley Girl gone awry?"

Then Ingraham got personal, too, taking a shot at McCain's weight. Again, mocking her: "Okay, I was really hoping that I was going to get that role in the *Real World*, but then I realized that, well, they don't like *plus-sized models*. They only like the women who look a certain way. And on this fiftieth anniversary of Barbie, I really have something to say."

McCain, who is hardly seriously overweight, easily deflected Ingraham's shots at her body size. Being slammed for carrying around a few extra pounds was nothing new to her, she acknowledged. "I have been teased about my weight and body figure since I was in middle school, and I decided a very long time ago to embrace what God gave me and live my life positively, attempting to set an example for other girls who may suffer from body image issues." Besides, she went on, "I have nothing to hide: I am a size 8 and fluctuated up to a size 10 during the campaign."

Then she very effectively fired back at Ingraham on two fronts. First, by accusing her of being even meaner than Coulter: "At this point, I have more respect for Ann Coulter than I do for Laura Ingraham because at least Coulter didn't come back at me with heartless, substance-less attacks about my weight." And then, with the cruelest cut of all, by calling attention to Ingraham's age: "Unfortunately, even though Ingraham is more than 20 years older than I and has been a political pundit for longer, almost, than I have been alive, she responded in a form that was embarrassing to herself and to any woman listening to her radio program who was not a size 0." Ouch!

Still, the merciless McCain wasn't through. Appearing on ABC's *The View*, she finished her opponent off with a final, feisty retort. Asked about her running feud with Ingraham, McCain said she had only four words for the outspoken talk show host: "Kiss my fat ass." Game, Set, and Match. McCain.

GET OFF THE BALCONY!

One other fight Laura Ingraham picked, but shouldn't have, concerned American journalists assigned to Iraq.

In February 2006, Ingraham herself made one highly publicized, eight-day visit to Iraq. Good for her. Although one could hardly argue she saw the "real" Iraq or was there to do the work of a real journalist. Just read her "Iraq Journal." As a prominent, conservative talk show host, she was treated like visiting royalty. She was housed on secure military bases and transported from base to base in heavily armored military vehicles or helicopters. When she left the base to visit Iraqi villages, she was accompanied by American troops assigned to her protection.

Excerpts from her diary:

Feb. 5—"In the middle of the night we were whisked off to an undisclosed location, and a few hours later flown to Baghdad by a great Air Force crew out of Alaska and a trusty old C-130."

Feb. 6—"This 24-hour period began with my hitching a late night Blackhawk ride up to Camp Taji, north of Baghdad."

Feb. 7—"I started the day with a pre-patrol briefing for an 18-soldier Humvee convoy to a local village near Camp Victory."

Feb. 8—"We left Camp Victory at 0530 in a very formidable-looking 4 Humvee convoy up to the International Zone in Baghdad."

Feb. 10—"We arrived via 'Rhino' (a.k.a. armored Winnebago with military escorts) back at Camp Victory at 0300."

Now, while it's noble for commentators to want to see the war zone for themselves, you must admit that Ingraham's visit to Iraq did raise an important question: Why the hell should American troops be pulled off the job they have to do in Iraq to protect and escort a radio talk show host? Isn't that an abuse of military resources and a waste of taxpayer dollars?

Unless, of course, the White House had approved the reassignment of the military as part of its propaganda campaign to convince the American people that we were actually winning the war in Iraq. But we would never, never suspect the Bush administration of being so devious. Nor would we ever accuse Laura Ingraham of being a willing puppet of any Bush propaganda machine. Never!

But, here's the rub. Having returned safely to the United States from her military cocoon in Iraq, Ingraham then had the audacity to blast those journalists who were assigned to Iraq full-time—some of whom had been there for years, and none of whom enjoyed the blanket military protection she did. She actually accused them of never getting off their hotel balconies. On March 21, she appeared on the *Today* show, following a report from Baghdad by NBC's Richard Engel, one of the very best and most fearless journalists in Iraq. Ingraham immediately challenged Engel's report, accusing NBC of "reporting only on the IEDs [improvised explosive devices], only on the killings . . . only on the reprisals" in Iraq, and for "reporting from hotel balconies" instead of in the field.

Nor did she back down when confronted with casualties among journalists in Iraq. Although she said "our hearts and prayers" go out to reporters like ABC's Bob Woodruff, who suffered near-fatal head injuries in January 2006, Ingraham insisted: "I will not change my view that giving context in this reporting is important." Even when two CBS crew members were killed by a car bomb in Baghdad on May 29, 2006, Ingraham defended her "hotel balcony" comments, saying "all the guys I talked to in Iraq were tired of it, and I was speaking for them." But the more Ingraham pretended that, having spent eight days in Iraq in the safe hands of the military, she knew more about the situation there than journalists who'd been in the country from the beginning of the war, the more she looked like a fool. Indeed, she was made to look like one by CBS reporter Lara Logan.

Appearing as a guest on CNN's *Reliable Sources* with Howard Kurtz on March 26, Logan first pointed out, in response to allegations by George Bush and Dick Cheney that the media were not telling the full story about Iraq by just reporting on daily car bomb attacks: "You can't travel around this country anymore without military protection. You can't travel without armed guards. You're not free to go, every time there's a school opening. . . . When journalists are free to move around this country, then they will be free to report on everything that's going on." As for Laura Ingraham's charge about reporting only from hotel balconies? Logan pounced: "Well, I think it's outrageous. Laura Ingraham should come to Iraq and not be talking about what journalists are doing from the comfort of her studio in the United States, the comfort and the safety. I don't know any journalist that wants to just sit in a hotel room in Iraq. Does anybody understand, that for us we used to be able to drive to Ramadi, we used to drive to Fallujah, we used to drive to Najaf, we could travel all over this country without having to fly in military helicopters. That's the only way we can move around here. So it's when the military can accommodate us, if the military can accommodate us, then we can go out and see. I mean, we just can't win. I think it's an outrage to point the finger at journalists and say that this is our fault I really do. And I think it shows an abject lack of respect for any journalist that's prepared to come to this country and risk their lives."

When Kurtz pointed out that Ingraham had recently been in Iraq for eight days the previous month, Logan sniffed: "Eight days!" Ingraham lost another battle, to another blonde. For the record, and just to put things in context: According to the Freedom Forum, sixty-eight journalists were killed covering World War II and sixty-six were killed during the ten years of the Vietnam War. Through the end of 2009, according to the Committee to Protect Journalists, 139 journalists were killed in hostile action in Iraq, plus fifty-one media workers (drivers, translators, crew)—making Iraq, by far, the deadliest and most dangerous conflict for journalists ever.

Note to Laura Ingraham: Of the 139 journalists who lost their lives in Iraq, none was killed on a hotel balcony.

FLIP-FLOP ON GAYS

To end on a more positive note, here's one more fight Laura Ingraham started, only later to admit that she was wrong.

As an undergraduate student at Dartmouth, Ingraham gained a national reputation for being notoriously antigay. She reportedly avoided restaurants that might employ gay waiters, lest one of them touch her silverware or breathe on her food and give her AIDS. (Do you think she actually demanded to know their sexual preferences before placing her order?)

Later, as editor-in-chief of *The Dartmouth Review*, she sent a reporter to a meeting of the Gay Students Association and then published an

article "naming names" of gay and lesbian students present and denouncing them as "cheerleaders for latent campus sodomites." Jeffrey Hart, faculty
adviser of *The Review* at the time, accused her of holding "the most anti-
homosexual views imaginable."

But then Ingraham had a "come to Jesus" moment on gay rights when
her brother Curtis came out of the closet with his partner, Ricky Smith,
who later died of AIDS. In an op-ed for *The Washington Post*, she apologized for the "callous rhetoric" of her undergraduate days and admitted a
change of heart: "In the ten years since I learned my brother Curtis was
gay, my views and rhetoric about homosexuality have been tempered, because I have seen him and his companion, Richard, lead their lives with
dignity, fidelity and courage." Until it hit home for her, she admitted, she
didn't understand the urgency for AIDS funding, the problems gay couples face with insurance, and the emotional strain of discrimination.

It would have been nice if, even before her brother surprised her with
his news, Ingraham had done a little homework about the millions of
American gays and lesbians who also lead their lives with "dignity, fidelity
and courage" and should be allowed to get married, have children, and
qualify for any job. But no, like too many conservatives—see also Dick
Cheney—Ingraham felt no need for tolerance until the hate impacted her
own family.

But still, her delayed conversion on this issue proves there may be some
hope left yet for Laura Ingraham. And, remember, she also likes dogs.

NEAL BOORTZ

Speaking of which, whatever happened to Neal Boortz? Did an old dog
learn a new trick? The self-described "Mighty Whitey" from Atlanta didn't
start out this way. I first got to know him as a colorful, yet thoughtful and
independent, voice from the South. That's why we used to invite him on
Crossfire. But, for whatever reason—probably to boost his standings among
conservatives—Boortz has morphed into just another right-wing attack
machine.

He calls himself a libertarian, to the dismay of many true libertarians. After all, he supported the war in Iraq, the war on terror, and the Patriot Act. And his daily targets are the same ones you hear beat up on by Rush Limbaugh, Glenn Beck, Michael Savage, and other right-wing bullies: all liberals, Democrats, politicians, Muslims, homeless, illegal immigrants, teachers, welfare recipients, hurricane victims, or minimum-wage earners. Same old, same old, same old.

In other words, Neal Boortz has jettisoned his reputation as an independent thinker and become just another predictable right-wing talk show host—trying hard, every day, to say something so outrageous it will catapult him into the top tier of conservative talk radio. And, Lord knows, he's said some mighty outrageous things.

He alone among conservative hosts, for example, has compared President Obama to a child molester. As he did on September 14, 2009, the first anniversary of the collapse of Lehman Brothers, when Obama gave a Wall Street speech on necessary reforms to the financial system. "Obama on Wall Street today," Boortz said on Twitter. "That's like sending a child molester to speak to a kindergarten class."

Maybe Boortz simply forgot that the Wall Street collapse occurred under George W. Bush, not Obama—and that Obama was just trying to make sure, through new regulations and legislation, that such an economic crisis didn't happen again. Or maybe he just couldn't resist a cheap shot.

DON'T YOU BELIEVE IT!

Fortunately, we never have to take Boortz seriously—because he himself warns us not to. He often reminds listeners that he is nothing but an "entertainer." And on his Web site he warns listeners: "Don't believe anything you read on this web page or, for that matter, anything you hear on 'The Neal Boortz Show' unless it is consistent with what you already know to be true, or unless you have taken the time to research the matter to prove its accuracy to your own satisfaction."

That's very comforting. So we never, for example, have to believe Neal

Boortz when he asserts that "global warming doesn't exist." We can simply ignore him when he asks, "Why is it so hard for so many people to understand that the whole thing behind the global warming scam, the climate change scam, it is now and it always has been an effort by the left to destroy capitalist economies?" Anybody who believes otherwise, says Boortz, is a "socialist" or a "communist." We don't have to believe Boortz because we've done our homework and we know the exact opposite is true.

We don't have to believe Neal Boortz when he tells his listeners that Bill Clinton, like Cheney Chief of Staff Scooter Libby, was indicted for and found guilty of perjury. It's simply not true. Clinton was impeached by the House, but he was neither indicted nor convicted of any crime. His only trial was in the U.S. Senate, where he was found not guilty.

We didn't have to believe Neal Boortz when he claimed that "Obama's health care plan is going to end up killing people." We know that when he said, "Especially among the ranks of the elderly, there are going to be people who die . . . Maybe tonight!"—all he was doing was sowing fear. Boortz, who knows better (after all, he can read), even spread the lie that Obama's proposal was a mandatory, government-run system where a federal government bureaucrat would choose between two people—which one gets health care and which one does not—and where consumers would be prohibited from buying their own health coverage from a private insurer. "No, you won't. Not in this country, you won't. Because it'll be a crime, it'll be illegal. You can't use your own money to buy health care in this country. You have to go through the government system." Of course, all Obama initially proposed was one, limited "public option" to compete with thousands of private insurance plans—each one of which already has an army of bureaucrats deciding which patients get insurance coverage and which ones do not.

We certainly didn't have to believe Neal Boortz when he expressed his support for the FBI's investigation of those who protested the beginning of the Iraq War in 2003. Among whom, I might add, were counted both myself and Pat Buchanan, at the time co-hosts of MSNBC's afternoon show *Buchanan and Press.*

The idea that Big Guv'mint should sic its police force on citizen

protesters is definitely not what one would expect from a so-called libertarian, nor even a true conservative. But Boortz defended the government's expanded police presence by questioning the patriotism of antiwar
protesters: "The FBI is investigating the backgrounds and organizational
methods of antiwar demonstrators in the U.S. Hopefully, that doesn't
come as a surprise to you. It is safe to assume that a large number of these
demonstrators are out there in the streets because they want America to
fail in its efforts to fight terrorism and its efforts to bring secular representative governments to Iraq and Afghanistan. Translated: Many of these
demonstrators are pro-Saddam and anti-U.S. So who wouldn't want them
investigated by the FBI?"

Who wouldn't want peaceful protesters investigated by the FBI? Libertarians, perhaps? Or anyone who believed in the First Amendment, like
all libertarians are supposed to. Finally, we don't have to take Neal Boortz
seriously when he blasts public school teachers, most of whom are members of their local teachers union. Most parents respect teachers and consider them heroes for the great work they do for very little money. Most
parents, but not Boortz. He must have been spanked by a teacher once,
because he thinks teachers are evil—even more evil than drug dealers.

"The single most dangerous entity, group of people in this country
right now, are the teachers unions," he told his audience. "They do more
damage to this country than all the drug pushers together. . . . If I had a
button right now, two buttons—push this button and it gets rid of all the
drug dealers; push this button, it gets rid of the teachers unions—I'm getting rid of the teachers unions."

Which is strange, even coming from Neal Boortz, because all the
teachers unions do is fight for teachers to get paid a decent salary, and not
have to settle for the minimum wage. And we all know what Boortz thinks
about those condemned to work for the minimum wage: "How incompetent, how ignorant, how worthless is an adult that can't earn more than
the minimum wage," he bellowed in 2006. "You have to really, really, really
be a pretty pathetic human being to not be able to earn more than . . . the
minimum wage."

Frankly, I think only a really, really, really, really, really pathetic human being would mock those Americans unlucky enough not to make more than the minimum wage. But I guess I just don't understand, because I'm not a libertarian.

But in Boortz's twisted world view, there are actually people worse than minimum wage earners. Some of them used to live in New Orleans.

HUMAN GARBAGE

I know. When I told you about Glenn Beck's attacking the families of victims of September 11, you didn't think anybody could stoop any lower, did you? Well, think again. Think Neal Boortz.

For some sick reason, Boortz was really bothered by Hurricane Katrina—but not for the same reasons all the rest of us were. He wasn't bothered by the miserable government response, nor by the rampant human suffering in the wake of the storm. No, he didn't care about the victims. He *blamed* the victims for not getting out of the hurricane's way!

Within days of the hurricane, he expressed his disgust for displaced residents of the Ninth Ward: "these Katrina refugees . . . so many of them have turned out to be complete bums, just debris." Who was responsible for those left homeless by the hurricane, most of whom were poor, black, and elderly? Boortz knows: "The primary blame goes on the worthless parasites who lived in New Orleans, who . . . couldn't even wipe themselves, let alone get out of the way of the water when that levee broke." And, for Boortz, the fact that so many were relocated to other cities was a blessing in disguise. "When these Katrina so-called refugees were scattered around the country, it was just a glorified episode of putting out the trash."

Even before Katrina, Boortz had called New Orleans "a city of parasites, a city of people who could not and had no desire to fend for themselves."

Following the storm, and once again going where no fellow right-wing talk show host would dare follow him, Boortz called the victims of Katrina—most of whom were poor, black, and elderly—"human parasites" and "deadbeats." Four years later, his attitude hadn't changed: "The last I checked, there were still 17,000 Katrina so-called refugees, you're right,

they're parasites, that are still living in hotels, motels, and various hurricane housing around the way." In fact, in June 2009, Boortz noted that
New Orleans was once again rated the murder capital of the United States,
in terms of murders committed per capita, by the FBI. Why? asked Boortz.
"Because the parasites are moving back to town."

What should happen to those Ninth Ward residents who were still not
back in their homes? Forget the Constitution. Boortz would take away their
right to vote. As he decreed in June 2009, "Everybody still living in a hotel
or a trailer after Hurricane Katrina, no votes. Can't vote again, ever, ever.
Can not vote again. Everybody living in Section 8 housing should not, nobody. . . . Nobody living in Section 8 housing should be allowed to vote.
And don't give me this 'elderly.' If you're elderly and living in Section 8
housing, you've done a piss-poor job of planning your life. No vote for you."

By the way, I visited the Lower Ninth Ward of New Orleans in October
2009, four years after Katrina. There's a good reason more people have not
moved back into their homes: because there are almost no homes there. I
saw block after block of nothing but slabs where homes used to be. I saw
many houses still standing in ruins, most of them with collapsed roofs, and
still bearing the markings painted on them by rescuers to indicate the presence of bodies or pets or toxic water. And, in the entire vast area, I saw
maybe a dozen new homes, in a sea of destruction. In late August 2009,
when President Obama marked the fourth anniversary of Katrina by re-
newing the federal government's pledge to continue to help rebuild the city,
Boortz was outraged. He immediately turned to Twitter and sent out the
following message: "Obama wants to rebuild New Orleans. Why? Build it
and they will come. They? The debris that Katrina chased out."

Somehow, I don't think Boortz would meet the definition of a compassionate conservative. Not in the way he treated victims of Katrina. Nor in
the way he trashed victims of the Virginia Tech massacre.

SILENCE OF THE LAMBS

On the morning of April 16, 2007, Virginia Tech student Seung-Hui Cho
stuffed two firearms and several clips of ammunition into his backpack

and headed for two university buildings, where he shot and killed twenty-seven students and five faculty members—the deadliest peacetime shooting by a single gunman in U.S. history, on or off a school campus.

As always after a tragedy, people were looking for answers and asking tough questions. Why didn't campus security shut down the campus after two people were killed in the first building and Cho had time to go back to his apartment, change his clothing, reload, and move on to the second killing ground? Why did Virginia's gun laws allow a young man who'd been diagnosed as mentally ill to buy two firearms—from the same dealer?

Many legitimate questions asked, but only Boortz blamed the victims themselves. Why did they just stand there and let themselves get shot, he wanted to know. Which is not only heartless, it's stupid. It's like asking those killed in an airline crash: Why'd you just go down with the plane, dummy? Why didn't you do something to save yourself?

Boortz first attacked the students killed on the day following the massacre: "How the hell do twenty-five students allow themselves to be lined up against the wall in a classroom and picked off one by one?" The next day, believe it or not, he even tried to turn it into a liberal conspiracy: "It seems that standing in terror waiting your turn to be executed was the right thing to do, and any questions as to why twenty-five students didn't try to rush and overpower Cho Seung-Hui are just examples of right-wing maniacal bias. Surrender—comply—adjust. The doctrine of the left." Come on! Isn't blaming liberals, or the victims themselves, for the murder of thirty-two individuals by a crazed gunman just a tad over-the-line? Even for Neal Boortz?

His abject callousness was further underscored as we learned more about the shooting. Contrary to what Boortz alleged, students were gunned down in the hallway and four different classrooms of Norris Hall. They were not lined up against the wall and "picked off one by one." Not only that, survivors told many stories of heroic attempts by both faculty and students to thwart Cho's killing spree, including: one professor who held the door to his classroom closed until most students could escape through the windows and he was killed himself; a student who barricaded the door to another classroom with a large table, saving the lives of all students in that room; a second professor killed after ordering her students to flee while trying to block the doorway to her classroom.

Once the facts were known and it was clear how wrong he was, did Boortz apologize to the victims and their families? Of course not. We're not supposed to take him seriously, remember? Not about Virginia Tech, and not about illegal immigration, either.

INVADERS FROM THE SOUTH

As we have seen, illegal immigrants are a favorite target of every conservative talk show host, from Limbaugh to Levin. Boortz is just more outrageous than most.

When the swine flu hit the United States in spring 2009, he at first blamed undocumented workers for spreading the disease. And he persisted in pushing that theory, even after the Centers for Disease Control reported that any connection to Mexico was due to American citizens who had traveled to Mexico, not Mexican citizens who traveled here. For Boortz, it was a public health conspiracy. "What better way to sneak a virus into this country than give it to Mexicans," he charged. "So if you want to get that epidemic into this country, get it going real good and hot south of the border. And, you know, then just spread a rumor that there's construction jobs available somewhere, and here it comes. Because we're not gonna do anything to stop them from coming across the border." Later, Boortz even joked that the CDC should rename the virus the "Fajita Flu."

Of course, like most conservatives, other than attacking or making fun of immigrants, Boortz offers no solid ideas of how to solve the problem of illegal immigration. Other than the classic nonstarter, that is: Oh, we could always build a three-thousand-mile-long, twenty-foot-high fence. Which would suit Boortz just fine: "I don't care if Mexicans pile up against that fence like tumbleweeds in the Santa Ana winds in Southern California. Let 'em. You know, then just run a couple of taco trucks up and down the line, and somebody's gonna be a millionaire out of that." In 2007, when he and other right-wing hosts rallied to kill George W. Bush's attempt at immigration reform, he signed on with extremists like Pat Buchanan who argued for rounding up all persons who are in the country illegally and shipping them back across the border. And, as they boarded the buses, Boortz would give them a goodbye present. He told his listeners: "During the warm-up hour of *The Neal Boortz Show,* we came up with a marvelous suggestion for solving two of America's problems at the same time: disposing of nuclear waste and doing something about the illegal aliens in this country. And that is, if the evil listeners to talk radio can just succeed in killing the amnesty bill, or if we can at least succeed in getting an amendment to the bill that says before you can get a visa to work here, you have to go home. Okay? Then all of the Mexicans who are here, as they leave the country we can give them a lovely parting gift, like they do on *Jeopardy!* We can give them a little—yeah, a little bag of nuclear waste from one of our nuclear power plants or maybe one of our nuclear military vessels."

It might even have a practical use, Boortz suggests: "Give 'em a little bag of nuclear waste as your lovely parting gift. AMF, which means 'Adios, my friend.' Send them all back across the border to Mexico. Tell 'em it's a tortilla warmer. You know, to put it in the tortilla box, and the tortillas stay warm. And then they will. And you'll be able to find them at night, too, because they'll glow."

Which might, in a *Saturday Night Live* kind of way, be funny. If you stripped away the ethnic slurs. And if Boortz were not serious. But he is.

In fact, here's another idea of what he thinks is a funny joke: "How many illegal aliens can you get in a Ford Excursion? Apparently about twenty-seven. Looks like a Mexican clown car. And you can actually roll that Ford Excursion on a back road in Arizona and only kill ten of them." And that's what passes for intelligent debate on conservative talk radio today. Isn't it sad?

However, no matter how willfully outrageous Levin, Ingraham, and Boortz are, they'll always be second-raters. It could be worse. Move one tier down the toxic talk pyramid, and you're suddenly among the wild-eyed rabble of local talk. That's where it really gets crazy.

At the local level, right-wing talk radio is a total free-for-all, where everyone's clamoring to get noticed by saying willfully stupid or offensive things. There are no rules—it's Thunderdome. Before we dive in, you have been warned.

HOMEGROWN TOXIC TALKERS

Legendary House Speaker Tip O'Neill once famously said, "All politics is local." And so is most news-talk radio.

We started by focusing on the big four nationally syndicated conservative talkers: Rush Limbaugh, Glenn Beck, Sean Hannity, and Michael Savage. Then we moved on to two others who've dabbled in both radio and TV, Bill O'Reilly and Lou Dobbs. And then we focused on the second tier of national radio talkers: Laura Ingraham, Mark Levin, and Neal Boortz.

There are a dozen or more other big national names, including: Hugh Hewitt, Michael Medved, Michael Reagan, Bill Bennett, Joe Scarborough, John Gibson, Fred Thompson, Dennis Miller, Michael Gallagher, G. Gordon Liddy, Blanquita Cullum, and Dennis Prager.

But they represent only a handful of more than 250 radio talk show hosts nationwide, the vast majority of whom are heard on only one local station.

In short, local talk show hosts form the bottom of the toxic talk pyramid. They are the real workhorses of the industry. They're the ones who fill up the airwaves on over 1,900 conservative talk stations from coast to coast. They're the weird voices you hear while driving your rental car late at night, as you scan the dial for something to keep you awake until you reach your destination. As talkers, they're usually just good enough to provide "local color," but not good enough that anybody outside their little twenty-five-square-mile patch would want to listen to them. Being local yokels, however, does not mean they are shrinking violets. Just the opposite. In talk radio, like every other field of endeavor, imitation is the cheapest and sincerest form of flattery. So the little boys and girls often go out of their way to sound as bad as the big boys and girls. And since all of them want to get national attention and move up the talk radio food chain, they sometimes say things that are even more outrageous than their national counterparts could get away with—which has, on more than one occasion, landed a few of them in trouble.

We don't have the space, and you don't have the time, to expose every right-wing nut on the radio. Or even those who are not nuts, just wrong.

Besides, you know who they are. Because, until there's a progressive talk station in every town and city in America, you can't escape them. They are legion. They pop up whenever and wherever you turn on the radio. Without even attempting to provide a complete list, the most outrageous of local conservative hosts, with a sampling of their more colorful comments, include the following:

- Ron Smith, Baltimore. On immigration: "The invasion of America continues and we're told it really doesn't matter, which just isn't true."
- Mark Davis, Dallas. On President Obama's Cairo speech: "I want an American president who looks out for American interests . . . and I don't know if we have one anymore."
- Lee Rodgers, San Francisco. On Sarah Palin: "Okay, here's Rodgers's take on Sarah Palin: Most of all, these liberal women resent the fact that she's good-lookin'. She's good-lookin'!"
- Roger Hedgecock, San Diego. On violence in Iraq: "The murder rate in Baghdad, the people being killed in Baghdad, is lower than the murder rate of Washington, D.C." Apparently,

Hedgecock doesn't count deaths of Iraqi civilians as "collateral damage."

- Barry Young, Phoenix. On the Virginia Tech massacre: "They allowed themselves to be shot one at a time. You gotta wonder why people would just stand there and be slaughtered."

- Mike Trivisonno, Cleveland. On the shooting at Success Tech High School: "When are we going to stop blaming society and start blaming the parents? Or just blame nature. Maybe humans have less potential than we think."

- John & Ken, Los Angeles. John on jury duty: "The truth is I don't trust juries. I don't trust twelve people who aren't smart enough to get out of jury duty. There's a lot of crazy people out there and many of them end up on juries."

- Erich "Mancow" Muller, Chicago. On Howard Dean and Democrats. He "ought to be kicked out of America and tried for treason. . . . Howard Dean is a vile human being. This guy is bloodthirsty. I'm telling you, I really think that every time you report another dead body in Iraq, they go, 'Hoo hoo, it's perfect.'"

- J. D. Hayworth, Phoenix. On assimilation: "The ever-so-successful process that used to be called 'Americanization' was a major movement in the early 1900s. . . . Henry Ford, a leader in this movement said, 'These men of many nations must be taught American ways, the English language, and the right way to live.' Talk like that today and our liberal elites will brand you a cultural imperialist, or worse. But if you ask me, Ford had a better idea."

- Howie Carr, Boston. On Bernie Madoff: "Maybe they can get Madoff to walk barefoot through the snow in New York City where he could run into one of those hot manhole covers and get electrocuted like the dogs often do."

- Bob Grant, New York. On African-Americans: "The U.S. has millions of sub-humanoids, savages, who would really feel more at home careening along the sands of the Kalahari or the dry deserts of eastern Kenya—people who, for whatever reason, have not become civilized."

Trying to catalogue every hateful, idiotic, or factually incorrect rant by local talkers would be a fool's errand—they never stop saying dumb stuff that isn't worth reading or hearing about. So let's just take a look at some of the worst right-wing talkers you might happen to encounter on your radio dial, were you to drive across this great citadel of free speech called America.

JAY SEVERIN, BOSTON

And you thought Massachusetts was a liberal stronghold? Think again.

Yes, the Bay State is the home state of John F. Kennedy, Tip O'Neill, Robert Drinan, and Paul Tsongas. It's represented in Washington by a pride of liberal lions: John Kerry, Barney Frank, Ed Markey, William Delahunt, Michael Capuano, and John Tierney. It's the battleground of the late, great Teddy Kennedy. It's the only state won by George McGovern in 1972.

Massachusetts is the bluest of all the blue states—except when it comes to talk radio (and Scott Brown). Funny thing, but true: There is not one progressive talk radio station in the entire liberal stronghold. Instead, Massachusetts residents are daily bombarded with some of the most strident and irresponsible voices in talk radio. Of whom by far the worst is Jay Severin.

Severin started out as a Republican political operative, working as a media consultant for many statewide and national campaigns, including the presidential campaigns of George H. W. Bush in 1980 and Pat Buchanan in 1996. Having run out of campaign options after becoming a Buchananite, he next turned loose his extremist political views on talk radio.

BLAMING MEXICANS

It's no easy task, getting suspended from your job as a conservative talk show host. As a group, they are, after all, paid to be outrageous. They constitute a gang of meanies who are generally allowed to make any ugly comments they want—as long as they're aimed at hated liberals, and not at fellow conservatives.

In other words, you have to be especially mean and nasty to get suspended from right-wing talk radio. Enter James Thompson Severino—formerly just old-fashioned "Jimmy" Severino, now known as Jay Severin. That's his stage name. Like Rush Limbaugh and Michael Savage, Severin, too, abandoned his real name for a more radio-friendly moniker.

As you might expect, Severin spends much of his airtime demeaning Democratic politicians. In his political pantheon, Al Gore is "Al Whore"—a man who, Severin declared, "would murder his daughter in order to become president." He branded Hillary Clinton a "lying bitch," a term he later said he regretted because "technically, it's a redundancy." He called Ted Kennedy "a fat piece of lying garbage" and constantly referred to Barack Obama as "Osama Obama."

As we've seen, these rabid, foaming-at-the-mouth attacks on liberals are par for the course in right-wing talk. They're the bread-and-butter of conservative talk show hosts. But, in the spring of 2009, Severin clearly stepped over the line.

That's when, without warning, the world was suddenly beset with a new, virulent strain of swine flu, believed to have originated on a pig farm in Mexico and quickly dubbed by the media as the Mexican Swine Flu. By June, cases had been reported in eighty-nine countries and the flu had claimed 468 lives worldwide—at which point, the World Health Organization declared the swine flu, or H1N1, a pandemic.

But the fact that it started in Mexico was all Jay Severin needed to know. He immediately seized on the swine flu as the latest salvo in a career built on bashing illegal immigrants. On April 30 he "informed" his radio audience:

"Now, in addition to venereal disease and the other leading exports of Mexico—women with mustaches and VD—now we have swine flu. . . . When we are the magnet for primitives around the world—and it's not the primitives' fault, by the way, I'm not blaming them for being primitives, I'm merely observing they are primitives—and when you scoop up some of the world's lowest of primitives in poor Mexico and drop it down in the middle of the United States—poor, without skills, without language, not share our culture, not share our hygiene, haven't been vaccinated. . . . It's millions of leeches from a primitive country come here to leech off you and, with it, they are ruining the schools, the hospitals, and a lot of life in America.

"Now, at this particular moment in history, they are exporting to us a rather more active form of disease, which is the swine flu."

Severin added that he wasn't surprised at this latest turn of events. After hordes of unclean people sneaking across the border for years, he insisted, we might have expected even worse: "We should, if anything, be surprised that Mexico has not visited upon us poxes of more various and serious types already, considering the number of crimaliens already here."

This was hardly the first time that Severin spread the myth that illegal immigrants come to the United States only to engage in criminal activity. Hence, his favorite slur: "crimalien" or "criminalien."

Just the week before news of the swine flu broke, he blamed the new Obama administration for not doing enough to secure the border: "The usual five thousand criminaliens that come across the Arizona border will probably be eight thousand tonight, and maybe tomorrow it will be 12,000, because even Mexicans are going to be trying to get out of Mexico at a greater rate."

Nor was this the first time Severin got in trouble for racist comments. In 2004, when one caller suggested that, rather than demonizing Muslims, Americans might be smarter to try to understand them, Severin retorted: "I have an alternative viewpoint. It's slightly different than yours. You think we should befriend them. I think we should kill them."

It was strangely discordant language coming from Boston's WTKK-AM, a conservative outlet that prides itself on offering political debate that is thought-provoking, but also "civil and respectful." On the swine flu, station officials finally had to acknowledge that Severin had crossed the line. Listener backlash was so widespread and so vehement they were forced to suspend him indefinitely.

Shed no tears for Severin. For him, "indefinitely" didn't last long. After a halfhearted apology, he was back on the air just one month later. True to form, on his first day back he called for the impeachment of President Obama.

"PULITZER" JOURNALISM

Severin's loyal listeners probably weren't surprised at his quick recovery. After all, it's hard to keep a Pulitzer Prize–winning journalist down!

Well, put it this way: It's hard to keep a man who *claims* to be a Pulitzer Prize–winning journalist down.

A "self-made man" in every sense of the term, Severin actually awarded himself a Pulitzer in September 2005 in response to a listener call about declining standards in journalism. As a broadcast journalist, Severin said he'd witnessed these falling standards himself: "But since journalism began, and up until the time at least that I took my master's degree from Boston University—and may I add without being obnoxious, up till and including the time that I received a Pulitzer Prize for my columns for excellence in online journalism from the Columbia School of Journalism, the highest possible award for writing on the Web—right up to and including that, you still had to practice journalism to be a journalist."

There you have it. Jay Severin won a Pulitzer Prize from Columbia for online journalism. Hoorah!

Except it's not true. Not even close.

The whole thing sounded fishy to *Boston Globe* columnist Scott Lehigh, who checked it out and spilled the beans:

1. There is no Pulitzer Prize for Online Journalism.
2. The Columbia School of Journalism has nothing to do with the awarding of Pulitzer Prizes.
3. And Jay Severin never won either a Pulitzer or an award from Columbia.

Confronted by Lehigh's column, Severin explained: "What I said was, there is a prize that my editor told me was the *equivalent* of the Pulitzer

Prize for Web Journalism." Which, again, doesn't exist. And, as you saw above, that's NOT what Severin said.

As for Columbia, the School of Journalism does, indeed, present an annual individual Online Journalism Award. But Severin never won it.

In 2000, Columbia did, indeed, award an Online Journalism Award to MSNBC.com for Web journalism "in collaboration." At the time, Severin was one of many columnists on the MSNBC site. But directors of the awards program told Lehigh the special Columbia recognition was for MS-NBC's site itself, and not for any individual contributor.

In other words, Severin made the whole thing up. But, as several newspaper articles pointed out, at least he graduated from Harvard Law School.

Oh, wait a minute. That's also not true. Severin never actually enrolled in Harvard Law School. While working toward a master's degree at Boston University, he did take a few classes at Harvard Law. That's it. Big difference. Except to Jay Severin, whose repeated reinventions are part of his makeup.

Next time, Jay, think bigger! Give yourself a Nobel Prize for Literature!

And, by the way, Severin didn't complete that master's degree from Boston University, either. (Well, you can't say he's not creative—at least in padding his résumé.)

MICHAEL GRAHAM: JAY SEVERIN WANNABE

Severin, however, is not without his dedicated followers, the most loyal of whom is Severin acolyte and fellow WTKK talk show host, Michael Graham.

Indeed, in one respect, Graham even exceeds Severin's success. An outspoken conservative, he's been canned for inflammatory remarks so often that he describes himself as "loud, obnoxious, and frequently fired." His job at WTKK, in fact, was his seventh radio posting in seven years.

The first case of Graham's "mouth working faster than his brain," as one former employer put it, came on his first professional radio job, on the mighty WBT in Charlotte, North Carolina. Just hours after the tragic

April 1999 shooting at Colorado's Columbine High School, Graham quipped: "They were targeting minorities and athletes—which, the athletes' part, is one minor benefit to this otherwise horrible story." Though meant as a joke, it wasn't funny. It fell flat. And it cost him his job.

His most recent, and most controversial, firing came in July 2005, from Washington, D.C.'s, conservative powerhouse, WMAL-AM. Graham stirred up a hornet's nest of protest when he blamed terrorism on Islam and repeatedly called Islam a terrorist organization. "The problem is not extremism," he told his listeners. "The problem is Islam. We are at war with a terrorist organization called Islam."

Despite howls of outrage from listeners and an official complaint filed by the Council on American-Islamic Relations (CAIR), Graham refused to back down. He continued his on-air attacks on Islam, and posted the following argument on the station's Web site: "If the Boy Scouts of America had 1,000 Scout troops, and 10 of them practiced suicide bombings, then the BSA would be considered a terrorist organization. If the BSA refused to kick out those 10 troops, that would make the case even stronger. If people defending terror repeatedly turned to the Boy Scout handbook and found language that justified and defended murder—and the scoutmasters responded by saying 'Could be'—the Boy Scouts would have been driven out of America long ago.

"Today, Islam has whole sects and huge mosques that preach terror. Its theology is openly used to give the murderers their motives. Millions of its members give these killers comfort. The question isn't how dare I call Islam a terrorist organization, but rather why more people do not."

The obvious fallacy with Graham's remarks, of course, is that he's comparing apples and oranges. Islam is a world religion. The Boy Scouts— even to those kids who really want their Eagle Badge—is just an organization. A better example would be comparing Islam and, say, Christianity. And nobody's been arguing that the crimes of a few Christian nut jobs should reflect on the religion as a whole. Put it that way, and Graham's remarks seem as absurd, intemperate, and hateful toward Muslims as, in fact, they are.

At first, WMAL's management defended Graham, insisting that all he was doing was "rattling the cage," like any good talk show host. But eventually, forced to choose between an unrepentant Graham and an unforgiving public, program director Randall Bloomquist—ironically, the same man who had earlier fired Graham from WBT—had the honor of firing him a second time.

For a local talk show host, Graham is exceptionally skilled at getting himself booked on cable television shows, but he's not always well received. In 2007, while Glenn Beck was still at CNN's Headline News, the Boston talker was invited to discuss a Clinton campaign commercial based on the famous last episode of *The Sopranos,* showing Bill and Hillary sitting together in a diner. Graham couldn't resist: "Didn't you at some point want to see, like, Paulie Walnuts, somebody come in here and just whack them both right there? Wouldn't that have been great? . . . Come on! Where's Big Pussy? Come on! Let's make it happen . . . I wanted that." Not even Glenn Beck could agree.

Like Pigpen in the *Peanuts* comic strip, Michael Graham just can't seem to stay out of trouble. So, in a way, Jay Severin's lucky. The way Michael Graham's going, he could end up making Severin look like a model citizen.

BILL CUNNINGHAM, CINCINNATI

You can't help but feel sorry for the people of Cincinnati. Not only are they forced to root for the Bengals, but for more than twenty-five years they've had to put up with the radical rants of conservative talk show host Bill Cunningham over WLW-AM 700.

Cunningham calls himself the "Voice of the Common Man." And you can prove you're a "common man" by going on his Web site to find out "What's Your Willie Thinking?"

Yet, even though he's just another predictable right-wing talking machine, Cunningham, like every other local radio host, yearned desperately for his fifteen minutes of national fame. He got his big break on February 26, 2008, when invited to introduce candidate John McCain at a Cincinnati campaign rally. Aiming to warm up the crowd for McCain, Cunningham three times denounced the senator's likely opponent as "Barack *Hussein* Obama"—the use of Obama's middle name an obvious implication that he was a Muslim or terrorist, or both.

McCain later repudiated Cunningham's remarks and pretended to be shocked by them. But why? Had his campaign bothered checking into Cunningham at all, they would have discovered that such personal attacks were part of his daily routine. In fact, Cunningham actually toned it down a bit for McCain.

For most of the campaign, he referred to the Democratic candidate as "Barack Mohammed Hussein Obama," even though "Mohammed" is in no way part of his name. Cunningham warned his listeners of the dangers ahead if "Barack Mohammed Hussein Obama can be elected the president of this country in these difficult terrorist times." After all, Cunningham falsely asserted, Obama "was raised in madrassas in Indonesia" and was a member of a "black separatist" and "black racist" church.

A month before the McCain rally, on Fox News, Cunningham tried to defend his butchering of Barack Obama's name by claiming he was just following the example of the Clintons. On *Hannity's America,* he explained: "I've had a couple individuals tell me that after the so-called white voters in Iowa and New Hampshire weighed in heavily, especially Iowa, for Barack Hussein Obama and then in New Hampshire, Hillary kind of made a little bit of a comeback. There has been a conscious effort by Bubba Clinton to smear and to slime Barack Hussein Obama on the race issue."

Which, of course, was nonsense. Led by Fox News, conservatives were the ones playing the race card in both directions: simultaneously calling Obama a racist for being a member of Reverend Jeremiah Wright's church, and calling Hillary Clinton a racist for daring to run against him. It didn't stop there. The very evening of McCain's Cincinnati rally, Cunningham gladly accepted an invitation to repeat his smears on national television. On Fox News, of course. Appearing on *Hannity & Colmes,* he referred to "Barack Hussein Obama" seven more times and insisted he had done nothing more that afternoon than give the McCain campaign what it demanded of him: "His people told me to give the faithful red meat. Give them red, raw meat." Now, suddenly, Cunningham complained, he was the victim of conservative political correctness: "What happened to me today is what's going to happen to conservatives for the next eight months if they bring up Barack Hussein Obama's name. Just say his name. All of a sudden, you're going to be electrocuted." But, in fact, Cunningham had done a lot worse than call Obama by his middle name.

OBAMA THE ANTICHRIST

Listening to Bill Cunningham, how could you not consider Barack Obama a dangerous man? After all, he was born to a "communist mother" and abandoned by his father. (Which, Cunningham says, is not unusual: "That's what black fathers do. They simply leave.") According to Cunningham, Obama was then raised by a "radical Muslim" from Indonesia, educated in an extremist Islamic madrassa, and rejected at the age of ten by both mother and stepfather and sent to live with his grandparents in Hawaii.

One might expect the very worst from someone with that background, and Cunningham does. In October 2008, he asked on his radio show: "Did you hear about this Khalidi tape where Obama is toasting a guy who wants to gas and fry Jews?"

Cunningham was referring to Rashid Khalidi, a Palestinian-American friend of Obama's and professor of Middle East Studies at Columbia University. Obama attended a reception for Khalidi in 2003 at which, reportedly—Horrors!—critical comments were made about Israel. But not by Obama. Not that there's anything illegal or un-American about criticizing the Israeli government, of course. In any event, both Khalidi and Obama have said publicly that, while friends, they do not agree on issues related to Israel.

But why would Cunningham let the facts get in the way. He jumped to the obvious conclusion, warning all Jews to vote for McCain "because Obama wants to gas the Jews, like the PLO wants to gas the Jews, like the Nazis gassed the Jews."

Win or lose, Cunningham warned, Obama's candidacy was perilous.

Not only did Jews have to worry about what might happen if Obama won the election, all Americans had to worry about the reign of destruction that would follow if Obama lost. "I think there will be one hundred cities burning if Barack loses," he predicted. "Yeah, that's what the black intelligentsia says."

All of Cunningham's paranoia boiled over in October 2008 when the Ohio secretary of state reported the number of new voters registered for the November election: 666,000. Cunningham made an immediate leap to the sinister symbolism of the number "666" in the Book of Revelation: "Around Ohio, the number is 666,000. Six-six-six. The mark of the beast."

Cunningham also gave credit for all new registrations in Ohio to the diabolical minions at ACORN. In fact, he was off by a wide margin (ACORN claimed 247,000 new Ohio registrants), but such an assertion allowed him to complete the circle of conspiracy: "Six-six-six. The mark of the beast. The great majority, of course, are registered by ACORN. The mark of the beast. And who is the beast? Who gave ACORN $800,000 as part of this criminal conspiracy? Who was the lawyer for ACORN? Who conducted ACORN seminars to tell ACORN employees and others how to cheat the system? Barack Hussein Obama. I may declare him to be the beast. Six-six-six. It could be the end of all days."

For Cunningham, of course, the term "the beast" was not just a euphemism. On October 18, he agreed with a caller that Obama might, in fact, be the Antichrist!

Just think. A few weeks later, in a flash of sulfur and brimstone, Cunningham's Antichrist was elected president of the United States. He's even won the Nobel Peace Prize. And the world hasn't ended yet.

WAGING WAR ON THE POOR

It's well known in Cincinnati that "Wild Willie" has no sympathy for the poor or the homeless. Or, to put it another way, he has no problem with them—as long as they stay out of sight. And don't hang around the courthouse and use the public bathrooms, for example. If they do, Cunningham has the perfect solution in mind. It's no good just arresting them, he insists.

More direct action is needed. "So if you take a big old cane, Singapore-style, and just beat the hell out of 'em, maybe five or ten swats. . . . They're gonna say, you know what?, I'm gonna quit being a homeless bum and I'm gonna stop peein' on the courthouse. . . . Taze 'em and cane 'em, inflict physical discomfort. Simply pain. Pain is a great motivator to refrain from certain forms of behavior."

Of course, in his warped mind, there's only one thing worse than being poor. And that's being fat. Which, he contends, most poor people are—because we give them so much free food. As documented by Media Matters for America, beating up on the poor is a recurrent theme of Cunningham's.

In late fall of 2008, for example, he questioned the need for annual Christmas food drives. After all, he complained, "we're about the only country in the world with fat poor people." And not just fat.

"Unlike many countries in the world," he told one caller, "we have fat poor people. We don't have skinny poor people. Ours are fat and flatulent."

Those poor people are fat, he says, simply because "they eat too much."

And in news that must come as a surprise to most poor families, who struggle merely to pay the rent and feed their kids, Cunningham announced that, since they get free food, the poor are able to spend all their disposable cash on electronic gadgets. "The poor community, so to speak . . . have cell phones, they have pagers, they have telephones, they have cars, they have HDTV, and they have those things because they spend no money on food, because it's all given to them for nothing."

The big difference between today's economic crisis and the Great Depression, Cunningham told his listeners, is that back in the 1930s the poor would sell apples on street corners. Today, they buy Apple computers.

Has this guy ever visited Over-the-Rhine or other poor neighborhoods of Cincinnati? I doubt he'd see many people sitting on their front steps, checking the latest stock quotes on their new MacBook.

But, for all those perceived reasons, Cunningham says any business-man would be crazy to open a grocery store in a poor neighborhood. People who live there won't shop there, because they can get all the food they want for nothing. "Why would a grocery store open in the poor community when everyone gets fed free and they eat too much?"

Obesity is, indeed, a big problem in America, across the board. And it is true that the poor are more likely to be overweight than wealthier Americans. But it's not because they're eating too much. It's because they're eating the wrong kind of foods. With less money to spend on food, they're forced to buy cheaper, high-calorie, high-fat foods. Lean meats, fresh fruit and veggies are out of their reach. So is daily exercise on the tennis court. In its own report on the rich-poor obesity issue, the *Seattle Post-Intelligencer* (that late, great, lamented newspaper) quoted one working low-income mother who admitted: "We didn't have enough to really go shopping, so we'd go to McDonald's. We just got junk food because it was so much cheaper and it was filling and it tastes good."

Still, Cunningham never lets the facts get in the way of a nasty right-wing attack. There's really nothing we can do to help the poor, he concludes. It has nothing to do with money. They're just not as good people as we are. He summed it up for one caller: "You know, people are poor in America, Steve, not because they lack money; they're poor because they lack values, morals, and ethics. And if government can't teach and instill that, we're wasting our time simply giving poor people money."

What a relief it must be for the poor of Cincinnati to know that their hardship has nothing to do with lack of money.

If it's true, as Jesus said, "For the poor you will always have with you" (Matthew 26:11), it's also true that, like the Pharisees, we will always have ignorant right-wing talk show hosts with us. Then again, the Bible also tells us to "suffer fools gladly" (II Corinthians 11:19).

BIGOTS AT THE ZOO

Like every other conservative talk show host, Bill Cunningham is always looking for threats to Western civilization as we know it: threats he can single-handedly tackle and thereby save humanity (or at least its straight, white, male members). But one of his strangest crusades was his campaign—against the Cincinnati Zoo & Botanical Garden!

In a momentary lapse of judgment, back in December 2008, zoo officials had formed a partnership with the new Creation Museum, located in nearby Petersburg, Kentucky. Visitors could get a reduced price if they purchased tickets for both the zoo's annual Christmas "Festival of Lights" and the museum's Christmas event, "Bethlehem's Blessings."

Scientists at the zoo and many zoo members complained about a clear contradiction between one institution that upheld the scientific theory of evolution and one that preached fervent creationism. It was hard for a scientifically based zoo to pretend that all of the magnificent animals it contained were created by God in one magic moment only five thousand years ago, as the Creation Museum aims to prove. Not to mention, it was also embarrassing for them to associate with a museum featuring one display of a triceratops with a saddle on its back. So directors of the zoo pulled the plug on their partnership with the Creation Museum—which caused Bill Cunningham to accuse them of being the worst bigots America had seen since the days of Bull Connor.

The zoo should have ignored complaints about its getting in bed with the Creation Museum, he insisted. But, oh no. "Instead of the zoo standing up against intolerance of Christianity and the bigots, they buckled under, and they did what every Bull Connor type has done since the days of Birmingham, Alabama: They allowed the passions of the mob and the opinions of the few to take the nation, or in this case the zoo, on a religiously bigoted course from which they had better get out of quickly."

This was no Sunday in the park controversy, Cunningham insisted. To him, this was the worst case of discrimination since the civil rights movement. "We cannot put up with a religiously based discriminatory organization and the bigots at the Cincinnati Zoo who would do this to the Creation Museum," he declared. And he couldn't understand why there wasn't more of a public outcry over what amounted to nothing less than a direct war on Christianity. "It would be an outrage if Islam or Muslims were targeted in such a fashion."

Obviously, Bill Cunningham has never listened to his colleague Michael Graham, who, as we just saw, never hesitates to target Islam.

But wait! According to Cunningham, it wasn't just about religion. It was also about race! "It's not necessarily about the museum; it's about publicly practiced bigoted racial discrimination against individuals who have a different faith set," he fumed. By discriminating against white Christians, zoo officials were "in the same category as the Ku Klux Klan." And then, assuming the mantle of Martin Luther King, Jr., Cunningham told the world: "Whether it's race discrimination or religious discrimination, it cannot stand." At which point, you expected him to stand and sing "We Shall Overcome."

Before calling out the National Guard, someone should remind Cunningham and his listeners (and our readers) that nobody was denied entrance to the zoo—and that the only "discrimination" was that some people were not able to buy a discount ticket to two unrelated, and contradictory, Christmas pageants. Even the animals in the zoo must have been confused—if they weren't already baffled by the saddle-bearing triceratops.

GUNNY BOB NEWMAN, DENVER

"Patriotism is the last refuge of a scoundrel." The great Samuel Johnson said it first in 1775, and it's still true today. Just tune in any day to "Gunny" Bob Newman on Denver's News Talk Radio 850 KOA.

Under the banner of the "Patriotic Resistance Movement," Gunny Bob fires off a staccato burst of hate at liberals, immigrants, Democrats, gays and lesbians, pro-peace activists, or anyone who disagrees with him. He says it's part of the "warrior legacy" he learned as a gunnery sergeant in the Marines. If so, it's a strange legacy—and certainly not one shared by all Marines—that teaches you to love America, but hate Americans.

After leaving the Marines, Newman set up his own security firm, became a national security commentator on Fox News, continued to write books on guerrilla warfare (he's published twenty-one), and started his radio talk show on 850 KOA, whose dominant theme can be summed up in one word: "paranoia."

BEWARE BLACK HELICOPTERS

For years, the paranoia you heard over talk radio, especially late at night, was fear of government agents swooping in by black helicopter to take our guns away. Or United Nations forces, secretly patrolling the United States in a very similar fleet of black helicopters. Recently, the fear of black helicopters was replaced, first by fear of a black candidate for president, and now a black commander-in-chief.

In fact, listening to Gunny Bob Newman during the 2008 presidential campaign, you might have gotten the impression he thought Barack Obama was running for dictator, not president. And, as a matter of fact, that's what he did think, and that's what he told his listeners. During the campaign, Gunny Bob called Obama a "sick freak" and a "pathological liar." In March 2009, he described the newly elected president as a "classically trained Marxist" whose aim was to turn the nation into "a socialist state with an all-powerful government that subjugates the people." In so doing, he suggested, Obama would be following the lead of "his ideological comrades": Hugo Chávez of Venezuela, Daniel Ortega of Nicaragua, and Fidel Castro of Cuba. He accused Obama of planning to achieve his goals through the creation of a "civilian military force." As a result, he warned, "absolute despotism could take place within four years." Already many Americans were worried about "how we're going to survive the Obamanista regime" and "whether the Constitution will survive."

And you thought I was exaggerating when I accused Newman of paranoia? This is the type of bizarre screed, totally un-rooted in reality, that you might expect from a loudmouth drunk at the bar, not an ostensibly objective talk show host with a media platform in a major American city.

GUNS AND GAYS

Naturally, Newman reinforced listeners' fears that Obama's immediate agenda was to seize their guns. According to Gunny Bob, Obama would

send Justice Department agents into private homes to make sure that firearms were properly stored—even though Obama had given no such orders
and is, in fact, supportive of Second Amendment gun ownership rights.

Like many conservatives, Gunny Bob also condemned Obama's executive order overturning the so-called Mexico City Policy of Ronald Reagan and, later, George W. Bush, which denied U.S. funding to any
international organization that included abortion as one option in its family planning program. But it was much more than a policy difference for
Gunny Bob. He accused Obama of practicing "eugenics"—just like, he
argued, Nazi Germany, the People's Republic of China, and Herod the
Great.

And it wouldn't stop there, warned Gunny Bob. Before we knew it,
Obama and "others on the radical left" would be funding "voluntary sterilization programs" in the Third World. Newman gets especially vitriolic
about Obama's promise to end the Pentagon policy of "Don't Ask, Don't
Tell"—adopted by Bill Clinton and Congress in 1994—thereby allowing
gays and lesbians to serve openly in the military. The outcome, he argued,
would be a disaster. Accepting gays in uniform would increase the risk
that members of the armed forces would contract the HIV virus, develop
AIDS, and then die "because they happened to get a transfusion from . . .
say, an openly gay person with a very active sexual, open lifestyle."

And, besides, he added, "If we have gays serving openly in the military,
according to the military, that is going to reduce their combat power. You
reduce combat power, casualties can go up."

All of which, Gunny Newman charged, meant nothing to the new
commander-in-chief: "This doesn't bother Barack Obama. It doesn't faze
him in the least. He doesn't care if a soldier or a Marine or a SEAL or
what have you gets HIV, becomes HIV positive, and then develops AIDS
and dies.

"Because to Obama," he continued, "what's most important is two
things, being politically correct—excuse me, three things: being politically
correct; functioning as a good leftist; and number three, paying back the
gay and lesbian lobby, which donated such staggering sums of money to his
campaign."

As always, Gunny Bob omitted certain pertinent facts. He never told his listeners that everyone applying for service in the armed forces is screened for HIV at enlistment, and every two years thereafter; that HIV positive applicants are excluded from service; or that members of the military who test positive for HIV while on active duty overseas are, by regulation, reassigned to the United States. Nor did he note that gays and lesbians have served with honor and distinction not only in Afghanistan and Iraq but in all of America's previous wars, and have greatly helped increase, not decrease, the military's combat readiness.

THE ALIEN PRESIDENT

For Gunny Bob, as with so many other conservative talk show hosts, the 2008 campaign was not just about beating up on Barack Obama. They also beat up on his wife, Michelle. How many hours, for example, were spent on right-wing talk radio and Fox News, discussing the famous "whitey tape," in which Michelle Obama allegedly expressed her disdain for "whitey"? In fact, the tape didn't even exist. Because she never said it.

But, as noted earlier, she did say something else they seized on: her remark about her renewed pride in America, thanks to her husband's campaign.

Now, I'm one of millions of white Americans who understood exactly what she was saying. It was, indeed, a proud moment to see America, for the first time, entertain seriously an African-American candidate for president. Right on!

But conservatives jumped on her comments, accusing her of being part of the "hate America" crowd. The Tennessee Republican Party featured Mrs. Obama's comments in a TV commercial warning voters they couldn't trust her husband to lead a country that both Obamas hated. And the same charge was repeated over and over again by Gunny Bob in Denver.

Finally the candidate himself stepped in. Appearing with his wife on *Good Morning America*, an angry Obama told ABC's Robin Wright: "If they think that they're gonna try to make Michelle an issue in this campaign, they should be careful. Because that I find unacceptable . . . I think these folks should lay off my wife."

Those comments sent hate mongers like Newman into orbit. For him, it was one more excuse to label Obama a terrorist. "Barack Obama is threatening those who challenge his vile wife," he told his radio audience. "Oh, really? . . . What is this clown, now? Some sort of a badass? What are you gonna do, Obama, come to Denver and try, key word 'try,' to whip my white ass?" At which point, I remind you, this is what conservatives accept and defend as legitimate debate on the issues. Gunny Bob continues with a racist slur and school-boy challenge: "Son [I'm sure he meant to call him "Boy"] . . . Son, you are not some sort of macho tough guy, trust me. You are just another blowhard, make-believe thug who wants to be the most powerful man on earth. You're a far-left, terrorist-hugging politician, not the bad-boy gangsta you want people to believe you are. Listen, sonny, why don't you grow a spine, and at least one cojone, and accept one of the many invitations I have extended for you to appear on *The Gunny Bob Show,* heard in thirty-eight states, many of which are rather important to your election plan? Oh, and if you ever do muster the courage to do so, we will definitely be talking about your wife and her myriad personal problems."

Needless to say, Obama did not accept his invitation. But, to tell the truth, he may not have been allowed anyway because—didn't you know?— Obama is not an American citizen! Yes, running out of substantive reasons for opposing Obama, Gunny Bob joined many conservative talk show hosts in jumping with both feet into the birth certificate conspiracy. Even after the Hawaii Department of Health produced his birth certificate— born August 4, 1961, at Honolulu's Queens Medical Center—and even though the U.S. Supreme Court refused even to consider the matter—the issue wouldn't die.

Political gadfly Alan Keyes, who lost the Illinois Senate race to Obama, filed a lawsuit challenging the legitimacy of Obama's presidency. An Army Reserve major at first volunteered for duty in Afghanistan, then demanded that his request be revoked because he could not serve under a commander-in-chief who was not an American citizen. The Army complied with his request! And nine Republican members of Congress signed onto a bill by fellow Republican, "big birther" Bill Posey (R-Fla.), that would require all future presidential campaigns to produce a copy of the candidate's birth certificate.

Meanwhile, conservative media commentators continued to fan the flames. Obama's birth certificate became Issue Number One for the conservative Web site WorldNetDaily (which also, *mirabile dictu*, publishes my weekly column). CNN's Lou Dobbs continued to insist there were still many unanswered questions about the circumstances of Obama's birth. And Watergate burglar, now talk show host G. Gordon Liddy called Obama an "illegal alien."

Rush Limbaugh took the issue one step higher. "Barack Obama has one thing in common with God. Know what it is?" he teased his listeners. "God does not have a birth certificate, either."

Once again, on this issue like many others, Gunny Bob Newman proved the most extreme. Not for him the garden-variety conservative theory that Obama was actually born in Kenya, his father's native land.

Newman claimed it was much more sinister: "He was really born in Iraq."

No explanation of how a white woman from Kansas and her Kenyan-born husband, living in Hawaii, managed to give birth to a son in Iraq. Nor any Iraqi birth certificate to prove it. But, what the hell? Why ruin a good conspiracy with the facts?

THE MUSLIM INVASION

But, of course! Now that we know Barack Obama was really born in Iraq, we realize what Gunny Bob was talking about when he predicted "an invasion of Muslim terrorists" as soon as Obama was elected president. We also understand why he wants to deny all Muslims their constitutional rights, whether they are American citizens or not.

"I want every Muslim immigrant to America who holds a green card, visa, or is a naturalized citizen, to be required by law to wear a GPS tracking bracelet at all times," he declared. "And the FBI and the NSA should monitor their phones and their e-mails, all communications—electronic—

at all times, as well as bug their places of work and their residences. If they don't like the idea, or if they refuse, throw their asses out of this country." Any other time, such an extreme proposal might have stirred up a lot of controversy. But, unfortunately for Newman in this case, George W. Bush beat him to it. Immediately after September 11, he ordered the NSA to monitor the phones and e-mails of *all* Americans, not just Muslims!

For Gunny Bob, even unleashing Big Brother on every Muslim in this country wasn't enough. We also, he decreed, had to prevent any more Muslims from coming here. "Call me kooky, but I think maybe it's time for a little moratorium on Muslim visas, period."

In typical fashion, Newman brushed off concerns expressed by human rights organizations like the Quakers' American Friends Service Committee (AFSC) over his wholesale trashing of the Constitution. His critics were nothing but "holier-than-thou, politically correct, anti–First Amendment, namby-pamby fools." And the AFSC itself was a "leftist, anti-America, anti-U.S. military hate group." God Save the Republic!

LOCAL TOXIC TALK

As already noted, as obnoxious as they are, the local talkers cited here are only the tip of the iceberg. There are hundreds of others like them, most flying under the radar and heard every day across the country.

We didn't even mention Denver's Mike Rosen, who routinely and deliberately makes the same "mistake": talking about the search along the Afghanistan-Pakistan border for "Obama bin Laden." And on one occasion even reporting that American soldiers in the mountains of Afghanistan had launched a special offensive to track down "Barack Obama."

Nor Minneapolis–St. Paul's Joe Soucheray, whose solution to Norm Coleman's embarrassing loss to Al Franken was to suggest banning almost all absentee ballots. "With the exception of the absent military, why should absentee voting be made available to anybody who wants to avoid the possibility of standing in line on election day?" So much for long-distance truckers, people who work two jobs, or the disabled.

And the list goes on and on. The point is, local right-wing talkers form the base of a huge pyramid of lies, at the top of which resides Rush Limbaugh, followed by Glenn Beck, Sean Hannity, and Michael Savage, followed by the second-tier gang, and so on all the way down. And often, due to market pressures or their craving for their own fifteen minutes of fame, local hosts say things that are even more vicious and stupid than we hear from their national role models. As soon as they do so, of course, they become the latest, if temporary, sweethearts of cable news. So much of what we hear every day from right-wing talk show hosts is so odious it makes you wonder: The American people are smarter, and more decent, than that. So how did these people get on the radio? And how do they stay on the radio?

Clearly, the free market itself would not produce or support such extreme political points of view or such offensive language. And indeed it does not.

As we will see in our next chapter, conservative talk radio is not the product of the free market at all. It is the creation of a huge, decades-old, well-funded, and carefully orchestrated conservative media machine. If you're brave, you might even call it a "vast, right-wing conspiracy."

HOW RIGHT-WING TALK WORKS

After reading this far, and probably even before cracking this book, you know that right-wing talk radio is a powerful and persistent force in America. But, I find, it's still largely unknown territory. *Terra incognita*, as they might say in Cambridge.

Everytime I have a conversation about talk radio, I get peppered with the same questions: Why are conservatives so successful on talk radio? Why are there so many right-wing stations? Why aren't there more progressive stations? And, especially, why can't liberals make it in the world of talk radio? Doesn't the failure of Air America prove that liberals don't know how to be successful talk radio hosts?

We'll dispel the myths about progressive talk radio in the next chapter. But first, let's examine what's behind the amazing success of conservative talk radio.

RADIO POWERHOUSE

We start with a brief survey of America's radio landscape.

The most authoritative study of talk radio today was conducted for the Center for American Progress and Free Press by a team of seven media specialists: John Halpin, James Heidbreder, Mark Lloyd, Paul Woodhull, Ben Scott, Josh Silver, and S. Derek Turner. In the interest of full disclosure, Paul Woodhull is my business partner in *The Bill Press Show,* and Mark Lloyd is now the chief diversity officer at the FCC, the Federal Communications Commission.

In their report, "The Structural Imbalance of Political Talk Radio," published in June 2007 and available online at americanprogress.org, they first establish three important findings:

1. IN THE INTERNET AGE, RADIO IS STILL BIG.

Even with all the people watching TV or surfing the Internet, radio remains popular. According to Arbitron, the national radio ratings company, 92.7 percent of Americans age twelve or older listen to the radio each week—"a higher penetration than television, magazines, newspapers, or the Internet." While radio listening hours have declined with the advent of television and the Internet, Americans still listened to some form of radio—news, music, sports, talk—an average 18.5 hours per week (!) in 2007.

2. NEWS-TALK RADIO HAS A HUGE FOLLOWING.

Of all the different radio formats—sports, finance, every type of music—news-talk radio is the second most popular in the number of stations and the number of listeners. Of some 10,506 total radio stations, more than 1,500 are news-talk. They reach almost 50 million listeners a week, comprising a 10.7 percent share of all radio listening.

3. CONSERVATIVE TALK RADIO IS KING.

A few lonely liberals like me have successful talk radio shows today. But, in terms of impact, there is still really no contest between conservative talk and progressive talk. For a representative sampling, the center experts examined the programming of 257 news-talk stations owned by the top five commercial station owners. They found that:

- 91 percent of the weekday programs are conservative, compared to 9 percent progressive;
- Every day, 2,570 and one quarter hours of conservative talk are broadcast over those same stations, compared to 254 hours of progressive talk. That equals ten conservative hours for every one hour of progressive talk;
- 92 percent of the stations do not broadcast a single minute of progressive talk programming.

Which, of course, leads to the big question: Why?

After all, we may not be a big liberal nation. But we're not a big right-wing nation, either. Fifty percent of Americans didn't vote for George W. Bush in 2004. Fifty-three percent didn't vote for John McCain in 2008. And neither of these figures counts the fact that half of the American population doesn't even bother to vote.

So why is 90 percent of talk radio devoted to conservative talk? Shouldn't those who voted for John Kerry or Barack Obama be equally served? Or, to put it another way, shouldn't talk radio be "fair and balanced"?

Clearly, today, it's not. Not even close. Again, the big question: WHY?

THE THREE FALLACIES

Three explanations are usually given: liberal talkers can't get good ratings; listeners don't want progressive talk; and Ronald Reagan started it all when he abolished the Fairness Doctrine. Not one of them is valid.

1. LIBERAL TALKERS CAN'T TALK THE TALK

This is the subject of our next chapter, but for now, and without trying to sound too defensive, let's just say this: The idea that there are no good liberal talk radio hosts, or that liberals somehow have never figured out how to master the format, is strictly nonsense.

There are several examples of highly successful progressive talk show hosts, including Stephanie Miller, Thom Hartmann, Ed Schultz, Mike Malloy, Randi Rhodes, and yours truly. And, as we will see, there are several reasons why they are not heard on more stations and in more parts of the country.

2. LISTENERS DON'T WANT PROGRESSIVE TALK

Now here, I must admit, there is a kernel of truth. But not the way conservatives always express it. The reason there are not hundreds of progressive radio stations, Limbaugh and others argue, is because there's simply no market for it. After all, radio is a for-profit business. If stations could make money off it, they'd put every possible progressive radio talk show host on the air. Since they can't, they don't. Simple as that.

No, it's not. Given the opportunity, there are lots of examples where progressive talk show hosts beat their conservative competition in the ratings and where progressive stations are making good money. But the opportunities are severely limited. More about that in short order. But this is also true: Conservatives do have an advantage among listeners for two reasons: the nature of talk and the choices available.

For starters, no doubt about it, talk radio is the perfect medium for conservatives because it's designed especially for two kinds of people: angry, white, older males, who make up the vast majority of talk radio's audience (67 percent); and people who can't think for themselves, and therefore need someone else to think for them. Or, as Jon Stewart said of, Glenn Beck, radio tells us "what people who aren't thinking are thinking."

Julia Child never wrote an easier recipe: To one outspoken, provocative, hate-filled person at the microphone, add any number of ignorant, angry, paranoid, nervous, and worried listeners who tune in every day to find out what to think and whom to hate—and voilà!, you have perfect talk radio.

For better or worse, liberals are more complicated. That's what makes them liberals. They embrace complexity and nuance. They don't want to be spoon-fed the issues, they want to debate the issues. They don't want to be told what to think, they want to be challenged to think—and even disagree. They may be liberal, but they're not necessarily always loyal. Talk show hosts can't even count on their coming back every day. Because they have minds of their own, and enjoy setting their own course.

Which gets to the question of choices. One choice, available everywhere, which greatly appeals to liberals because of its smart, in-depth, and consistently independent reporting and analysis is public radio. It's well documented that NPR programs like *Morning Edition, All Things Considered,* and others cut deeply into the potential listening audience for progressive talk radio. According to Arbitron, the top radio ratings service, public radio listeners "overindex" for Democrats at 110 and "underindex" for Republicans at 90. In other words, the percentage of Democrats who listen to public radio is higher than the percentage of U.S. citizens who are Democrats. Conversely, the percentage of Republicans who listen to public radio is lower than the percentage of U.S. citizens who are Republicans. But public radio listening is not something that Rush Limbaugh or Sean Hannity ever have to worry about.

3. ABOLISHING THE FAIRNESS DOCTRINE WAS THE CAUSE

As Richard Nixon might say, and once famously did, "Let me make one thing perfectly clear": Despite all the cries of warning you hear from right-wingers about a left-wing conspiracy to take away their microphones, nobody in any position of power today advocates bringing back the Fairness Doctrine. There is no legislation pending in Congress to do so. Nor have President Obama's appointees to the FCC shown any interest.

What cannot be denied, however, as we have seen, is that there is a huge imbalance between left and right in talk radio today—and abolition of the Fairness Doctrine is partly responsible.

Actually, the Fairness Doctrine gets a bad rap. As painted by conservatives, it was nothing short of Soviet-style government censorship. In reality, it was nothing of the sort. It was relatively harmless, and painless—and it even did a lot of good.

According to the history pages of the Museum of Broadcasting, the Fairness Doctrine, adopted by the FCC in 1949, was nothing but "an attempt to ensure that all coverage of controversial issues by a broadcast station be balanced and fair." What's wrong with that? In the spirit of Fox News, aren't conservatives supposed to believe in broadcasting that is "fair and balanced"?

In practice, the FCC required two things of radio stations. One, as a public service and as part of their broadcast schedule, they were required to cover the major controversial issues of the day, on which they were also required to reflect all points of view. Which meant—to take a purely hypothetical example, of course—for news-talk stations, they could not feature all right-wing hosts, all the time. Two, if stations endorsed a candidate, ballot initiative, or legislative measure, they had to provide time for the opposition to respond.

It was hardly an onerous burden. Stations lived with it, followed it, and thrived in both ratings and revenue. On several occasions in California, I remember being asked to tape a rebuttal to a radio or television station's editorial position for or against a state ballot initiative. At the time, it was just the way business was done.

But that was still considered too much of a burden by the get-rid-of-all-regulation crowd that came to Washington with Ronald Reagan. They convinced him the policy was an infringement on free speech guaranteed by the First Amendment. And his appointees to the FCC effectively killed

the Fairness Doctrine in 1987 by announcing they would no longer enforce it. Now free of all restrictions on content, program directors rushed
to Rush, who made his national radio debut one year later. The news-talk
format exploded from four hundred stations in 1990 to 1,400 by 2006. By
that time, there were few moderate voices heard on talk radio anymore.
Hosts were either extreme right or extreme left—the vast majority, as we
have seen, extreme right.

Unfortunately, while dumping the Fairness Doctrine did open the doors
to a highly profitable expansion of news-talk radio, especially on the AM
dial, it also served to undermine the level of civil discourse around political
issues. As a nation, we are more poorly served by talk radio without the Fairness Doctrine. For the most part, instead of a vibrant, informative, balanced
debate on the most important issues facing us as a people, we are met by
loud, not-always-so-well-informed, highly partisan, screaming voices on the
right and left. And that's not how public airwaves should serve the public.

There, in fact, is the central argument that always gets lost in any discussion about the Fairness Doctrine. It was based on a still very solid
principle: that America's airwaves belong to the public. They belong to *us*.
Radio and TV owners were granted a license to broadcast over the public
airwaves, but only for a limited time—and, most significantly, they were
given that license for free. The bandwidth they borrowed from the American public was worth billions of dollars, and yet they paid NOTHING for
it. In return, since they're operating over "public" airwaves, they are, or
were, given only one condition: that they broadcast in the "public interest."
In other words, that they serve the general public, not just one slice of the
public, no matter how large or how small. And that—not on every program,
not even once an hour, but at some time in their broadcast schedule—all
points of view be welcome.

That principle was valid then, and it's still valid today. Indeed, Section
315 of the Communications Act still requires commercial broadcasters "to
operate in the public interest and to afford reasonable opportunity for the
discussion of conflicting views of issues of public importance." But, alas,
without the willingness of the FCC to enforce the regulation, for all practical purposes the Fairness Doctrine no longer exists.

There have been isolated calls to "bring back the Fairness Doctrine," but they have been largely ignored or roundly criticized. On my radio show, Michigan senator Debbie Stabenow once suggested it was time to "consider" restoration of the Fairness Doctrine as one option for guaranteeing some balance on the radio airwaves—and she received so many hateful phone calls and e-mails her office systems crashed.

But, truth be told, bringing back the Fairness Doctrine is not the best solution to the problem, for at least three reasons. First, because its time has come and gone. In its original form, it was a policy that worked well in the golden days of radio and television, when there were only three television and radio networks, but would never work today when there are hundreds of cable channels, multiple radio networks, and countless blogs or Web sites, all pumping out news, analysis, or opinion. It would be impossible to apply or enforce. A Fairness Doctrine designed for the 1950s could no more work in this age of the new media than could a television set designed for the 1950s. You might as well try to bring back black and white TV.

Second, the political will to restore the doctrine is just not there. Republicans, still convinced it's a direct assault on the First Amendment, will never support it. And not even all Democrats will dare enter those shark-filled waters, for fear of getting eaten alive. Which is why President Obama, picking his battles carefully, has said this is one he does not want to fight. Without his direction, the Obama FCC, led by Chairman Julius Genachowski, will never consider restoration or enforcement of a dusty, antiquated, and yet still very controversial policy.

But the third and most important reason is that even restoration of the Fairness Doctrine would not get to the heart of the problem: which is less one of content, and more one of ownership.

RIGHT-WING OWNERS RULE

Let's cut right to the chase: The number-one reason conservatives overwhelmingly dominate talk radio today is because *that's what conservative owners demand*—even if they lose money in the process.

We saw, above, the one-sided, right-wing tilt in talk radio programming today. Why is there such an imbalance? Because only five owners control the majority of the talk radio airwaves. And that's what they want.

Again, the Center for American Progress/Free Press study lays out the facts. At the time the study was published in 2007, five companies together owned the largest number, the most powerful, and the most highly rated of all news-talk stations.

All five companies offer listeners full-time, lopsided, conservative programming. On their news-talk stations, three of the five, in fact, offer zero progressive talk. Here they are:

- Clear Channel—145 stations—86 percent conservative
- CBS—30 stations—74 percent conservative
- Cumulus—31 stations—100 percent conservative
- Salem—28 stations—100 percent conservative
- Citadel—23 stations—100 percent conservative

Since the study was published, Citadel purchased those radio stations previously owned by Disney, giving it exclusive control of conservative talk stations in top markets like New York, Chicago, San Francisco, and Los Angeles. And you wonder why it's so hard for a liberal to make it as a talk radio host? The deck's stacked against him or her from the beginning.

While most pronounced among stations owned by the Big Five, a significant imbalance in programming also exists, regardless of ownership, among all sixty-five news-talk stations in the top ten markets: 76 percent conservative talk versus 24 percent progressive talk.

But that's not all. The problem created by ownership of so many stations nationwide is compounded by two additional factors: the ability of one company to own multiple stations in the same city, thereby destroying any chance for real competition; and their ability to own the biggest radio shows themselves, in addition to radio stations. So guess whose shows are automatically booked on all the biggest stations?

Don't mean to beat a dead horse, but I repeat: You wonder why it's so hard for a liberal to make it big-time as a talk radio host? The deck is stacked against him or her from the very beginning.

Again, the key is ownership. Indeed, I would argue that, far more damaging to diversity in talk radio than effective abolition of the Fairness Doctrine in 1987 was passage of the Telecommunications Act of 1996, signed into law by President Bill Clinton. That legislation hurt in two ways. It both erased the limit on the number of radio stations any one company could own nationwide and increased the limit any one company could own in the same market, from two to eight. Previously, companies were restricted to owning twenty-eight stations nationwide and two stations in any one market. Today, those regulations have been greatly relaxed. As a result, Clear Channel, for example, was able to expand rapidly from its forty stations to over 1,200. On the national level, allowing one company to own an unlimited number of stations gives a huge advantage to nationally syndicated programming, the vast majority of which is conservative. This may be easier to understand once you know how talk radio works economically.

In this modern world, talk radio is almost medieval in its business model. With few exceptions, no money changes hands. It's all done on a barter basis, much like a fifteenth-century farmer trading two chickens for a new pair of boots.

In this case, the syndicator approaches a radio station owner and offers three hours of a big, nationally recognized radio show in return for three hours of time on the station. The station owner, in turn, trades three hours of time for three hours of programming. Then, to seal the deal, the syndicator reserves x number of commercial spots that his sales force can sell to national advertisers, and keep the money. The local station gets the rest of the commercial spots, which they sell to local advertisers. That's the way most radio deals are structured, and that's why Rush Limbaugh, Sean Hannity, Michael Savage, and others can boast so many affiliates—because they give their show away for free! Since they get it for free, why wouldn't five hundred stations air Rush Limbaugh's show? The fact that he can boast so many local affiliates is more a tribute to the "free (literally) market" than to his talents.

For the record, it is also true that, in a very few cases, and only in major markets, some shows are actually able to charge stations for the right to carry their programming. But, again, those are exceptions, not the rule.

For the network and for the local station, the barter system is a win-win. The syndicator picks up another outlet at no cost, plus increased revenue from national advertisers. The local station gets a big-name talent at no cost, plus increased revenue from local sponsors. Not only that, with no local talent in-house, the stations carry very little overhead. Except for one engineer and the sales staff, they can get by with no salaries to pay, no studios to build, no real estate to rent. How sweet it is.

For the big companies, it's even sweeter when they own multiple stations in the same market: usually, that means one big 50,000-watt signal, and several smaller, 3–5,000-watt signals. Having shut out any competition in the same market, they are then free to make whatever corporate decisions serve their own purposes, and always do.

The first trick is to dedicate the most powerful, 50,000-watt signal exclusively to conservative talk. That helps reinforce the myth that listeners demand right-wing talk, because it's always heard on the most powerful stations. Listeners, however, have nothing to do with it. It's strictly a corporate decision.

Having established the 50,000-watt blowtorch as the home of conservative talk, the Big Five owners have one more trick up their sleeve: giving the shows they own maximum exposure on the stations they own. In the trade, it's called "vertical integration." Take Clear Channel, for example. Clear Channel not only owns 145 news-talk radio stations (of its total 1,200). It also owns Premiere, the number one syndicator of conservative talk radio—which, in turn, syndicates *The Rush Limbaugh Show, The Sean Hannity Show, The Glenn Beck Program,* and other conservative programs.

Follow the money. Naturally, Premiere-owned programs get top booking on Clear Channel–owned stations, and nobody else stands a chance.

But even that's not all. Once having secured the biggest stations, strongest signal, and best slots for conservative talk radio, owners either refuse to air progressive talk on any of that same city's other talk stations—again, reinforcing the myth that there's no consumer demand for progressive talk—or, as was the case of Washington, D.C., they assign progressive talk to the weakest signal of the group of stations, which is either inaudible at certain hours of the day or in some parts of the city, or both.

For a couple of years, for example, my show was carried by Washington's lone progressive talk station, 1260 AM, the weakest sister of three stations formerly owned by Clear Channel and later purchased by Washington Redskins owner Dan Snyder. While I enjoyed being on the air in the nation's capital, it was frustrating that the station's signal could not be heard in downtown Washington. Consequently, every day I was flooded with calls and e-mails from listeners who were enjoying the show while driving in from the suburbs, only to hear nothing but static once they crossed into the District. Most accused the Bush White House of zapping the airwaves to prevent my criticism of him from being heard in the capital. And there was no way I could convince them otherwise. George Bush wasn't the culprit, Dan Snyder was.

Now, here's the shocker, and what most people refuse to believe. In many cases, station owners are so committed to conservative talk, they're willing to lose money on right-wing talk rather than give progressive talk a chance.

RIGHT-WING OWNERS IGNORE THE BOTTOM LINE

Warning! For this part of our discussion, you're going to have to suspend belief. Because what I'm about to tell you totally defies logic. It's hard to believe it's true, but it is.

Ready? Here it is: Conservative radio station owners are not always driven by the bottom line. Time and time again, they have shown that, in their zeal to push conservative talk and bury progressive talk—they are even willing to lose money doing so!

I know what you're thinking: That can't be so. That's not the way American businessmen work. They don't care about politics or public policy. All they care about is the bottom line.

Yes, that's the accepted wisdom. Except it's wrong, wrong, wrong.

Believe it or not, conservative station owners have, in more than one market, proven that they are willing to lose money rather than give progressive talk radio a chance.

CASE NO. 1: MIAMI

For years, Miami had one of the most successful progressive talk stations in the nation: Clear Channel's WINZ. Their lineup included Stephanie Miller, Ed Schultz, and Randi Rhodes. And they were getting good ratings. Yet in 2008, Clear Channel suddenly pulled the plug on all progressive talk and converted the station into sports talk—even though the Miami market was already saturated with sports talk stations. WINZ immediately plummeted in the ratings and in revenue. But Clear Channel's management didn't care. They chose sports jocks on the air over those pesky liberals.

CASE NO. 2: SAN DIEGO

Chalk up the same experience in "America's Finest City." Yes, it's a conservative, Navy town. But San Diego also has a big, lively, active, liberal constituency. I know. I've worked there many years. And, along with other progressive talk show hosts, I appeared on KLSD and got good ratings. No matter. Again, Clear Channel pulled the plug on progressive talk and replaced it with sports talk, even though there were already several successful sports talk stations in the same market. The station immediately sank in the ratings and never recovered. But Clear Channel didn't care. They were more than willing to pay the price of keeping liberals off the air.

CASE NO. 3: CINCINNATI

Third verse, same as the first—and second. This time, station WCKY in Cincinnati, once a ratings-success progressive talk station, became another losing sports talk outlet.

CASE NO. 4: AKRON

For me, this one really hits home. WARF-AM in Akron was the first radio station to carry *The Bill Press Show,* even before we were syndicated nationally. Twice, we took the show to Mike's Place, a great family restaurant in nearby Kent, for live broadcasts before hundreds of fans, even at six o'clock in the morning. Stephanie Miller, Ed Schultz, Randi Rhodes, and others enjoyed equal success on the station. But the ratings bonanza of so many progressive talk show hosts must have made Clear Channel executives nervous. In 2006, local managers were ordered by headquarters to cancel all progressive talk show hosts in the entire state of Ohio and replace them with—what else?—sports!

CASE NO. 5: WASHINGTON, D.C.

As mentioned above, the experience in Washington was different, but equally frustrating. In 2005, Dan Snyder, owner of the Washington Redskins, was looking for a radio station he could buy in order to broadcast his football games. The only one available was a strong, 10,000-watt Clear Channel station. But Clear Channel would only sell him their one big station if Snyder would agree to buy two smaller signal stations at the same time. Money never being a problem with Dan Snyder, he bought all three. And to manage his three stations, he created a new company, Red Zebra Radio.

As Snyder had planned, Red Zebra turned the biggest of the three into Washington's official Redskins station, broadcasting sports talk and football. The station with the second-strongest signal was maintained as a conservative talk station. And, wouldn't you know it, the third, weak sister, of the bunch, 1260 AM, was dedicated to progressive talk—with *The Bill Press Show* starting the day from 6–9 A.M.

Even though, as discussed earlier, the signal could not be heard in much of the listening area, particularly downtown Washington, it was important to be on the air in the nation's capital—for the quality, as well as the quantity, of listeners. I often heard from senators, members of Congress, White House and congressional staff, and key lobbyists who listened to the show during their morning drive.

And we had a large, general listening base as well, which we proved on January 18, 2009, at President Obama's inauguration—filling George Washington University's 1,500-seat Lisner Auditorium for a rollicking, three-hour, special inaugural broadcast featuring talk show hosts Stephanie Miller, Ed Schultz, Al Sharpton, Randi Rhodes, and yours truly; and guests Governor Brian Schweitzer, Laborers' Union president Terry O'Sullivan, and House Majority Leader Steny Hoyer.

I really felt proud after that special inaugural broadcast. For the first time, we had put progressive radio on the map in Washington. Imagine my surprise then, just two weeks later, when I received a call from Bruce Gilbert, general manager of Red Zebra Radio, informing me they were dropping the progressive format. Because of the barter system described above, it was costing them almost nothing to run 1260 AM. But Dan Snyder figured he could spend even less if he simply ran canned financial advice programming all day. Again, he didn't care about ratings or revenue—and he certainly had no commitment to progressive talk—as long as he was making money on his football station.

Washington thus became one more case study of owners suppressing progressive talk and keeping liberal talk show hosts off the air in America's major markets, even if it cost them money to do so. For them, it appears ideology counts as much as profit.

THE RIGHT-WING MESSAGE MACHINE

As powerful as it is, the success of conservative talk radio is not the full measure of the dominance of conservatism in America today. It is only one manifestation of it. The conservative message machine is well oiled, well funded, and well organized—and it didn't happen by accident.

How conservatives started from nowhere and grew to dominate political discourse in this country is an amazing story. And nobody has tracked it better than Rob Stein, former Clinton Treasury Department official and founder of the liberal donors organization, Democracy Alliance.

In September 2003, I had breakfast with Stein at the Four Seasons hotel in Georgetown. Over cheese omelets and croissants, he flipped through the print version of his PowerPoint presentation, "The Conservative Message Machine Money Matrix." I remember being stunned. This is exactly what liberals needed to know—and needed to replicate.

After watching Republicans consolidate their gains in Congress in the 2002 midterm elections, Stein said to himself: This doesn't make any sense. America's not a right-wing country. Most Americans don't agree with conservative policies. So how did conservatives build such a powerful and effective political message machine?

Powerful, indeed. We're talking a message machine fueled by more than eighty nonprofit organizations and think tanks, all funded by a handful of conservative family foundations and wealthy individuals to the tune of $400 million a year. Every morning, they churn out the message of the day to a vast network of radio stations, talk show hosts, cable television producers, columnists, and right-wing bloggers—all of whom have been recruited, subsidized, and supported by the same funding sources.

Now you know why they all sound the same: because they're talking from the same talking points!

Again, as Stein discovered, that vast network didn't just pop up spontaneously. It was very carefully planned, funded, coordinated, and executed—and it didn't just happen overnight. The movement actually began in the early 1970s, when the U.S. Chamber of Commerce commissioned Lewis Powell, former head of the American Bar Association and member of eleven corporate boards, to prepare a memo on how to save capitalism and promote conservatism. What became known as the Powell Memorandum, entitled "Attack on the American Free Enterprise System," warned that, unless conservatives rallied together to prevent it, liberals would soon destroy the free market system itself. And with amazing insight, Powell sketched out an action plan that is still being followed today.

They needed to confront liberalism everywhere, Powell advised conservatives, with particular emphasis on developing and spreading conservative principles through a well-organized message machine. And the whole movement would require a level of financing available only if conservative foundations and individuals were willing to pool their resources in common cause. And so they did.

Two years later, Richard Nixon named Lewis Powell to the Supreme Court. But his memo remained the blueprint according to which the modern conservative movement was slowly and methodically built. The Coors Brewing and Richard Mellon Scaife family foundations provided the seed money. The Heritage Foundation and other right-wing think tanks provided the ideas. And soon a vast network of media outlets spread the message. It was all integrated from top to bottom.

At the top of the pyramid, as intended, is the most visible element of the conservative movement: its vast media machine, built by design. Following Powell's advice, leading conservatives raised the funds and founded the think tanks to pump out the research. They bought the stations and formed the networks to propagate the ideas. Later, with the emergence of the new media, they backed creation of early conservative blogs. They also recruited, subsidized, trained, and found jobs for right-wing talk show hosts and bloggers.

Stein estimates that in those eighty conservative organizations and think tanks are some 36,000 people, all trained on how to shape issues, develop a message, and use every available media outlet to deliver that message. It's a veritable army of propagandists, pumping out conservative doctrine every day—and providing conservative talk show hosts the content they need to fill their allotted three hours of radio.

So there you have it. Now you know why right-wing radio is so powerful today. The near-monopoly on conservative ownership of radio stations, combined with a vast conservative message machine, has created its own parallel universe of talk radio, a veritable media powerhouse, much more conservative than the nation at large.

Now here's the sad part. That conservative juggernaut is made even more powerful by the fact that, next to it, liberals have almost nothing: few stations, few owners, and only the very beginnings of a message machine.

Where there are eighty conservative think tanks, there are at best only a handful of progressive research organizations, including the Center for American Progress, the Economic Policy Institute, and Citizens for Tax Justice.

Where there are five big conservative radio networks, which own hundreds of stations, there is not one progressive radio network.

Where there are 1,700 news-talk stations, over 1,600 of them feature nothing but conservative talk show hosts. There are at most sixty progressive talk stations in the entire country.

Fair and balanced? My ass!

FIXING THE PROBLEM

If what's heard on the public airwaves is indeed going to reflect the ideas and values of the general public, and not just one far-right slice of them, then something must be done to correct the current imbalance in talk radio programming. Since the public airwaves are regulated as a public utility by the FCC, that first means some degree of government intervention.

Knowing that they now enjoy an unfair competitive advantage, conservatives warn that liberals plan on bringing back the Fairness Doctrine. Indeed, right-wing talk show hosts have made a veritable industry out of convincing their listeners that, not only is the Fairness Doctrine coming back, but it will force all conservative talk show hosts off the airwaves. Of course, they will resort to anything to keep the natives restless—and convince them to keep sending money to conservative organizations in order to "preserve freedom of speech."

But—pure hogwash!—the truth is just the opposite. First, as we've seen above, the Fairness Doctrine contained no restrictions on content, conservative or liberal. It simply required that there be a mix of voices. Second, there are no plans or pending legislation to restore the Fairness Doctrine, and President Obama has already said he would oppose any such effort. Quite simply, right-wingers are ranting deliriously about a threat that does not exist.

As with any real threat to the First Amendment, the answer lies in more speech—in this case, more speech on the airwaves—not less. But also, at the same time, making sure that local needs are met and diverse opinions are aired.

Rather than restoration of the Fairness Doctrine, what makes more sense, according to the authors of the Center for American Progress report—and what they recommend—are changes in FCC regulations governing ownership of media outlets.

Under the FCC's current rules, in the largest markets with forty-five or more commercial radio stations, one business entity may own or control up to eight commercial radio stations. In a market with fourteen or fewer commercial radio stations, a single business may own or control up to five stations. To achieve the goal of greater diversity, the CAP report recommends that the FCC rules be revised as follows:

- On the national level, ownership by any one business entity should not exceed 5 percent of the total number of AM and FM broadcast stations.
- On the local level, no one entity should control more than 10 percent of the total commercial radio stations in a given market; which translates into . . .
- No more than 4 commercial stations in large markets (45 or more stations);
- No more than 3 stations in mid-markets (30–44 stations);
- No more than 2 stations in smaller markets (15–29 stations);
- Only 1 station in the smallest markets (14 or fewer stations).

At the same time, the center report authors recommend shortening the term of a radio station license from eight to three years, and requiring stations to file more frequent reports with the FCC on how, as a licensee, they are fulfilling their legal responsibility to serve the general public.

One additional step toward breaking the conservative monopoly on talk radio would be to sever the ties between ownership of broadcast outlets and ownership of content providers. Imagine the dilemma faced by local radio executives of programming "in the public interest" when forced to choose between a program provided by their parent company or programming provided by an independent or competing company. The bottom line will always trump the public interest here.

We have seen companies like Clear Channel cancel progressive talk in order to install a sports outlet that will carry sports programming provided by Premiere, owned by Clear Channel. Even if the station does worse in the ratings, the local executive gets credit for being a good, loyal team player by supporting the parent company's programming. As we explained earlier in this chapter, the local radio station gives commercial inventory (x number of spots per hour) to the program provider. In the case of Clear Channel, they would rather offer those spots for lesser-rated programming owned by their own company than offer them to another provider for programming that more listeners would want to hear.

It's that deadly combination of few owners, all conservative, who own and control both almost all stations and programming in every major market that so tilts the radio marketplace in favor of right-wing talk and against progressive talk.

To be sure, those few changes recommended above would not automatically bring about the end of the overwhelming advantage enjoyed by conservative talk on the airwaves today. But they would create an environment where it would at least be possible to hear a greater diversity of voices—and where progressive talk radio would have a fair opportunity to establish itself as a viable, financially successful, ratings-successful, market-driven alternative. For all the reasons seen, that opportunity simply does not exist today. In order for progressive talk radio hosts to take advantage of that opportunity, however, they will need the support of the progressive donor community—support that, to date, has been mysteriously and sadly lacking.

In 1971, by warning of the collapse of capitalism, Lewis Powell was able to energize conservatives to build a combined and powerful research-outreach-broadcast machine that has dominated American media, electronic and print, for the last thirty years.

Today, progressives need to build an equally all-encompassing and powerful message machine. What's appalling is not so much the fact that progressives lag so far behind conservatives in this department. It's that progressives have barely begun to respond. Too many progressives, who should know better, don't understand either the importance of the media or the conservative media juggernaut they are up against.

Believe me, I know. As creator of my own radio show and partner with Ed Schultz, Stephanie Miller, Thom Hartmann, and others in building a national progressive radio presence, I have spent hundreds of hours trying to convince wealthy liberal donors of the importance of creating a powerful progressive media machine to offset the right-wing blockhouse. Too often, it's like trying to sell ice to Eskimos.

These are good, smart, generous people. But they'd rather give their money to candidates. They prefer rubbing elbows with political celebrities at fund-raising dinners. They take pride in getting face time with a senator—or president!—and having their calls returned. As for the importance of the media in creating long-lasting political power, they just don't get it. Those liberal individuals and labor leaders who do get it, God bless 'em, are few and far between.

Until that changes, unfortunately, conservatives will continue to rule talk radio, and liberals will lag far behind.

In fact, given their vast deficiency in resources, it's amazing that progressive talk radio, in its brief existence, has enjoyed as much success as it has . . . as we will see next.

9

PROGRESSIVES FIGHT BACK!

How times have changed on the radio.

Not so long ago, there was not one nationally syndicated progressive talk show host.

Today, that situation is dramatically different and vastly improved. As we have seen, conservatives continue to dominate the airwaves. But over the last few years, there has emerged a growing gaggle of liberal talk show hosts, now heard in almost every major market in the country. And we are doing just fine, thank you. Our numbers include:

Syndicated by Dial Global Radio Network: Ed Schultz, Stephanie Miller, Thom Hartmann, and yours truly, Bill Press.

Syndicated by Westwood One: Randi Rhodes.

Independently syndicated: Mike Malloy.

And, of course, we proudly count one United States senator among our ranks: former Air America talk show host Al Franken.

And, in addition to Ed Schultz, one more MSNBC anchor: former Air America host Rachel Maddow.

Progressive talk radio is still in its infancy, but we've been at it long enough to shatter three common and related myths you hear from know-nothing conservatives:

1. Liberals can't do talk radio.
2. Nobody wants to listen to progressive talk radio.
3. Liberal programming can't make money on talk radio.

All three statements are demonstrably false.

PROGRESSIVE TALKERS

The first charge is laughable on the face of it. After all, if there's one thing liberals know how to do, it's talk, talk, talk. Hasn't that been the right-wing knock on us from the start?

The idea that liberals could not succeed on talk radio probably got started because—without naming any names—the first few lefties who appeared on the national airwaves crashed and burned. This happened for two reasons: They didn't have wide distribution; and, frankly, some of them just weren't very good. It's a far different situation today.

Ed Schultz is a powerful talk show host. So are Stephanie Miller, Randi Rhodes, Mike Malloy, Ron Reagan, and Thom Hartmann, among others. And I like to think I also do a decent job. In terms of sheer talent and talk radio skills, our gang can hold its own against any lineup of conservative talk show hosts. And our shows are just as entertaining and even more informative, yet far less inflammatory.

Unfortunately, the myth that liberals can't hack talk radio was has only been further fueled by Air America's filing for bankruptcy in 2006, and then again in January 2010, which had nothing to do with Air America's on-air talent, and everything to do with Air America's fiscal mismanagement.

More on Air America in just a moment. But the only reasons there have not been more successful progressive talk show hosts is because, for a long time, nobody would hire them and, still today, there are relatively few stations willing to put them on the air.

The world of talk radio is a lot like the way congressional districts are set up. It used to be that it didn't matter so much if you were a Democrat or Republican, you could get elected to Congress based on the strength of your ideas. But no longer. With strictly partisan reapportionment supported by both parties, there are now clearly defined Republican seats and just as clearly defined Democratic seats. And don't dare try to run in a Republican seat if you're a Democrat.

Similarly with talk radio. It used to be that talk stations would offer a smorgasbord of political opinions. A morning news team might be followed by a right-wing mid-morning host, followed by a libertarian, followed by a liberal. However many opinions there were on any given issue, you'd hear them all on that same station at some point during eighteen hours of live broadcast. But no longer.

Today, for the reasons we outlined in the last chapter—mainly, the right-wing politics of network owners—the vast majority of radio stations are programmed all-right and far fewer all-left. That being said, those station managers who are willing to air progressive talk have a small but impressive roster of talk show hosts to choose from.

ED SCHULTZ

America's first nationally syndicated progressive talk show host. As I pointed out in Chapter 5, not so long ago Schultz was the top local radio host in Fargo, North Dakota. Today, he's the top progressive radio host in the country in number of broadcast stations and he's still known for delivering "straight talk from the heartland." In spring 2009, in addition to radio, he began his own nightly show on MSNBC. A champion of working-class Americans, those "who take a shower after they get home from work," Schultz calls himself a "gun-totin', red-meat-eatin' lefty." He's the king of progressive talk.

STEPHANIE MILLER

Born to politics, but on the other side of the aisle. Her father, Bill Miller, was Barry Goldwater's running mate in 1964. But Stephanie's a true-blue, certified liberal—and a gifted entertainer. She has successfully translated her wacky brand of stand-up comedy to talk radio. She and her sidekicks daily offer at once the most informative and most entertaining of progressive talk shows, with a lively mix of listener calls, interviews with big-name guests, and lampooning of outrageous comments from the previous day's right-wing radio and TV shows. If laughter is the best weapon, Miller is the most lethal of all progressive talk show hosts.

THOM HARTMANN

If Miller is the most comic of today's progressive talk radio hosts, Thom Hartmann's the most cerebral. And the most knowledgeable. The author of nineteen books, Hartmann brings to each show the insights gained from his experience as an entrepreneur, psychotherapist, founder of children's hospitals around the globe, and radio disc jockey. He launched his radio show in 2002 from Vermont, later moved to Portland, Oregon, to join KPOJ-AM, stepped into Al Franken's slot on Air America in February 2007, and then joined Dial Global. Two years later, *Talkers Magazine* named him the most listened to progressive talk radio host in the nation.

RANDI RHODES

Don't get into an argument with Randi Rhodes unless you're on her side. She is a take-no-prisoners kind of talk show host: passionate, colorful, outspoken, in your face, and convincing. But she's also known for doing so much homework preparing for her show that she knows the issues better than anybody. An Air Force veteran, Rhodes had already been doing political talk radio for ten years—the number-one talker in West Palm Beach, Florida—before she joined Air America, where she soon became their most popular host. Fired by Air America for off-the-air comments about Hillary Clinton, she joined Nova M briefly, and is now syndicated by Premiere Radio Networks, the syndication arm of Clear Channel.

MIKE MALLOY

What Randi Rhodes is to late afternoons, Mike Malloy is to late nights: wild, angry, no-holds-barred, emotional, and a hell of a lot of fun. Plus extremely well informed. Mike started out in Atlanta and Chicago, before joining the early lineup of Air America. When Air America went bust, he came back to life on the short-lived Nova M network, but is now independently syndicated and commands a large and loyal following. Malloy's an unabashed liberal, who hates phonies of either party. Perhaps the most colorful and outrageous of all progressive hosts, Malloy had his most fun on-air when George W. Bush was in the White House. Where Bush loved giving other people nicknames, Malloy had a few for him, including Knuckle Nuts, the Unelected Idiot, President Bunny Pants, and Cinco de Moron.

RON REAGAN

Yes, his father was *that* Ronald Reagan, but you'd never know it from listening to *The Ron Reagan Show*. The son of the conservative icon is as liberal as they come and showed his independent streak at an early age, informing his parents when he was twelve that he was an atheist and would no longer be going to church with them. A gifted dancer, Ron was accepted by the famed Joffrey Ballet and danced at the Met. But politics and the media proved a stronger attraction. I first met him when he was an intern at KABC-TV in Los Angeles. He went on to host shows for BBC, the Animal Planet network, and MSNBC, having become more openly political once his father had left the White House. After starting out on radio at Seattle's KIRO-AM, Ron's three-hour evening show is still heard in Seattle, on 1090 AM, KTPK. In 2004, he electrified the nation with his speech at the Democratic National Convention in support of federal funding for stem-cell research, a cause his mother, former First Lady Nancy Reagan, had long championed.

ALAN COLMES

Alan Colmes was already a popular stand-up comic and radio talk show host when he was hired as a liberal commentator by Roger Ailes at Fox News in 1996. For the next thirteen years, he earned his liberal stripes up against Sean Hannity, five nights a week, on *Hannity & Colmes*. If Fox were really "fair and balanced," he'd still be there. During that time, Alan was often slammed for not being tough enough on Hannity. In his book, *Lies and the Lying Liars Who Tell Them*, Al Franken made fun of him by deliberately printing his name in small letters. The truth is, had Colmes been more aggressive, he'd never have been allowed on Fox and there would have been no liberal counterpart to Hannity, just as there is none today. So, no matter how polite, give him credit for hanging in there. As successful as he was on television, however, radio continues to be Alan's first love. His nightly show is syndicated nationally by Fox News Radio.

PROGRESSIVE RATINGS SUCCESS

As has been oft stated, right-wing talk dominates the airwaves. Where the left-leaning format has been tried, however, progressive talkers have proven themselves successful—even up against the best-known right-wingers.

In Portland, Oregon, Thom Hartmann, broadcasting over KPOJ-AM 620, perhaps the most successful progressive station in the country, regularly beats Rush Limbaugh, heard in the same time slot over KPOJ's sister station, 1190. And that's not because Portland is such a liberal mecca. Yes, the city of Portland itself is a progressive stronghold, but it's only the hole in the donut. Four out of five counties in the Portland listening area voted for George W. Bush in 2004 and 2008. Hartmann beats Limbaugh in that market because he consistently delivers a better, more intelligent show.

Ed Schultz, the very first nationally syndicated progressive talk radio host, was another overnight ratings success in the Portland market. When he joined KPOJ's lineup in the spring of 2004, the station's numbers sky-rocketed.

In radio, the critical ratings measurement is called AQH Share, or "average number of listeners per quarter hour." That's a key indicator because the more listeners per quarter hour, the more stations can charge for commercials. Before Ed Schultz, KPOJ was earning a 0.1 AQH share, or 1,000 listeners per quarter hour, in his noon–3 P.M. time slot. Within three months, Ed had boosted their ratings to a 6 AQH, or 60,000 listeners—an increase of 5,900 percent. Who says progressive talk radio doesn't work?

Stephanie Miller soon followed Schultz to national syndication and ratings success. Her unique brand of off-the-wall political news and commentary was just what liberals needed to survive the dreadful Bush years (and enjoy the Obama years!). In less than a year, she vaulted to the number-two position in Los Angeles morning talk radio, one of the toughest and most competitive time slots in the country, beating out veteran talkers Adam Carolla, Doug McIntyre, and Laura Ingraham. She repeated that success in Seattle, Madison, Tucson, Minneapolis, Asheville, San Francisco, and many other markets around the country.

For years, Randi Rhodes has been Rush Limbaugh's worst nightmare, because she has consistently cleaned his clock in the ratings—starting in Rush's adopted hometown of West Palm Beach. Head-to-head against Limbaugh on a sister Clear Channel station, she consistently beat him in the key twenty-five- to fifty-four-year-old demographic. When Clear Channel merged the two stations, she followed Limbaugh—and outpaced him even more. That success propelled her to Air America and national syndication where she quickly became Air America's number-one most highly rated host, even though all the publicity went to Al Franken and Janeane Garofalo. She even jokingly referred to herself as Air America's "Unknown Host."

PROGRESSIVE MONEYMAKERS

As progressive talkers have thrived, so have the stations that carry them. Both, of course, are essential for successful talk radio of any stripe. Without good talent on the air, a station will fail. Absent a station with a strong signal, good management, and an aggressive sales staff, not even the best talent can survive. But the combination of good talent and good management has created many success stories for progressive radio around the country. Here are just a few:

PORTLAND—KPOJ-AM

Portland, Oregon, is known for many things—including Powell's, perhaps the best bookstore in the country. It's also known, thanks to the vision of KPOJ-AM program director Mike Dirkx, for being the birthplace of progressive talk radio.

Stuck with an underperforming AM station as part of Clear Channel's Portland cluster, Dirkx realized he needed to try something new and different. Neither sports talk nor guy talk had worked on the station, and the market couldn't absorb any more right-wing talk, so Dirkx decided to give progressive talk a shot.

At about the same time, Air America was trying to get off the ground. The timing was perfect. In March 2004, KPOJ became Air America's first affiliate and was an immediate success. Within weeks, it had zoomed to number four in the market. Within months, Clear Channel stations in Miami, Los Angeles, San Francisco, Albuquerque, Detroit, Denver, and other major markets had followed Portland's lead. Plus Madison, as we will see next.

Dirkx started out with Air America's roster of talk show hosts, plus Ed Schultz in midday. But as Air America dropped its original shows, he reached out to other talkers, including Stephanie Miller, Randi Rhodes, and myself. In 2005, Thom Hartmann moved to Portland to host KPOJ's morning show, in addition to his own midday Air America program.

Today, KPOJ is America's longest-running and most successful progressive talk station, making money for Clear Channel for the last few years. It got started at the right time and in the right market. But it's also enjoyed dedicated leadership and staff, which believed in progressive talk and worked hard to make it succeed.

MADISON—WXXM-FM

The story of what was happening on Portland's KPOJ was not lost on other Clear Channel stations around the country. One man watching closely was Mike Ferris, operations manager of Madison, Wisconsin's, 92.1 FM, "The Mike." In the spring of 2004, having enjoyed little success with either alternative rock or soft rock on the station, Ferris suggested to his Clear Channel bosses that they try to duplicate Mike Dirkx's success in Portland—only to be told he was, basically, crazy.

By the end of the summer, however, when Portland's progressive talk continued to climb in the ratings, Ferris tried again—and this time succeeded. In September 2004, 92.1 switched to all-progressive talk with the standard Air America lineup of Al Franken, Randi Rhodes, and Rachel Maddow. Later, program director Brian Turany and Ferris added Ed Schultz and Stephanie Miller. Clear Channel ran full-page ads and billboards, promoting the new format. Madison's a great college town. All those students and professors provide a built-in audience for progressive talk, and the station enjoyed immediate success for the next two years. In every department but one: sales. Sponsors were hard to get, because they feared alienating some customers by advertising on liberal political talk shows. So Ferris reluctantly announced the station was switching to sports at the end of 2006. And that resulted in one of the greatest success stories in progressive talk radio.

No sooner had Clear Channel's announcement hit the airwaves than angry listeners complained of a right-wing conspiracy. They circulated petitions, held rallies, collected signatures, sent letters and e-mails to corporate headquarters, lined up new sponsors. In brief, they did everything effective protesters should do—and it worked! Madison liberals raised so much hell that Clear Channel reversed its position and kept progressive talk on the air. Today "The Mike," with an all-progressive lineup and still under the leadership of Mike Ferris and general manager Jeff Tyler, is one of Madison's top-tier stations, holding its own in ratings, attracting new sponsors, and making money for Clear Channel.

Again, who says liberals don't listen to talk radio? Remember Madison.

MINNEAPOLIS–ST. PAUL—KTNF-AM

Minnesota Democrat Bill Luther lost his seat in Congress as part of the nationwide Republican surge in the 2002 midterm elections. Rather than just get mad, he decided to get even. He recognized that Republicans won largely because they had a powerful message machine—and the Democrats had none. So he determined with Janet Robert, his then-partner and now wife, to do something about it.

Robert and Luther first leased three hours of time on a local Minneapolis station, during which they aired Al Franken's Air America show. Franken, after all, was a favorite native son. As his show began to attract both audience and sponsors, Robert and Luther leased four more hours in order to add Ed Schultz and a local host to the lineup. At which point, just as progressive talk in the Twin Cities was starting to show results, the station was sold out from under them and they were left with no broadcasting platform.

Welcome to lesson number one of talk radio, which all progressives have learned the hard way: UNLESS YOU OWN THE STATION, YOU ARE SCREWED. OR SOON WILL BE.

Fortunately for them, another local station, KTNF 950-AM, popped up for sale at the same time. Having first tried and failed to convince wealthy Democrats to invest in the project, Robert used her own funds in October 2004 to buy KTNF—and start from scratch to build a new progressive talk station. It was a tough, uphill battle, hard to convince business sponsors to advertise on a station that only reached the Minneapolis–St. Paul metropolitan region, not the outlying counties, and which broadcast a progressive message. One potential sponsor told Robert: "If I advertised on your station, I could not face my friends at the country club."

But with the help of labor unions and Indian tribal councils, Robert managed to keep on the air, cover her operating expenses, and begin attracting advertisers who wanted to reach a loyal, grateful, committed progressive audience. By January 2009, five years later, KTNF was turning a profit: a financially successful, independently owned and politically powerful progressive talk station. KTNF will always have bragging rights as the station that launched the political career of Senator Al Franken.

ASHEVILLE—880 AM

Another success story, this one from the South, and another Clear Channel station. Like Portland, Asheville, North Carolina, was stuck with a lackluster AM station, then called "Easy 880," broadcasting easy listening music, attracting no audience, and making no money. Then the year 2004 brought an exciting presidential election and a revolutionary new experiment in progressive talk out of Portland. Bingo! Brian Hall, who had just moved from sales manager of Clear Channel's Asheville group of stations to program manager, saw the opportunity and pounced. On September 13, 2004, he went on the air with a whole new sound, "880 The Revolution." Early "revolutionaries" were Al Franken, Ed Schultz, Stephanie Miller, and Randi Rhodes, followed later by me.

880 was immediately well received by listeners in "The Paris of the South" and remains a huge success. It has met or exceeded its budget every year, its revenues continue to grow, and the station continues to attract loyal new listeners and advertisers—especially now, with Barack Obama in the White House.

Bottom line: It's been proven over and over again that progressive talk can make money—indeed, is already making money—on stations with a good signal, a dedicated sales staff, and strong talent.

In response to those who still blindly insist that progressive talk radio won't work, I am reminded of G. K. Chesterton's famous retort to those who made the same claim about Christianity. "The Christian ideal has not been tried and found wanting," he noted, "it has been found difficult and left untried."

In fact, given its success, it's surprising that progressive talk radio didn't develop sooner and had such a rocky start.

THE WORLD OF PROGRESSIVE TALK

Once upon a time, there was no progressive talk radio. Period. And, as we've seen, that wasn't so long ago.

Some old-timers may remember an earlier, valiant, but unsuccessful attempt to build a national progressive talk radio network under the unfortunate name of the i.e. America Radio Network (i.e., for information and entertainment). Owned and funded by the United Auto Workers union, i.e. America actually had a pretty good run, 1996 to 2004, and featured some top-flight talent: Thom Hartmann, Mike Malloy, Peter B. Collins, Jim Hightower, Nancy Skinner, Peter Werbe, and Doug Stephan. But they didn't have enough outlets to turn a profit, and the union was soon losing a reported $75,000 a month. In December 2003, UAW president Ron Gettelfinger announced he was pulling the plug.

So, once again, there was nothing but right-wing voices on talk radio, until . . .

The change began with a bomb dropped at a media gathering in New York in October 2003. Addressing the New Media Seminar sponsored by *Talkers Magazine*, Gabe Hobbs, head of news talk radio for Clear Channel, stunned his audience by announcing that the nation's largest radio network—which, until then, had fielded nothing but conservatives on its 1,200 radio stations—was ready to embrace progressive talk. In the world of talk radio, that was the equivalent of George W. Bush announcing he'd scheduled a sex-change operation.

The reasoning behind their decision was straightforward, Hobbs explained: Conservative talk radio was no longer a growth industry. The market had been saturated. The only way to grow was to reach out to that vast, and as yet unserved, audience—namely Democrats and Independents, people on the left or in the middle. Clear Channel wasn't going to do anything radical, Hobbs hastened to add. It didn't plan to abandon conservative talk on its biggest stations. But it would experiment with progressive talk on its second- and third-tier stations in certain markets.

Hobbs's announcement opened the floodgates for progressive talk radio by providing a network of potential stations across the country willing to hire good liberal talkers. But where were they going to find the good liberal talkers?

Into the breach stepped Jones Radio Networks. In January 2004, they launched *The Ed Schultz Show* in national syndication, followed by Stephanie Miller and, a year later, Bill Press. (Jones was bought by Triton Media in June 2008, and its radio syndication became part of Triton's Dial Global division.)

As noted above, five months after Hobbs had given the green light, Portland's KPOJ became the first Clear Channel station to switch to a full lineup of progressive talk, beginning its new format on March 31, 2009 . . . Which just happened to be the very same day a new national progressive talk radio network called Air America was launched in New York.

Ask anybody. If they'd heard anything at all about progressive talk radio, all they'd heard about was Air America. For most Americans, the two were one and the same: Air America *was* progressive talk radio; progressive talk radio *was* Air America.

That was simply not the case. As we've seen, Air America was but one brand of progressive talk. They were not the first ones out of the box, and they were not the biggest provider of progressive talk radio. But they definitely had have the best-known brand in progressive talk—and therefore deserve a special look.

AIR AMERICA

Someday they'll erect a monument to Sheldon and Anita Drobny. They're the father and mother of progressive talk radio. And they had the vision to create Air America.

Successful business leaders and active Democrats, the Drobnys were enjoying a quiet life in Chicago until their favorite radio host, Mike Malloy, was fired. Angry over the silencing of one more liberal voice, they decided to do something about it. They pulled their friends together, started raising venture capital, formed AnShell Media, and hired Atlanta radio guru Jon Sinton to create a national progressive radio network.

Sinton went to work, raising money, hiring writers, locating studio space, and rounding up talent—starting with comedians Al Franken, Janeane Garofalo, and Lizz Winstead, and longtime successful talker Randi Rhodes. Unable to raise sufficient capital themselves, the Drobnys sold AnShell to advertising executive Evan Cohen and his business partner, Rex Sorensen, who renamed the company Progress Media. Mark Walsh was hired as CEO. Sinton remained as president. Cohen soon announced he'd raised $30 million, and Air America went live on March 31, 2004.

Give Cohen credit for one thing: No new business venture has launched with a greater flurry of glowing publicity. Air America and Al Franken made the cover of *The New York Times Sunday Magazine*. Cable television covered their first day broadcasts. Newspapers across the country ran stories about the revolution in talk radio: Liberals on the air! For the first time! Who will be the new Rush Limbaugh of the left? Liberals nationwide hailed the presence of a new radio network with the avowed mission of blocking George W. Bush's reelection. The Air America brand was solidly established.

Unfortunately, Cohen was better at getting publicity than raising money or managing a company. Turns out he hadn't raised anywhere near $30 million. Within two weeks of its launch, Air America lost two of its biggest affiliates, Chicago and Los Angeles, over money problems. Two weeks later, Walsh quit the company and, in another week, Cohen and Sorensen were forced out by remaining investors.

At which point, Air America almost went out of business. They couldn't even meet payroll. On-air talent went without a paycheck so writers and producers could get paid. For a while, Al Franken took on the task of raising new funds from wealthy Democratic donors. Somehow, the network survived, but its money woes were compounded when it was revealed that

Cohen had arranged $875,000 in loans to Air America from the Gloria Wise Boys and Girls Club, at a time when he was also serving as director of development for the Bronx-based community organization.

Air America, meanwhile, gained a new CEO, legendary music producer Danny Goldberg. But its financial problems continued, and in October 2006, it was forced to file for bankruptcy under Chapter 11. Air America agreed to pay back the ill-gotten Boys and Girls Club loans, but that didn't help their bottom line. In business deals unrelated to Air America, Cohen was later indicted for money laundering by the state of Hawaii. In March 2007, the company was sold to Green Family Media, headed by real estate mogul Stephen Green and his brother Mark Green, former New York City public advocate. To manage their new enterprise, the Greens hired former Clear Channel executives Bennett Zier and Bill Hess.

Air America's financial problems were serious. But even more serious was its loss of on-the-air talent. One by one, Air America's big names either drifted away or were let go. Al Franken left to run for Senate. Janeane Garofalo left to focus on her acting career. Randi Rhodes and Mike Malloy were dropped. Rachel Maddow gave up her radio show for MSNBC.

DIAL GLOBAL

For a while, there was one other player in progressive talk radio.

When Air America filed for bankruptcy the first time, Sheldon and Anita Drobny refused to just sit by and watch their baby fail. Yet once again they went out to shake the money tree and raise the investment capital necessary to keep the progressive network alive. Even though their fund-raising efforts were successful, Air America's directors refused to relinquish control of the company. So the Drobnys decided to form their own company, Nova M, instead, and compete directly with Air America.

Nova M got off to a great start, signing up veteran talkers Randi Rhodes and Mike Malloy and establishing a home base at KPHX-AM 1480 in

Phoenix. After just a couple of years, however, money ran out and the Drobnys were forced to shut down the new network.

Meanwhile, Jones Radio, which, as we saw earlier, was first out of the box with Ed Schultz, had enlarged its progressive radio portfolio, and continued to go strong. Jones was purchased by Triton Media, owner of Dial Global Radio Networks, in 2008. In addition to music, and conservative talkers Neal Boortz and Michael Smerconish, Dial Global also syndicates *The Ed Schultz Show*, *The Stephanie Miller Show*, *The Thom Hartmann Show*, and *The Bill Press Show*.

Dial Global is the major provider of progressive talk radio today, and the only national syndication company and network to make a serious commitment to finding outlets for both conservative and progressive radio talk show hosts.

MEDIA MATTERS MATTERS

There's one other important player in the world of progressive talk radio. In fact, I couldn't do my own show—or this book—without them. And that's a great organization called Media Matters for America. Yes, it sure does.

Media Matters was founded, and is still led, by my friend David Brock, whom I first met when he was a staff writer for *The American Spectator* and the darling hatchet man of the far right wing. As the man who first reported on state troopers procuring paramours for Arkansas governor Bill Clinton (never proven) and author of a blistering book on Anita Hill, David still has a lot of sins to atone for. But he's already off to a damned good start.

His book on Anita Hill having been so well received by conservatives, Brock was recruited and paid a sizable advance to write a similar hit piece on First Lady Hillary Clinton. In researching that book, however, he learned that Hillary was not the evil witch conservatives painted her to be. His book, *The Seduction of Hillary Rodham*, actually turned out to be a pretty fair analysis of Clinton's strengths and weaknesses—which was the last thing Washington's conservative establishment wanted out of Brock. As he related it to me, he knew that he was now persona non grata among conservatives, shortly after his Hillary book was published, when he was summarily dis-invited from a dinner party hosted by leading Federalist Society lawyer Ted Olson and his late wife, conservative commentator Barbara Olson.

Nobody knew better than Brock how the conservative message machine worked. And nobody understood better than he how Democrats suffered from having no message machine at all. So he decided to try to level the playing field. With the assistance of John Podesta, founder of the Center for American Progress, and with funding from a new group of liberal donors banded together as the Democracy Alliance, Brock launched Media Matters for America in May 2004, just in time to influence the 2004 presidential election.

In short, Media Matters is the liberal watchdog over the right-wing media. While producing occasional excellent in-depth analyses of trends in the media, its primary mission, and most valuable contribution, is to monitor dozens of hours of conservative radio and TV broadcasts daily, spot right-wing lies as soon as they air, expose them to the rest of the media, and immediately counter them with the truth, posted on its Web site, www.mediamatters.org.

It's an invaluable rapid-response service: something that conservatives have been provided for years by their Media Research Center, run by L. Brent Bozell, but which progressives never really enjoyed until the advent of Media Matters. In its short life, Media Matters has already eclipsed the Media Research Center in reach and influence. Media Matters, for example, was the first to publicize widely Don Imus's characterization of the Rutgers women's basketball team, "That's some nappy-headed ho's there."

Take it from me. I depend on Media Matters and use its material on my radio show every day, and I know the same is true of other progressive talk show hosts. But the greatest proof that Media Matters is doing its job are the loud and angry screams from conservative hosts whenever Media Matters catches them in the act.

Rush Limbaugh, who has featured on his Web site a picture of Stalin wearing a Media Matters insignia, regularly accuses Media Matters of being nothing but a "Hillary Clinton, George Soros, DNC front group" (the organization has never received any funding from Soros, but so what if it did?). Their sole purpose, he argues, is "to take things out of context here and misreport and cast aspersions."

Michael Savage, true to form, is much more hateful in his comments about the researchers at Media Matters, calling them "the Brownshirts of our time." They also represent, claims Savage, "a fascist front group" and a "gay, fascist Web site." Pulling out all the stops, Savage has also called them a bunch of "yokels and drunks," "cretins," "rat snitches," "snitch perverts," "scum," and "punk coward psychotics." Do you think maybe Media Matters got under his skin?

More troubling, Savage threatened to sue Media Matters under California's anti-stalking legislation and post the names and photographs of Media Matters staff on his Web site. His lawyers must have counseled him against it, because he never followed through on either threat.

For his part, Mark Levin often lashes out at "you morons at Media Matters, the criminal front group."

After they published his ugly comments about immigrants and minimum wage workers, Neal Boortz attacked Media Matters, calling them "Media Morons" and "Media Myrmidons." He accused David Brock, whom he dubbed "the illegitimate bastard child of Hillary Clinton and George Soros," of "waiting for one little statement that you can take out of its total context and just go on a rampage with, with your Web postings, and see if you can pull that Don Imus thing off all over again."

Lou Dobbs, who was called out by Media Matters for his obsession with President Obama's birth certificate, lashed back by calling the group a "partisan bunch of hacks" and made an on-air plea to Obama: "Would you do me a favor? Call off your attack dogs like Media Matters."

Bill O'Reilly is notoriously thin-skinned, and he shows it whenever some of his more outrageous comments are duly reported by Media Matters. He's denounced them as a "far-left, character assassin group" and the "propaganda arm" of the "far-left smear machine." He's targeted

Brock as "the biggest villain in the country." And Media Matters nailed O'Reilly for so many lies during the 2008 presidential campaign that he finally announced: "Any of the presidential candidates who can deport those swine, I'm voting for them."

Naturally, Glenn Beck also complains about "the liberal hit squad." Having nothing new to say, he simply repeats the number-one Fox News lie about the organization: "Media Matters goes after a conservative like Rush Limbaugh, but they refuse to confess their extreme liberal agenda, or the fact that the majority of their funding comes from billionaire activist George Soros." Again, Media Matters gets zero funding from Soros, but again, so what if it did?

There's no reason for right-wing talk show hosts to tie themselves in knots over Media Matters, for there is one easy way to get Media Matters off their backs: Simply tell the truth. Or, get used to being called out for telling lies.

Thank God for Media Matters for America!

DON'T COUNT NPR

You can't really talk about who's part of progressive talk radio without talking about who's not. And that includes NPR.

Everybody knows that NPR stands for National Public Radio. But it also stands for "Not Progressive Radio."

Don't get me wrong. I'm a big NPR fan. I tune in often. Robert Siegel, Nina Totenberg, and Linda Wertheimer are personal friends. *Car Talk* is, in my humble opinion, the best show on the radio. And *Wait, Wait . . . Don't Tell Me!* is a close runner-up.

But as I noted earlier, NPR is not the same as progressive talk, no matter how many times conservatives try to make that argument. It's their standard, predictable response to any complaint about the lopsided, right-wing bias of talk radio: "We don't need progressive talk radio because liberals can always listen to NPR." Or, variation on the same theme: "It doesn't matter that there are so few progressive talk stations, because liberals have NPR."

Nonsense! Repeat after me: NPR is *not* progressive talk. It's *public* radio, for one. Which has a totally different funding source—taxpayers, foundations, or listeners—and a different goal: to inform and entertain, but not to make a profit. By contrast, progressive talk, like conservative talk, is a form of commercial talk radio, totally funded by commercial sponsors, which—in addition to informing and entertaining its listeners—is also geared to making as much profit as possible.

Not to mention the difference in programming. You may hear a liberal commentator on NPR once in a while. But you will easily hear just as many, if not more, conservative or middle-of-the-road commentators. What you will *never* hear on NPR is what you hear all day long on conservative or progressive talk: a host spending three hours bashing leaders of one political party or the other.

Do a lot of liberals listen to NPR? Yes, because they're more open-minded than most conservatives and more interested in NPR's lengthy, factual, in-depth news reporting than the quick, bullet-point news flashes you get from most so-called news stations.

Does NPR take a lot of listeners away from progressive talk radio? Yes, again. For the same reason. Plus, liberals don't have the same crying need most conservatives suffer from to hear their political biases repeated, if not beat to death, hour after hour, day after day.

The point is: NPR does not take the place of progressive talk radio. No way. It simply does not meet the listening needs of liberals who are looking for good, entertaining, and informative political talk radio featuring hosts who share their liberal opinions and advocate the causes they believe in. That choice, available to conservatives in every hamlet, town, and big city in America, is available to liberals in only a relative handful of cities and, usually, on that city's weakest radio signal.

Put it this way. Only 47 percent of Americans voted for John McCain, but they control 95 percent of talk radio. Most of the 53 percent of Americans who voted for Barack Obama—and don't want to listen to Rush

Limbaugh or Sean Hannity—can't find progressive talk radio anywhere on their radio dial. At least not on ground stations. Which is why more and more of them are going extraterrestrial.

SIRIUS XM

One place where progressive talk radio hosts are already able to get around the conservative ownership monopoly and compete fairly with right-wing talk show hosts is on Sirius XM satellite radio—where consumers, not owners, decide what they want to listen to, and are willing to pay for.

The same opportunity exists for conservative hosts, of course. But that's the point. Satellite radio's the only level playing field in talk radio.

Even before the merger, both XM and Sirius offered listeners a choice in talk radio: Talk Left and Talk Right. That's still the case in the new, combined company, announced in 2007 and approved by the FCC in 2008. Though now one company, Sirius XM, they still operate as two independent satellite services, each offering multiple listening options for everything from music to sports to politics: XM, over 170 channels; Sirius, over 130. And each offers a channel devoted exclusively to progressive talk, and one devoted exclusively to conservative talk.

For syndicated talk radio shows, the economic benefits of being carried on satellite radio are nonexistent. Since it is commercial-free, Sirius XM offers no advertising revenue stream to talk shows it carries. All revenues raised from listener subscriptions go to overhead—or to pay Howard Stern.

But being heard on Sirius XM is great for "branding" and for attracting new listeners. Sirius XM claims it is unable to determine how many listeners are tuned into any one of its channels at any hour of the day. Still, it is probably safe to assume that, with their combined 18.5 million subscribers, there are more people listening to progressive talk radio at any time on satellite radio than on all progressive talk stations combined. And more and more are simply picking up the phone.

GRAB THAT PHONE

There's one other place where technology has created a level playing field in talk radio, and that's the iPhone.

Industry experts predict that it won't be long before the radio as such becomes an unnecessary appliance. People will still listen to the radio, mind you. They just won't listen to the radio on their radio, they'll listen to the radio on their phone, either at home or in the car. In fact, it's already happening. The iPhone has a radio application, by which listeners can connect to any radio station carrying their favorite show, and listen live. Plus most talk radio shows today, including mine, post a podcast, a commercial-free version of their program, on iTunes, enabling fans to download the show to their iPhone and listen to it anytime, anywhere they want. Even over and over again. The popularity of podcasts as the most convenient way to listen to favorite radio shows is growing rapidly. Michael Harrison, publisher of *Talkers Magazine*, predicts that the podcast and the exclusive content provided on podcasts represents the future of talk radio, and that radio appliances, as we now know them, will soon be obsolete.

As with satellite radio, cell phone technology doesn't discriminate between progressive talk and conservative talk. The same opportunities exist for each. But that's a big improvement over the imbalance that exists today on commercial talk radio because of the control exercised by so few conservative owners.

New technology, then, is clearly working in favor of progressive talk radio. Someday, maybe not in our lifetime, but someday, the ready availability of talk radio outside traditional, ground-based, commercial radio stations—where listeners, not station owners, decide what goes on the air—will be the norm. But until then, there's only one way that progressive talk radio can thrive and survive. Liberals have to stop complaining about how many radio stations are owned by conservatives—and start buying their own.

FUTURE OF PROGRESSIVE TALK

Based on the ratings success enjoyed by Al Franken, Rachel Maddow, Ed Schultz, Thom Hartmann, Stephanie Miller, Randi Rhodes, Mike Malloy, and others, I am convinced there's a bright future ahead for progressive talk radio. And based on the business success of Portland, Madison, Minneapolis, Asheville, and other markets, I believe that progressive talk can succeed anywhere in this country. There will always be a market for progressive talk radio, and there's a growing one today.

In fact, all indications are that the glory days of conservative talk are in decline, and the golden age of progressive talk is just beginning.

For progressive talk to really take off, there is one thing necessary. Not restoration of the Fairness Doctrine. Not any edict of the FCC. Not even putting Rush Limbaugh in jail. The one thing necessary is a change in ownership of radio stations. And that's something that only liberals can do for themselves.

I can't tell you how many times fellow liberals have complained to me about Rupert Murdoch. Oh, he's terrible, they whine. He has too much power over American media. He owns the *New York Post*. He owns *The Wall Street Journal*. He owns News Corporation, which owns Fox News. And he wasn't even born in this country. We have to do something about him. To which, I reply: Stop complaining about Rupert Murdoch. He's a brilliant and successful businessman. Yes, his control of so much of America's media is a problem. But the solution is not to shut down Rupert Murdoch. The solution is to find our own Rupert Murdoch, or group of Rupert Murdochs, to get into the media business, buy up a chunk of it, and devote it to a progressive political message.

Come to think of it, that's why conservatives are always accusing groups like Media Matters of being a "Soros-funded operation." Because they're secretly afraid that George Soros, or someone like him, would actually step forward and put up the funds to build a progressive talk radio network of stations. Alas, so far, Soros has shown little interest.

If the secret in real estate is location, location, location, the secret in media is ownership, ownership, ownership. Only when wealthy liberals recognize the importance of the media in winning and protecting political power . . . Only when they're willing to put their own money on the line . . . Only when they control, through ownership or long-term lease, a network of stations across the country, will progressive talk show radio ever be close to competing with conservative talk.

Ownership! Until wealthy donors step up to the plate and start buying and building their own network of progressive talk stations, no matter what lip service they might give to media reform, they are only kidding themselves.

Ownership! Until liberals—and there are lots of liberals as wealthy as Rupert Murdoch out there—until liberals buy their own radio stations, progressive talk radio will always be the poor, neglected stepsister of right-wing talk.

If wealthy liberals were really serious about building long-term political power for Democrats, they would forget about giving money to individual candidates—and put all their money into building a progressive media empire. Aesop never wrote a clearer fable. Which doesn't mean Democrats will ever get it right. Conservatives are counting on them not to.

CONCLUSION:
AMERICA'S TOWN MEETING

Finally, a few words about the contribution of talk radio and the importance of getting it right.

One thing for sure: Right-wing or left, talk radio's here to stay. As long as there are traffic jams and debates over issues around the dinner table, listeners will tune in to talk radio: to listen, to learn, to laugh, and to participate. After all, it's the only chance many people have to voice their opinions publicly—and anonymously, if they care to. Nobody really knows if "Vernon from Washington, D.C." is really Vernon from Washington or Mark from Bend, Oregon. Yes, people can—and do—express their political opinions anonymously on the Internet, in blogs, chat rooms, and so forth. But a lot of people don't have the time, or know-how, to express their opinions electronically, and talk radio will always be a more direct and more communal medium.

No doubt, talk radio will continue to grow and expand, adapting to new technologies and new opportunities. The only questions are: Will talk radio continue to be as one-sided as it is today? And will so much of it continue to be so mean and ugly?

As I stated at the outset, I'm a big champion of talk radio, whether talk show hosts come from the left, right, or middle. Indeed, the more I listen to talk radio, and the more hours I spend behind the microphone, talking about the issues and taking calls from listeners, the more I value and appreciate both the power and the promise of the medium.

My experience as a host has taught me two things about talk radio. First, after voting, there's no better way to involve people in the workings of democracy. By offering good, lively talk radio, both on the left and the right, and by giving people the opportunity to weigh in and voice their opinions, we are performing a very valuable public service. There is no better democratic (small "d"!) platform available anywhere, so easily accessible to so many people at the same time.

We also offer an important service by providing people someplace where they can feel at home in an increasingly complex and confusing world. Jack Swanson, program director of KSFO and KGO in San Francisco, and one of the most gifted (and colorful!) radio executives in the country, put it this way: "You know what people want most in the world, besides love? People want to be told, 'You're right.' Whether you're here at conservative KSFO or at liberal KPFA in Berkeley, the core value is the same." Listeners, in other words, know there's one place on the dial where they can find themselves among friends—whether it's friends on the right, or friends on the left. And that place is talk radio. Listening to talk radio by themselves, at home or in the car, they suddenly don't feel so lonely.

But . . . Here's the second lesson, I believe: Talk radio is not really serving the public when it gets so ugly and when it remains so overwhelmingly one-sided.

Talk radio has already had enormous influence over America's political process. Unfortunately, as we hear from listening to most conservative talk show hosts, that influence has mostly been in a negative direction: tearing people apart, exploiting divisive issues, pitting one group against another, and denying honest differences of opinion. That's the perversion of toxic talk, which has seriously damaged the level of political discourse in this country.

As Americans, political debate is not only protected by the Constitution, it is part of our nature. It's in our blood. We learned the value of robust discussion of the issues from our Founding Fathers and Mothers. But at the very heart of that debate lies the premise that unites us as Americans: We all want what's best for this country, we may just differ on how to get there. Unfortunately, that essential premise gets lost on right-wing talk radio. Instead, it's all us versus them. I'm right, you're wrong. Or, worse yet, I know what's right for America—and you're un-American if you think otherwise. There's no room for dissent, no room for honest differences of opinion, no room for thought. And anybody who disagrees with me, from the president of the United States on down, is a pinko, commie, racist, socialist, moron, Nazi, idiot, or worse. That kind of talk radio—as practiced by Rush Limbaugh, Glenn Beck, Sean Hannity, Michael Savage, Mark Levin, Laura Ingraham, Neal Boortz, Lou Dobbs, and others—violates every rule of civil discourse and does a disservice to our democracy. It is fundamentally un-American. And Americans deserve better.

Americans deserve to hear more than a right-wing chorus on the radio, too. We are, after all, a great and diverse nation. And, to reflect that diversity, we need a wide-open sounding board on the radio. The greater the mix of voices, the better talk radio mirrors what America's all about, and the better it is for listeners and for the country. In order to become informed citizens, people need to be exposed to more than just one point of view.

Talk radio's been called "America's front porch." I like to think of it as "America's town meeting." In colonial times, it was easier to keep people informed and achieve consensus—admittedly, in part because so many Americans were excluded from full citizenship. Town fathers just called a meeting to present the facts, debate the issues, and make a decision. Today, it's almost impossible. Our cities are so big, people are so busy, issues are so complex, the electorate is more diverse, and special interests are so powerful that it's hard to convince people to bother to vote, let alone get involved in the political process.

Few people have time for town meetings anymore. And fewer and fewer people take time to read the daily newspaper or watch the evening news. But whether driving to work or puttering around the kitchen, everybody has time to listen to talk radio. It's the easiest and most direct way to engage the voting public today: not only informing them of the issues, but giving them the opportunity to join the national debate.

That's what so great about talk radio. You don't need a master's degree or consulting contract. You don't need to learn how to make your own Web site. You don't have to pay a fee. You don't have to leave the comfort of your own home, office, or car. To participate, all you need is a set of ears. And an opinion—and who doesn't have plenty of those? With one set of ears, one opinion, and one phone call, anybody can join the national conversation on any issue, and be listened to and taken as seriously as any other caller.

With its capacity to empower every listener fully, and empower all of its listeners equally, talk radio can be the most democratic form of communication. But talk radio will never achieve its full potential so long as it's overwhelmingly dominated by right-wing ministers of hate.

We need to fumigate our airwaves of toxic talk by ensuring there are more diverse opinions to be heard on the radio, all around the country. The solution to a problem like Rush Limbaugh and his horde of thin-skinned bullies is twofold. First, we must point out, time and time again, how right-wing radio hosts are misrepresenting the truth and mischaracterizing their enemies. That's the role of progressive talk show hosts. Eternal vigilance is the price of a free and functioning civil society. In order to respond to the wave of lies cascading from right-wing radio, we also must fight fire with fire and build and support a national progressive media and radio network that can stand up to the right-wing money machine.

Our Founding Fathers knew that the best response to bad or wrongheaded ideas are better ones, aired in open debate. Free speech and impassioned but civil argument have always been the American way. But the right-wing stranglehold on radio has threatened our ability to conduct an

honest political debate, and its intolerance of opposing arguments has polluted and diminished our politics.

In short, we have let the airwaves—and our political system—be consumed with a poisonous cloud of toxic talk. Now's the time to get active,
get involved, build a powerful progressive media machine, and help clean
up the air.

ACKNOWLEDGMENTS

"With a Little Help from My Friends"

The Beatles said it best. Like them, with a little help from my friends and co-workers, I've had a great ride in the magical world of talk radio.

For me, it all started at KABC, 790 AM, Los Angeles, where I was hired by program director Wally Sherwin to guest host for Michael Jackson and Ray Bream, both first-class talk show hosts. Michael was lucky to discover Lyle Gregory, one of radio's most talented producers, who became a lifelong friend. It was especially exciting to join what I still remember as the best morning show I ever heard: *The Ken and Bob Company,* led by Ken Minyard and Bob Arthur (later replaced by Roger Barkley). The real star of the show was engineer "Waco Pat." Their philosophy was "EGBOK"—"Everything's going to be OK." And, after listening to their wacky show, you just knew everything would be. My job was offering morning commentary, which I did, in my underwear, from my little pad in the Hollywood Hills. Later, thanks to new program director Michael Fox, I also enjoyed sparring (fully dressed) every afternoon with Bill Pearl, on a show appropriately called *The Dueling Bills*—until Grinch George Green fired us both. When I joined KABC, it was the king of talk radio in Los Angeles. By the time I left, it had started to slip (no cause and effect, I hope) and was soon overtaken by KFI-AM 640, home of Rush Limbaugh, Dr. Laura, and Bill Handel. Looking to provide a little balance to an otherwise all-conservative lineup, program director David Hall hired me to host a weekend show on Saturday and Sunday afternoons. Under the banner "Bill Press, True American," we livened up weekend listening with the help of three top-notch producers: Johann Beckles, Marc Germain, and Tim Kelly. Marc went on to host his own successful shows on KFI, KABC, and KTALK—known as "Mr. KFI," "Mr. KABC," or simply "Mr. K"—before creating Talkradioone.com. He was succeeded by the talented and zany Tim Kelly, who could turn out a song parody faster than I could give the station call letters.

My time at KFI overlapped with two climactic events in Los Angeles: the Rodney King verdicts and O.J.'s acquittal. KFI was then located in the heart of Koreatown, one of the areas hardest hit in the Rodney King riots. To be sure of staying on the air, we secretly relocated the entire station to the home of a station engineer in the San Gabriel Mountains, where we bunked out and broadcast for several days. During the O.J. riots, we stayed on location. But I remember one night, while National Guard troops patrolled the streets, when an officer warned us not to leave our studio because a sniper was firing at the building. Exciting times, indeed.

Of all the radio professionals I have worked with, both before and after KFI, David Hall was the youngest and the best. He taught me to have confidence in myself, not to be afraid to share my personal emotions and experiences with listeners, and, most of all, to relax and have fun on the air. He was always supportive, ready with a critical or positive comment, and full of ideas on how to improve my broadcast.

The entire time I was doing television and radio in Los Angeles, my wife Carol and I also maintained our home in Inverness, in Marin County. Which gave me many opportunities to join the team at San Francisco's legendarily successful KGO-AM 810—starting back when the great Jim Dunbar was still its lead anchor. Ronn Owens, one of the best and most successful talk show hosts in the country, often honored me by asking me to fill in for him—an assignment in which, like Ronn, I benefited greatly from working with first-class producer Marc Silverman. I also subbed for the late Pete Wilson, and made frequent guest appearances on the morning and evening news. I still feel part of the KGO family, thanks to general manager Mickey Luckoff, program director Jack Swanson, an extraordinary radio talent, his assistant Trish Robbins, and news directors Greg Tantum and Ken Berry.

Soon after moving to Washington, D.C., in 1996, I began appearing on WMAL-AM 640, serving as a fill-in host and offering occasional commentary on the Chris Core program. In 2002, program director John Butler created a new morning show by inviting me and conservative Jane Norris to team up with WMAL veteran Andy Parks in kind of a right/left/center combo. The hours were abominable, 5–9 A.M., but we delivered a fun, lively show—until Chris Berry arrived as the new general manager. Fired again!

It being obvious by now that the only way I could keep a job in talk radio was to be my own boss, I teamed up with business partner, Paul Woodhull, and made a syndication deal with Amy Bolton, senior vice president of affiliate sales for talk radio at Jones Radio Networks (later purchased by Dial Global Radio Network). After persuading a few good friends to invest in Bill Press Partners, LLC, we launched *The Bill Press Show* in June 2005 in one market: Akron, Ohio. We were soon picked up by Sirius Satellite Radio (and, later, XM), thanks to their creative program director Dave Gorab.

A big thanks to Paul Woodhull and Amy Bolton and her affiliate relations team at Dial Global, including Jessica Sherman, Debbie Greenbaum, Ramona Rideout, and Donna Harrison. Another big thanks to all the sales staff at Dial Global, led by Eileen Decker, John Murphy, and Donelle Brown, who do a great job attracting advertisers to air their spots on our show.

I am especially grateful to our investment partners for their confidence in me and in the profit potential of progressive talk radio: Joe Azrak, Mike Barnes and Joan Pollitt, Sam Bleicher, Richard Blum, Eli Broad, Mark and Susie Buell, Alan Davis, Al Dwoskin, Louise Gund, Irwin Jacobs, Greg Keever, Ben Lap, Norman Lear, Ira Lechner, Jonathan Lewis, Charles and Kathy Manatt, Ron and Joy Mankoff, George Marcus, Chase Mishkin, Milan Panic, Pat and Bernice Patterson, Robert and Allison Price, Sol

Price, Sandy and Jeanne Robertson, Fred and Kathy Rotondaro, Lynn Schenk and Hugh Friedman, Steve Silberman, Richard Spohn, Andy Tobias, and Dick and Sue Wollack. Thank you, one and all.

As a longtime proud union member, I am also most grateful to those national labor leaders whose unions sponsor *The Bill Press Show*: Terry O'Sullivan and the Laborers Union of North America; Tom Buffenbarger and Rich Michalski of the Machinists Union; Mike Sullivan and Vince Panvini of the Sheet Metal Workers Union; Gerald McEntee and Lee Saunders of AFSCME; Joe Hunt of the Ironworkers Union; and James Hoffa of the Teamsters. Nobody's been a stronger supporter of progressive talk radio, from the beginning, than our great labor unions and their members, America's working men and women.

On *The Bill Press Show,* I'm lucky to work every day with two talented radio professionals: executive producer Peter Ogburn and assistant producer Dan Henning. My thanks to both for making me almost sound good—and to Stevie Lee Webb, our regular go-to guy for production help. And thanks also to those who joined the show briefly before moving on to other pursuits: Christy Harvey, Jonathan Levy, Jeff King, Nate Lurie, Lesley Lopez, Mark Pacheco, Danielle Tiley, and Kate Petty. Democratic strategists Rich Masters, Peter Fenn, Jamal Simmons, and Chris Kofinis are invaluable parts of the team, as frequent guests or fill-in hosts. A special thanks to them, as well as to all those members of the House and Senate who regularly make themselves available for interviews so early in the day. They honor us every time they make an appearance on the show.

There may not be many national progressive talk show hosts, but the few who do broadcast every day are world-class. I'm proud to be in the company of Ed Schultz, Stephanie Miller, Thom Hartmann, Randi Rhodes, Ron Reagan, and Mike Malloy—and I'm in awe of their strong voices on the air. Like them, I've also had the pleasure of working with some of the brightest people in talk radio around the country, including: Mike Dirkx in Portland, Janet Robert in Minneapolis–St. Paul, Harvey Wells in Chicago, Robin Bertolucci and Don Martin in Los Angeles, Brian Hall in Asheville, Tim Wenger in Buffalo, Mike Ferris in Madison, Peter B. Collins in Monterey, Mike Keane in Palm Springs, Doug Lang and Paul Van Erem in

Seattle, Tom Quinn in Reno, John Scott in San Francisco, Kris Olinger in Denver, and Til Levesque and Todd Thomas in Detroit. Thanks to all.

Directly or indirectly, every progressive talk radio host owes a special debt to Sheldon and Anita Drobny, founders of Air America. They've been especially generous to me with their advice, for which I thank them. And a special word of thanks to radio exec Ron Hartenbaum, who finds time to help steer *The Bill Press Show* in the midst of his many other radio responsibilities.

Agents get a bad name. Which is too bad, because most of us couldn't survive without them. In radio and television, I benefited enormously from the guidance and counsel of George Bane, George Hiltzik, and David Katz. True professionals. As is my book agent, Ron Goldfarb. Much more than that, he's also a wonderful friend and adviser. Carol and I cherish whatever time we get to spend with Ron and his wife Joanne.

None of us in talk radio, liberal or conservative, would be where we are today without the visionary leadership of Michael Harrison, founder and publisher of *Talkers Magazine*. Michael understands the industry, and sees its future, better than anyone. He is the ultimate radio professional: devoted to the medium and the people who work in radio, not to any one format or brand of politics. Under Michael's direction, *Talkers* is the voice of American radio. He also sponsors a great annual forum, bringing together radio professionals from all parts of the country for an exciting exchange of ideas. Bravo, Michael.

Even if you just skimmed this book, you know I could not even have started it without the strong support and outstanding research of the great team at Media Matters for America. Rush Limbaugh, Michael Savage, Glenn Beck, Sean Hannity, and Bill O'Reilly consider them the enemy. I consider them our heroes. With Media Matters, founder David Brock changed the landscape of American media—for the better!—giving us a vigilant, aggressive watchdog, working full-time to expose the lies of the right wing and report the truth. In addition to David, I'm grateful for the direct assistance of Eric Burns, Karl Frisch, Eric Boehlert, Jamison Foser, and all the hardworking staffers at Media Matters.

To Media Matters, credit for helping create the book. To Thomas

Dunne and the talented crew at St. Martin's Press, all credit for producing it. In addition to Tom, a political junkie and delight to work with, special thanks to senior editor Rob Kirkpatrick, director of publicity Joe Rinaldi, editorial assistant Margaret Smith, and members of their staff.

Finally, one more time, two people without whom writing this book would have been impossible. For research assistant Kevin Murphy, this is the fifth book we have produced together. His insights and editing skills just keep getting better and better. And, of course, aside from me, the long hours at the word processor were hardest on Carol, who put up with them with her usual grace and patience, knowing that, someday, it would all be in print. And here it is. Thank you, Carol.

INDEX